VICTORIAN SOUNDSCAPES

⚞ VICTORIAN SOUNDSCAPES ⚟

JOHN M. PICKER

OXFORD
UNIVERSITY PRESS

2003

OXFORD

UNIVERSITY PRESS

Oxford   New York

Auckland   Bangkok   Buenos Aires   Cape Town   Chennai
Dar es Salaam   Delhi   Hong Kong   Istanbul   Karachi   Kolkata
Kuala Lumpur   Madrid   Melbourne   Mexico City   Mumbai   Nairobi
São Paulo   Shanghai   Taipei   Tokyo   Toronto

Published by Oxford University Press, Inc.
198 Madison Avenue, New York, New York 10016

www.oup.com

Oxford is a registered trademark of Oxford University Press

Library of Congress Cataloging-in-Publication Data
Picker, John M.
Victorian soundscapes / John M. Picker., date.
p. cm.
Includes bibliographical references (p.) and index.
ISBN 0-19-515190-9; 0-19-515191-7 (pbk.)
1. English literature—19th century—History and criticism. 2. Sounds in literature.
3. Sound—Recording and reproducing—Great Britain—History—19th century.
4. Speech in literature. 5. Sound in literature. 6. Voice in literature.   I. Title.
PR468.S68 P53 2003
820.9'356—dc21   2002035906

1 3 5 7 9 8 6 4 2

Printed in the United States of America
on acid-free paper

⚓ ACKNOWLEDGMENTS ⚓

A T THE University of Virginia, where I began and wrote most of this book, several close listeners and readers deserve special thanks for their encouragement and counsel. Michael Levenson and Paul Cantor graciously read and helped me revise drafts of the chapters. Karen Chase, Herbert Tucker, Stephen Arata, and Bernard Carlson lent their ears and support as the project took shape, and Ralph Cohen and Stephen Cushman provided inspiration beyond the confines of it that influenced it all the same. I also would like to thank the Harvard English Department, chaired by Larry Buell. As I finished the book in Cambridge, Lynn Festa, Marjorie Garber, Oren Izenberg, Barbara Johnson, Ann Wierda Rowland, Elaine Scarry, Marc Shell, Werner Sollors, and especially Leah Price responded with enthusiasm and advice.

Over the last few years, primarily through the Victorian Literature and Culture seminar at the Humanities Center at Harvard, I have gotten to know, in their capacities as exemplary speakers, writers, editors, and auditors, James Eli Adams, Nancy Armstrong, Gillian Beer, Jim Buzard, Kate Flint, Andrew Miller, Lillian Nayder, John Plotz, and Helen Small, all of whom, in one way or another, had an impact on this project. Lisa Gitelman, Ivan Kreilkamp, and Emily Thompson have been my major partners in the recovery of acoustic culture. It is a privilege to acknowledge the foundational scholarship that has influenced my thinking and writing, especially the work of Kathleen Tillotson, Raymond Williams, and Richard Altick (to name just three), although in this I am hardly alone.

I thank many current and former residents of Charlottesville for keeping me company and for the opportunities that they have given me to sound off: Mara Amster, Candace Caraco, June Griffin, Chris Krentz, Anne McIlhaney, Dee McMahon, honorary Virginian Jason Mezey, Ana Mitric, Ken Parille, Dan Philippon, Steve Ramsay, Lisi Schoenbach, and Lisa Spiro. Danny Siegel, Virginia Zimmerman, Johnnie Wilcox, Michelle Allen, and Corey Brady kept me thinking about noise long after our Dickens seminar had ended. Thanks also to the respondents to my queries on the VICTORIA list and to list manager Patrick Leary, who has more than once supplied the answers; to Richard Bebb for information on early audio recordings; to Susan Amster for publication advice; to Anna Henchman for assistance with the bibliography; and to my students at Harvard, who have put these ideas to the test in the classroom and tutorials.

This book would not have materialized without the diligence of Elissa Morris, who skillfully guided it through the publication process. I express gratitude to the readers of the manuscript for Oxford University Press for their comments and recommendations, most all of which have been incorporated into the book. Also at Oxford, I thank Jeremy Lewis for his assistance with the manuscript and my belated additions to it, and Stacey Hamilton for her attention and patience on matters related to production. I gratefully acknowledge the Clark and Cooke funds from Harvard and DuPont, Bradley, and GSAS fellowships and Thomas J. Griffis prizes from Virginia that enabled me to conduct research for and assemble the manuscript.

Annotations to Charles Babbage's copy of *The Ninth Bridgewater Treatise* are quoted by permission of the Houghton Library, Harvard University. My experience at Houghton benefited from Susan Halpert's expert knowledge of the collections and her ability to turn up unexpected finds related to Victorian illustrators. Letters from the Babbage Correspondence and the Gladstone Papers are quoted by permission of the British Library. Unpublished materials related to Thomas Edison and George Gouraud are quoted courtesy of the Thomas A. Edison Papers. I thank Jerry Fabris at the Edison National Historic Site for providing copies of archival audio materials. The typescript of Wilkie Collins's letter to George Gouraud is quoted courtesy of Mrs. Faith Clarke, the great-granddaughter of Wilkie Collins and Martha Rudd. The manuscript of Charles Dickens's prospectus and dedication for his Cheap Edition is cited by permission of the Berg Collection of English and American Literature, the New York Public Library, Astor, Lenox and Tilden Foundations, and I thank Isaac Gewirtz and Stephen Crook at the Berg Collection for their assistance in locating the manuscript.

A number of people have helped me to track down the images used in the book, and in this regard I want to thank Brigitte Istim at the Punch Library, London, Anne Battis and Ben Weiss at the Burndy Library, Dibner Institute, MIT, Cyndie Burgess at the Armstrong Browning Library, Paul Johnson at the Public Record Office, and Gary Pietronave at EMI Archives. Unless otherwise credited, the illustrations are reproduced from the Collection of the President and Fellows of Harvard College.

Parts of the book were presented at several conferences and seminars over the last five years, and I thank the participants, in particular those who attended the lively "Acoustic Victorians" panel at the 2001 Narrative conference in Houston, for questions and suggestions that helped me to rethink and refine much of what follows. Portions of the introduction and chapters 1 and 4 have been published in different form in *New Literary History* 32 (2001) and the *American Scholar* 71 (2002), and I am grateful to John Bethell, Anne Fadiman, and the readers of these essays for their curiosity and commentary. Chapter 2 incorporates "The Soundproof Study: Victorian Professionals, Work Space, and Urban Noise," from *Victorian Studies* 42 (1999/2000): 427–53, reprinted with permission of the editors and Indiana University Press.

I owe my greatest thanks, finally, to my family, whose musical and analytic inclinations echo in what follows, and to the people I am fortunate to have in my audience: David Caplan, Mark Duckenfield, Jeffrey Feldman, Mark McWilliams, and especially Whitney Espich, who heard it all before everyone else did.

ᕔ CONTENTS ᕕ

⚑ ILLUSTRATIONS ⚑

VICTORIAN SOUNDSCAPES

INTRODUCTION
The Tramp of a Fly's Footstep

HEARING THINGS

IN AN 1827 article titled "Experiments on Audition," Charles Wheatstone, musical instrument maker, King's College physics professor, and co-signer of the 1837 patent on the electric telegraph, described with little fanfare a rudimentary, nonelectric amplifier of faint sounds that he dubbed a "microphone."[1] Just over a half-century later, in 1878, a Kentucky music professor named David Hughes revived Wheatstone's term for his own invention of the carbon microphone. As W. H. Preece, the electrician for the British Post Office, put it at the time in public lectures, Hughes's device opened up new areas of acoustic inquiry: "The microphone is an instrument which acts towards the ear as the microscope does to the eye. It will render evident to us sounds that are otherwise absolutely inaudible. I have heard myself the tramp of a little fly across a box with a tread almost as loud as that of a horse across a wooden bridge. There was a remarkable sound that accompanied the tramp of Mr. Fly, and a facetious friend of mine told me he thought the noise was occasioned by the neighing of the proboscis of the fly."[2]

Meanwhile, George Eliot, writing in the voice of the cynic Theophrastus Such in her final published work, was more restrained about what she called the "microphone which detects the cadence of the fly's foot on the ceiling, and may be expected presently to discriminate the noises of our various follies as they soliloquise or converse in our brains."[3] The tread of a fly was just the starting point for a writer in *The Spectator* who anticipated that it now would be possible "to hear the sap rise in the tree; to hear it rushing against small obstacles to its rise, as a brook rushes against the stones in its path; to hear the bee suck honey from the flower; to hear the rush of the blood through the smallest of blood-vessels, and the increase of that rush due to the slightest inflammatory action."[4] Such were the more imaginative uses for new powers of listening that would attend to "the roar on the other side of silence," as Eliot famously had written in *Middlemarch* (1871–1872). Or, as Preece put it in his 1878 lectures, it now could be confirmed that "all in this room, every one's body while I am speaking, is alive with sound."[5]

Five years later, in 1883, in what now is Indonesia but then was the colonial domain of the Dutch East India Company, the eruption on the volcanic island of Krakatoa caused one of the greatest natural disasters to date and created the loudest sounds ever documented. In their official report, members of the Royal Society noted that the noise of the August eruption traveled nearly three thousand miles to Rodriguez Island in the Indian Ocean, where the chief of police recorded that "several times during the night of the 26th–27th reports were heard coming from the eastward, like the distant roars of heavy guns" (see figure I.1).[6] A journalist at the time provided a more immediate analogy: if a resident of Philadelphia "should earnestly insist upon his having heard an explosion in San Francisco, *three thousand miles away*, he would receive a pitying smile, and his listener would silently walk away."[7] With such booming sound effects and the months of dazzling English sunsets that resulted from the debris it scattered, Krakatoa eventually surfaced in the writings of Alfred Tennyson, Gerard Manley Hopkins, A. C. Swinburne, John Ruskin, and even the likes of R. M. Ballantyne, who immortalized the noise and the volcano in his 1889 novel *Blown to Bits*: "It is no figure of speech to say that the *world* heard that crash. Hundreds, ay, thousands of miles did the sound of the mighty upheaval pass over land and sea to startle, more or less, the nations of the earth."[8] It is worth pausing to note the imperial overtones of this event: the empire strikes back here with a violence that is distinctly aural.

From the tramp of a fly's footstep to the roar of a volcanic blast, the Victorian soundscape was so varied and vast as to be too much for one pair of ears to apprehend. The juxtaposition of technological developments and natural forces as wildly different as the microphone and Krakatoa suggests at the outset that this was a period of unprecedented amplification, unheard-of loudness. It was, to use Preece's words, an age "alive with sound": alive with the screech and roar of the railway and the clang of industry, with the babble, bustle, and music of city streets, and with the crackle and squawk of acoustic vibrations on wires and wax—yet alive as well with the performances of the literary figures who struggled to hear and be heard above or through all of this.

4

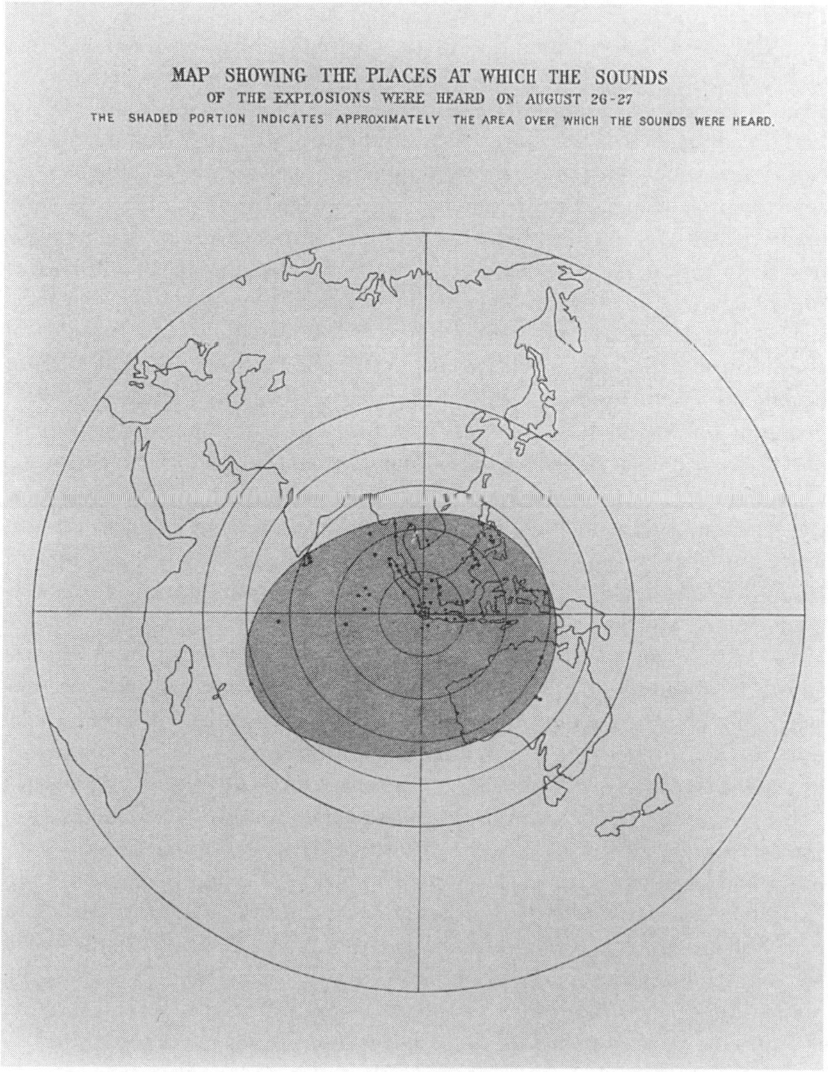

FIGURE I.1. VISUALIZING AN AURAL PHENOMENON: THE THREE-THOUSAND-
MILE RANGE THAT SOUNDS FROM THE KRAKATOA ERUPTION TRAVELED, AS
SHOWN IN A MAP PREPARED FOR THE OFFICIAL REPORT OF THE ROYAL
SOCIETY. PLATE 16 FROM *The Eruption of Krakatoa and Subsequent
Phenomena: Report of the Krakatoa Committee of the Royal Society*, ED. G. J.
SYMONS (LONDON: TRÜBNER, 1888), BETWEEN PP. 88–89.

In doing so, they endowed the acts of sounding, silencing, and hearing with broad physical and symbolic significance. At midcentury, besieged by street noises that interrupted his writing, Thomas Carlyle invested in a plan to construct a soundproof study at the top of his house. But once it was finished, he found it difficult to work there, claiming the shock of stray sounds had become even worse than before. In her fiction, George Eliot invoked the motif of acute hearing to suggest the perceptive capacity a truly sympathetic character might possess. Yet to her central character Theophrastus, the microphone appeared to promise more distraction than edification. Carlyle built a silent room that turned out to be an echo chamber, and Eliot lived long enough to see her literary metaphor of an idealized receptive sensibility become a literal condition of everyday existence. As the growing body of recent scholarship on nineteenth-century photography, optics, and visual culture indicates, the gaze acquired a new degree of importance in this period, but the era also experienced a rise in close listening.[9] In more ways than one, Victorians were hearing things. A serious consequence of this, as Carlyle and Eliot found out, was the recognition of ambient sound as ubiquitous and inescapable and its endowment with new material and figurative meanings. What the avant-garde composer John Cage discovered more than a half century later, Victorians already knew: that "there is no such thing as silence."[10]

To revive a term that they themselves first gave wide currency, theirs was an age of "auscultation," not only in the medical sense initiated by the stethoscope (invented by Laennec in 1816) and perfected by the microphone, of amplifying the sounds of the heart, lungs, and other organs in order to identify illnesses more accurately, but also in the sense of careful listening to a world at large — and in flux.[11] It was during this period that physicians became, in Jonathan Sterne's words, "virtuoso listeners," and "speaking patients with mute bodies gave way to speaking patients with sounding bodies."[12] When Lydgate uses a stethoscope on Casaubon in the late 1820s to early 1830s world of *Middlemarch*, this procedure corresponds with Eliot's stethoscopic intent to amplify the silent roar of others' heartbeats and minds in the years on the other, earlier side of the First Reform Bill and Victoria's reign, even as it stages the belated incursion of modernization into English medicine.[13] If earlier nineteenth-century doctors were the first to diagnose their patients with sophisticated methods of auscultation, then Victorian writers and artists became the first to diagnose their culture with such attentive soundings. Charles Dickens hinted at as much through the words of the stonemason "Stony" Durdles, who describes his unusual hearing abilities to the choirmaster and possible murderer John Jasper in *The Mystery of Edwin Drood*, published in 1870:

> "Now, look'ee here. You pitch your note, don't you, Mr. Jasper?"
> "Yes."
> "So I sound for mine. I take my hammer, and I tap. . . . I tap, tap, tap. Solid! I go on tapping. Solid still! Tap again. Hallao! Hollow! Tap

again, persevering. Solid in hollow! Tap, tap, tap, to try it better. Solid in hollow; and inside solid, hollow again! There you are! Old 'un crumbled away in stone coffin, in vault!"

"Astonishing!"[14]

Such was the power of nineteenth-century hearing that for Stony Durdles, telegraph-like taps of auscultation led to a corpse: appropriately enough, as it turned out, for this discovery occurred in the story the author died writing. Exhausted from literary production, but especially from his public reading tours, where thousands thronged to hear the voice of the Inimitable, Dickens at the end of his career found himself not only the towering practitioner of Victorian close listening but also the greatest victim of it. A decade before the debut of the phonograph, Dickens had used his lecture circuit to perfect and maintain a technology of oral presence. The tours transformed him into a re-producing speech machine, as his perpetual need to repeat himself fed and appeared to sanction his audiences' incessant desire to hear the same old hits again and again—primarily *A Christmas Carol*, which, in countless renditions on stage, film, radio, television, and not least, sound recordings, still returns each year, to haunt and bless us, every one.

The first chapter of this book opens with a work of natural theology pub-lished the year of Victoria's accession to the throne, and the final chapter closes with a painting trademarked in the year of her death. Her reign delin-eates the chronological reach of this volume because her subjects extended the range and depth of close listening and came to understand it in ways that still resonate with the aural experience of modernity. In four case studies, I in-vestigate the two major roles that hearing played in Victorian culture: as a re-sponse to a physical stimulus and as a metaphor for the communication of meaning. I examine the close relationship between Victorian sciences and technologies of sound, on the one hand, and literary and cultural representa-tions of sound, voice, and hearing, on the other. This argument works to turn the approach to the Victorian gaze on its ear, by offering an approach that it-self turns to and on the ear.

AN AUSCULTATIVE AGE

BEFORE Victoria was crowned queen, before *The Pickwick Papers* began appearing in monthly parts in 1836, Dickens and his contemporaries found themselves the inheritors of the Romantics' preoccupation with the sublime force of the music and quiet of nature. One only has to think of the frequency of the metaphor of the Aeolian harp in Romantic poetry to recog-nize the centrality of natural sound to the Lake Poets. In *The Friend*, Samuel Taylor Coleridge wrote that hearing "the thunders and howlings of the break-ing ice" on the Lake of Ratzeburg one winter night convinced him that "there are sounds more sublime than any sight *can* be, more absolutely suspending the power of comparison, and more absolutely absorbing the mind's self-consciousness in its total attention to the object working upon it," while William Wordsworth went on to equate the capabilities of the ear with those of the eye in his long poem from 1828, "On the Power of Sound."[15] The Romantic poets' preference for the rough music of nature over the refined performances of concert halls and salons was echoed by Charles Lamb in his "Chapter on Ears" (1821), later collected in his *Essays of Elia.* "I have no ear," Lamb claimed as Elia, adding that he had "sat through an Italian Opera, till, for sheer pain, and inexplicable anguish," he had "rushed out into the noisiest places of the crowded streets" to console himself with sounds he "was not obliged to follow, and get rid of the distracting torment of endless, fruitless, barren attention!" Only outside on the streets could he take "refuge in the unpretending assemblage of honest, common-life sounds."[16] By his twenty-sixth birthday, Dickens owned not one but two well-thumbed copies of the works of, in his words, "the original, kind-hearted, veritable Elia."[17] It was Lamb's step across the threshold from the opera house into the hubbub of London street life, the bustle that Elia's ear interpreted as a "paradise," that helped set the precedent for Dickens and his fellow urban journalists to attend to and begin to archive the new "common-life" sounds of the Victorian city.

Several publications by scientifically inclined figures in the 1820s and early 1830s sounded the first hints of a larger cultural shift toward close listening. Among his many other investigations, Wheatstone, beginning in 1823, published a series of eclectic aurally centered articles with such titles as "New Experiments on Sound."[18] By that time, William Hyde Wollaston—physicist, chemist, discoverer of palladium and rhodium, and inventor of the *camera lucida*—had made, in an article titled "On Sounds Inaudible by Certain Ears" (1820), the earliest claim for the relative receptivity of ears to high-pitched frequencies. One story has it that Wollaston, attempting to ascertain whether some people could hear high notes that others could not, played on pipes while hiding behind the stacks in Sir Henry Bunbury's library and watched to see which readers jumped or winced at certain pitches.[19] Through such eccentric methods, Wollaston explored "the other side of silence" a half-century before George Eliot invoked the ability of "hearing the grass grow and the squirrel's heart beat" as a metaphor for her doctrine of sympathy and lamented that "the quickest of us walk about well wadded with stupidity" (189). One of Wollaston's most distinguished students, the astronomer-physicist-chemist John Herschel, completed an article on "Sound" for the *Encyclopaedia Metropolitana* in 1830, which synthesized previous studies and influenced, among other works of the early 1830s, the physicist David Brewster's writings on acoustic and musical illusions in his *Letters on Natural Magic Addressed to Sir Walter Scott* (1832) and mathematician Mary Fairfax Somerville's survey of sound in her best-selling *On the Connexion of the Physical Sciences* (1834), which went through ten editions. These writings were widely consulted by readers from all walks of life, not just scientists. (The word "scientist" would be coined in 1840, when William Whewell did so in his *Philosophy of the*

Inductive Sciences.) These writings predate the kind of specialization that came to dominate the professions later in the century and instead were intended for a broad audience eager for self-education. Neither dilettantes nor amateurs in the negative sense, the authors saw no conflict in their work between scientific investigations and humanistic investments: after all, Wheatstone also made musical instruments, Herschel wrote (and published) poetry, and Brewster addressed his letters to Scott, his fellow countryman and favorite novelist. Although the situation would change, the realm of sound was neither an exclusive nor yet a too technical one.[20]

Among the most compassionate of early nineteenth-century expositors of aural experience was William Wright, the self-proclaimed "surgeon aurist extraordinary" to nobility, from Queen Charlotte to the Duke of Wellington, whom he outlived. Wright dedicated an early work to Wellington and, in a pamphlet published after the duke's death in 1852, disclosed that Wellington's hearing in his left ear had first been damaged by gunfire and then completely lost after an earlier doctor's botched treatment.[21] To that noisy stanza from Tennyson's ode (which, in 1890, the laureate himself recorded by shouting into a phonograph), Wright's admission of the duke's hearing loss lends an unintended irony:

> Where shall we lay the man whom we deplore?
> Here, in streaming London's central roar.
> Let the sound of those he wrought for,
> And the feet of those he fought for,
> Echo round his bones forevermore.[22]

This is a eulogistic roar and echo, after all, which the military hero, even had he been alive, would have only half heard. Beginning in 1817 with *An Essay on the Human Ear*, Wright published a number of books on the physiology of hearing and treatments for deafness, but his work is dominated by outrage at those, like Wellington's earlier doctor, who advocated caustics, mercurials, "acoustic drops," and other absurd remedies to "cure" it. The poet Thomas Hood sent up the entire enterprise in "A Tale of a Trumpet" (1841), his comic poem about a peddler's sale of a speaking trumpet (the amplifying predecessor to Hughes's microphone), which happens to be possessed with the power to let users eavesdrop on whispered rumors and hushed-up scandals. Hoping to undo her deafness, an old woman buys it and delights in suddenly hearing all the gossip in the neighborhood. After dutifully spreading everyone else's secrets, she gets her comeuppance when the town condemns her as a witch and drowns her. Then, as now, there was much money and risk to be hazarded in schemes designed to clear the impaired or indifferent ear; as Hood put it, "But think what thousands and thousands of pounds / We pay for nothing but hearing sounds."[23] Surgeon aurist Wright's critiques, however, were more explicit and severe. As late as 1858 (seven years after the Great Exhibition, that defining display of Victorian progress in industry, science, and commerce), in a long digression in his *Fishes and Fishing: Artificial Breeding of Fish, Anatomy of Their Senses, Their Loves, Passions, and Intellects*, Wright paused once more to castigate "most of the regular professors of aural surgery," whose methods proved "not only perfectly *useless*, but *highly injurious*, and *too often fatal*."[24]

Undeterred by such risks from their desire to listen and hear, Victorians in their scientific and technological discoveries and literary innovations went a long way toward dispelling, or at least redefining, the mysteries of hearing and sound. This book analyzes the stages by which they sought to transform what Romantics had conceived of as a sublime *experience* into a quantifiable and marketable *object* or *thing*, a sonic commodity, in the form of a printed work, a performance, or, ultimately, an audio recording, for that most conspicuous legacy of Victorianism, the modern middle-class consumer. This period gave rise, after all, to the electric telegraph and the microphone, the telephone and the phonograph, technical apparatuses such as Hermann von Helmholtz's vowel resonators and John Tyndall's singing flames, and specialized short-hand systems like Isaac Pitman's phonography and Alexander Melville Bell's Visible Speech, all of these, in one form or another, means to make manifest and manipulate formerly intangible, unruly vibrations.[25] The pivotal figure in the conquest of vibration was the German physiologist Helmholtz, who crafted the bridge between Romantic and Victorian aural sensibilities, be-tween the lyric power of the Aeolian harp and the electric current of the tele-phone. As the physicist James Clerk Maxwell put it in his 1878 Rede Lecture,

> No man has done more than Helmholtz to open up paths of commu-
> nication between isolated departments of human knowledge. . . .
> Helmholtz, by a series of daring strides, has effected a passage for him-
> self over that untrodden wild between acoustics and music—that Ser-
> bonian bog where whole armies of scientific men and musical men of
> science have sunk without filling it up. We may not be able even yet to
> plant our feet in his tracks and follow him right across.[26]

I examine Helmholtz's cultural affinities with and influence on George Eliot and others in more detail in chapter 3, but for now it is enough to say that his special force lay in his willingness to preserve the romance of sound waves—in one of his favorite images, their elusiveness and mystery evoked those of far-off ocean waves he surveyed from a high cliff—even while he dissected their pitches and harmonics like so many laboratory specimens. Helmholtz fed Victorians' curiosity, and fueled their speculation, about the workings of the ear. "We want to know why certain sounds affect us in certain ways, and the want will no doubt be satisfied," a contributor to one of the journals Dick-ens had launched and edited wrote. "The human ear is being continually per-fected. . . . The growth of aural discrimination will be accelerated as the nerv-ous sensibility of our race advances, and those who follow us will hear sounds, simple and compound, that are imperceptible to us."[27] I argue that although science and technology seemed to lay open the workings of sound, music, and voice right under their ears, Victorian writers found in these new truths a basis for wonder, inspiration, and even romance, and they also found new questions to ask as they positioned these discoveries in their increasingly decadent, uncanny world.

Consider for a moment the connections between acoustic technology and British poetry, which extend back to the later nineteenth century, that is, over six decades before Dylan Thomas made the first commercial recording for Caedmon in 1952. As England's aged poet laureate, Tennyson seemed a logical subject for voice recording when the "perfected" version of Edison's phonograph arrived in London in 1888. Two years later, one of the inventor's assistants carried a phonograph all the way to the poet's home on the Isle of Wight to capture him reading excerpts from *The Princess* (1847) and "The Charge of the Light Brigade" (1854). Who would have imagined that the eighty-year-old Tennyson would warm to the new technology? But he did, and recordings preserve his thanking the assistant for showing him (in a mock American accent) "Edison's my-*rack*-uhlis invention." He arranged to keep the machine and went on to record about a dozen poems in full or part, periodically replaying them for himself and his guests during the last two years of his life. In my final chapter, I examine Tennyson's motivation to embrace the phonograph. For all that physiologists would do to measure, quantify, or demythologize what it meant to hear, Tennyson's case is one of several I consider that reveal the persistent, deeply personal effects of sound waves on a skilled ear.

NUISANCE AND RESONANCE

THIS BOOK opens with two chapters devoted to sounds as discerned outside professional dwellings—in the streets and public spaces of Victorian London—and follows with two chapters on the place of sound inside, in the drawing rooms and parlors of middle-class homes. It moves from the public sphere to the private to examine the ways in which sound interpenetrated the two, as, for example, in the case of the street noise that interrupted the labors of writers and artists working in their homes. At the same time it moves from the figurative potential of sound to its noisy reality, to show how the terms of aurality penetrated Victorians' thoughts about themselves and their relation to the world, even as that world grew more cacophonous. This book argues that the development of Victorian self-awareness was contingent on awareness of sonic environments, and that, in turn, to understand how Victorians saw themselves, we ought to understand how they heard themselves as well. Aural dimensions of Victorian science, domesticity, and technological innovation register the emergence of this self-awareness and the means by which sound ostensibly was disciplined and made concrete by the end of the century.

In their scope and detail, Dickens's works constitute an important touchstone for Victorian sound. My opening chapter analyzes the soundscape of *Dombey and Son* (1846–1848), the novel that most profoundly reflects the changes brought about by the railway boom of the 1840s. I show how the period of *Dombey* ushered in Dickens's desire to broadcast his words ever more widely in print and performance, to cross the waves and enter homes like a decades-too-early radio signal. My argument brings together the natural theology of Charles Babbage and the history of the mid-Victorian book to make the case that Dickens's development as novelist and public reader has a particular kind of acoustic significance, one rooted in his own sense of the literal and figurative power of his authorial voice.

To harness that power, however, he had to compete with a more pressing, because more physical, problem of sound: that is, the increasing volume of street noises that undermined his and so many other urban dwellers' writing labors. The argument of my second chapter draws upon journalism, political tracts, petitions, editorials, and cartoons to explore the threat that ubiquitous street noise, and the Italian organ grinders who produced it, posed to artistic, literary, and intellectual professionals in the middle of the century. I show how the material presence of sound in Victorian urban life had material consequences in the lives of, among others, Carlyle, Babbage, Dickens, and, not least, his illustrator John Leech. Theirs are cases that, viewed in isolation, have appeared unfortunate, pathological, or just strange, but when considered collectively attest to the precarious professional status that domestic confinement conferred on these "brain-workers" and others like them.

Chapters 3 and 4 present the literary and cultural consequences of the mechanical fulfillment of Babbage's aural philosophy, as adapted by Dickens in chapter 1 and challenged by street musicians in chapter 2. Figurative and literal manifestations of sound unite in the third and fourth chapters, which cover the period from the 1860s and 1870s through the fin de siècle, when writers as well as scientists were concerned with what Eliot's common-law husband George Henry Lewes called "the physical basis of mind." Helmholtz's new understanding of the physiology of hearing sympathetically resonated not only in Eliot's fictional project, especially the strained silences and stifled speech of *Daniel Deronda* (1876), but also in the technological and psychological discoveries that occurred alongside it. These developments echoed Eliot's investment in the lingering presence of the human voice, at the same time that they showed the consequences of what Geoffrey Winthrop-Young and Michael Wutz refer to as "the coincidence of psychology and Edisonian technology" over the last quarter of the nineteenth century, and in particular, the more complicated presence of sound in literature as a result of technological change.[28]

The closing chapter takes up the literary and cultural impact in Britain of one of the great inventions of the last quarter of the century, the phonograph—or, as a writer in *Nature* put it, no doubt with London's besieged "brain-workers" in mind, "the phonographic barrel-organ, which will doubtless by and by take the place of that instrument of torture which makes the lives of delicate-eared artists and *littérateurs* miserable."[29] The fierce vocals of Tennyson's final verses, the metallic whispers of Bram Stoker's classic *Dracula*, and what Joseph Conrad called the "sinister resonance" of his beating

Heart of Darkness are considered as products of the new babble culture that reigned within the old wired world.[30] These and other authors addressed the place of the writer and his or her work in a city, and increasingly a globe, criss-crossed, as journalist Henry Thompson put it in 1901, by "Voices! Voices! The voices of a mighty multitude, year in and year out, holyday and holiday, noon and night, flow[ing] over our heads and under our feet in a ceaseless, silent chorus."[31]

Tradition has largely demanded allegiance to one of two camps concerning the value of sound in literary and linguistic study. On the one hand, there are those, most notably Walter Ong, who have defended orality as primal, communal, and a potent remnant of an acoustic past all but decimated by the shift to print and visual culture.[32] On the other hand, there are those such as the poststructuralist Jacques Derrida, who effectively banished voice and sound to the lower depths of much literary critical work by emphasizing the grammatological qualities of language, the sense that nothing is outside of or separable from its written text, over the phonocentric assumptions of those like Ong.[33] Yet when set against a broader canvas, as Jonathan Rée writes, these debates can seem "actually rather inane."[34] They ignore a third position, which maintains "that the aural and written modes of language are equivalent but simply differ, both deriving from the ontologically prior nature of language itself."[35]

The chapters that follow do not remain bound by the esoteric confines of such terms and positions as Ong's and Derrida's. Instead, they step outside this debate, to the extent that it still is one, to consider the more palpable questions of how Victorians interpreted sound in newly amplified forms, as voice, noise, vibration, music, and electric echo, and how it worked within but, often at the same time, against their acts of writing. The impetus for such an approach, and the source of the title of this book, can be traced back to Murray Schafer's influential *The Tuning of the World* (1977), which first demonstrated the need and methodology for this kind of attention with an ear-opening study of sonic environments throughout history and across cultures.[36] Schafer used the word "soundscape" to refer to "any portion of the sonic environment regarded as a field for study" and wrote that "the home territory of soundscape studies will be the middle ground between science, society, and the arts" (274, 4). Concerned as he was with environmental acoustics, noise pollution, and acoustic design, and with formulating such concepts as clairaudience (exceptional hearing ability), sound imperialism (when sound power is sufficient to dominate a soundscape), and the earwitness (a literary figure who records the soundscapes of his or her own time and place), Schafer undertook an ambitious interdisciplinary task long before they were fashionable. His effort was a harbinger of the work those engaged not only in cultural and literary studies but also in ecocriticism and acoustic ecology would be doing in the coming decades.[37]

The faint murmur of soundscape studies being published around the period of Schafer's book—and, for that matter, when I began my research on this one in the early 1990s — has risen to a steady hum. Not surprisingly, many of these volumes, which include pioneering anthologies as well as several monographs, have focused on the twentieth century.[38] The scope of such projects, however, has broadened to include investigations of the workings of sound in contexts as diverse as early modern English drama, the behavior of nineteenth- and twentieth-century French concert audiences, and Edison-era silent and sound film.[39] The rappings of spiritualism and lashings of slavery have received extensive attention by scholars of eighteenth- and nineteenth-century American soundscapes, who have demonstrated the challenge and value of restoring premodern soundtracks, or of performing, if you will, a kind of acoustic archaeology on the (ostensibly silent) records of the distant past.[40] Most important for the purposes of this book, the eminent Victorianist Peter Bailey issued a long overdue manifesto-of-sorts for scholars who seek to understand noise, and especially Victorian noise, as more than a mere nuisance or background phenomenon — a call that I answer in chapter 2.[41] His voice joins others in a like-minded appeal for narratives of what Steven Connor identifies as "the auditory self," that is, "an attentive rather than an investigatory self, which takes part in the world rather than taking aim at it."[42] I do not see these social qualities as necessarily incompatible, however. The stories told in this book are of figures at once attentive and investigative, those who both contributed to and, consciously or not, hoped to control, even to dominate, their acoustic worlds.

"Worlds," I should clarify, and not "world." The subjective nature of sensation was of central interest to the Victorians. It seems appropriate to steer away from a monolithic conception of a singular Victorian soundscape toward an analysis of the experiences of particular individuals listening under specific cultural influences and with discernable motivations, if that is the word, for hearing as they did. In Dickens's case, for one, aurality and imaginative power were inseparable. In 1872, George Henry Lewes, who knew about the effect of the mind on the senses, wrote: "Dickens once declared to me that every word said by his characters was distinctly *heard* by him; I was at first not a little puzzled to account for the fact that he could hear language so utterly unlike the language of real feeling, and not be aware of its preposterousness; but the surprise vanished when I thought of the phenomenon of hallucination."[43] How to explain the hallucinatory implications for Dickens's hearing, and for hearing Dickens, is where I turn first.

⚝ I ⚝

"WHAT THE WAVES WERE ALWAYS SAYING"

Voices, Volumes, *Dombey and Son*

Hear Dickens, and die; you will never live to hear anything of its kind so good.

—From a review of a public reading by Dickens

BABBAGE AND DICKENS: A LIBRARY OF AIR

ON 24 May 1837, Princess Victoria, less than a month before becoming queen of England, turned eighteen, and Charles Babbage, mathematician and inventor of the machine considered the first modern computer, published a volume in London entitled *The Ninth Bridgewater Treatise: A Fragment*. Making a present of a copy to the princess "on the most important," Babbage wrote to her, "of the anniversaries of your natal day," he claimed to offer the book "in defense of Science and for the support of Religion."[1] Like the author himself, the *Treatise* was hard to classify.[2] Brief, fragmentary in design, and published without compensation, the work nevertheless was among the most important early Victorian contributions to the debate over natural theology and an eccentric pre-Darwinian attempt to reconcile spiritual phenomena with scientific reasoning.[3] The argument of the *Treatise* centered on Babbage's attempt to show by way of analogy to his calculating machine known as the Difference Engine that miracles such as the appearance of new species could be rationally interpreted, if changes in organic life over time were seen as an elaborate equation series designed by the Creator. Babbage conceived of God as a programmer, and miracles were "the exact fulfilment of much more extensive laws than those we suppose to exist," the equivalent of the outcome obtained from a pattern of equations—or, in contemporary terms, the output of a computer program—written and performed by the Almighty.[4]

Bold and, to modern ears, odd as this theory is, it has tended to overshadow an even more speculative chapter of the *Treatise*, one on sound. In the ninth chapter, entitled "On the Permanent Impression of Our Words and Actions on the Globe We Inhabit," Babbage draws in part on the work of Pierre Laplace and William Wollaston, to claim that pulses of air emitted by the voice, even after they become inaudible to human ears, remain in one form or another permanently etched on the earth's atmosphere: "The waves of air thus raised, perambulate the earth and ocean's surface, and in less than twenty hours every atom of its atmosphere takes up the altered movement due to that infinitesimal portion of the primitive motion which has been conveyed to it through countless channels, and which must continue to influence its path throughout its future existence" (35).[5] In a central analogy, the atmosphere becomes the repository for voices from all time, and Babbage compares the voices etched on air to words printed on a page:

> Thus considered, what a strange chaos is this wide atmosphere we breathe! Every atom, impressed with good and with ill, retains at once the motions which philosophers and sages have imparted to it, mixed and combined in ten thousand ways with all that is worthless and base. The air itself is one vast library, on whose pages are for ever written all that man has ever said or woman whispered. There, in their mutable but unerring characters, mixed with the earliest, as well as with the latest sighs of mortality, stand for ever recorded, vows unredeemed, promises unfulfilled, perpetuating in the united movements of each particle, the testimony of man's changeful will. (36)[6]

For Babbage, the air acts as a giant scroll or phonograph, permanently recording voices that, he concedes, only God possesses the knowledge to replay.

Responses to this passage ranged from dismissive to enthusiastic. The eminent geologist Charles Lyell privately confided to Babbage that he considered it "farfetched," while Thomas Hill, the twentieth president of Harvard and author of a "supplement" to the *Treatise* titled *Geometry and Faith* (1849), claimed it inspired "a thrill of mingled admiration and fear," and Henry P. Babbage, Babbage's youngest surviving son, wrote after his father's death that it "contains the earliest statement that I have seen on the principle of the 'conservation of energy.' . . . it is distinct and clear as to simple force and sets it forth in a way that startled many and was not long in being followed up."[7] One "startled" reader who followed this chapter up was Charles Dickens, a good friend of Babbage. Dickens owned a first edition of the *Treatise*, and it made such an impression on him that he cited it in a speech delivered in 1869, less than a year before his death, and more than three decades after the *Treatise* had been published: "It was suggested by Mr. Babbage, in his *Ninth Bridgewa-*

ter Treatise, that a mere spoken word—a mere syllable thrown into the air—
may go on reverberating through illimitable space for ever and for ever, seeing
that there is no rim against which it can strike: no boundary at which it can
possibly arrive."[8] Over two decades before giving that speech, however, Dickens had alluded to the ninth chapter in a major novel. In a curious aside in
Dombey and Son (1846–1848), he describes the socially mobile Sir Barnet Skettles as "like a sound in air, the vibration of which, according to the speculation
of an ingenious modern philosopher, may go on travelling for ever through
the interminable fields of space."[9] Dickens paraphrases that key passage from
the ninth chapter of the *Treatise* and allows readers to surmise that the "ingenious modern philosopher" is Babbage.[10] His *Treatise* forms the starting
point for my discussion of Dickens because it left a surprising imprint on
Dombey and Son and the novelist's subsequent professional life. *Dombey* is, on
its own terms, a novel dominated by and absorbed with the effects and intelligibility of sounds and voices. However, I want to suggest that the presence of
Babbage's theory of aural permanence in this earlier novel and once again in
a late speech constitutes a framework for understanding Dickens's development as an author, performer, and publishing innovator. Alongside the writing
of *Dombey*, he hit upon his own means to achieve stratospheric success, but
this would be on Babbage's terms, in which the valuable words of "philosophers and sages" mix with all that is "worthless and base" to move through "illimitable space." *Dombey* and Dickens's career from this juncture on became
an echo chamber, so to speak, for the ideas that the "ingenious modern
philosopher" expressed about the diffusion of voice.

Interpreters of *Dombey* regularly classify it as Dickens's breakthrough
book. The author's seventh novel, they claim, represents his first "serious"
fiction, in which he demonstrated new depths of plotting and construction
and more sophisticated writing, organization, and social criticism than he
displayed in his previous endeavors. Kathleen Tillotson's commentary from
1954 remains the consensus view: "*Dombey and Son* stands out from among
Dickens's novels as the earliest example of responsible and successful planning; it has unity not only of action, but of design and feeling."[11] As evidence
for this argument, scholars from Tillotson on refer to the celebrated July 1846
letter to his close friend and biographer John Forster, in which Dickens outlined with unprecedented foresight what he hoped to accomplish in the
novel. The critics reiterate: as Dickens created *Dombey*, so *Dombey* created
Dickens, and the professional novelistic career was realized by the singularly
ambitious work.[12]

But like many assertions about Dickens's life and canon, this one invokes
a narrative of mythic proportions that has tended to obscure a more complicated reality. For while it is generally agreed that the novel was Dickens's first
to involve a complete set of number plans, significant strands of the plot
nonetheless remained underdeveloped at the outset. Dickens admitted as
much when he wrote in that famous letter to Forster that he would "carry the
story on, through all the branches and off-shoots and meanderings that

come up."[13] In this spirit, Dickens substantially altered major developments that "came up" among central characters once serialization was under way. It is well known, for instance, that Dickens originally had intended Walter Gay, the novel's young *naif* who sails away for much of the story only to reappear just in time to marry Florence Dombey and live happily ever after, to suffer humiliations and gradually waste away, as Dickens put it, "from that love of adventure and boyish light-heartedness, into negligence, idleness, dissipation, dishonesty, and ruin."[14] When Forster protested, Dickens changed his plan, turning Walter into the Prince Charming with whom readers are familiar. Perhaps the author's greatest change of mind affected the portrayal of Edith Granger, the senior Dombey's second wife, whom Dickens had planned to make an outright adulteress and to have die for her sins. Her character proved so compelling, however, that Dickens's correspondent Lord Jeffrey insisted the author uphold her moral righteousness and deny any possibility of physical intimacy between Edith and James Carker, Dombey's nemesis: "Note from Jeffrey this morning, who won't believe (positively refuses) that Edith is Carker's mistress."[15] Dickens here also gave in, altered his plot to allow Edith to survive untarnished, and seized the opportunity to heighten audience sympathy for a figure who remains one of his strongest female characters.

What the evidence makes clear is not that *Dombey* was a slapdash production—far from it—but that it was not as fully formed in its initial stages, or single-minded in its execution, as numerous arguments might lead one to believe. In fact, the construction of *Dombey* was more laborious and collaborative for Dickens, particularly in its early phases. Over two years elapsed between the appearance of the final number of *Martin Chuzzlewit* and the first of *Dombey*, an unusually long duration for an author who early on had established such a high rate of productivity. The period was marked by shorter publications (two Christmas stories, *Pictures from Italy*), restless travel, and ongoing feuds associated with Dickens's founding, editorship, and ultimate abandonment of the fledgling *Daily News*. "Vague thoughts of a new book are rife within me just now," Dickens wrote from Devonshire Terrace early in this period, "and I go wandering about at night into the strangest places, according to my usual propensity at such a time—seeking rest, and finding none."[16] He wandered not only about dark London streets, but also, one suspects, about "the strangest places" within his imagination, where the plans for *Dombey* took shape while questions of professional identity and productivity perpetually dogged him. As others have noted, these years were partly a time, after disappointing sales of *Chuzzlewit* and against a backdrop of professional distractions, for the task of regrouping on Dickens's part, as he refined his technique of writing novels and reflected, with Forster, on what it would take to keep readers devouring them.

Yet at the same time as *Dombey* developed out of these concerns over reception, it also became absorbed with working through them. *Dombey* demonstrated Dickens's uneasy relationship with acts of writing and communication, a relationship that became most charged during this period in his career. The strain of composing the novel punctuated the letters to Forster: "I have been hideously idle all week," Dickens wrote to him, and later, "You can hardly imagine what infinite pains I take, or what extraordinary difficulty I find in getting on FAST." Then, "I am working very slowly," and again, "Could not begin before Thursday last, and find it very difficult indeed to fall into the new vein of the story." For Dickens in Lausanne, far away from the crowded streets of London and trying to write *The Battle of Life* simultaneously with *Dombey*, anxious self-doubt became acute:

> I am going to write you a most startling piece of intelligence. I fear there may be NO CHRISTMAS BOOK! . . . I don't know how it is. I suppose it is the having been almost constantly at work in this quiet place; and the dread for the *Dombey*; and the not being able to get rid of it, in noise and bustle. . . . But this is certain. I am sick, giddy, and capriciously despondent. I have bad nights; am full of disquietude and anxiety; and am constantly haunted by the idea that I am wasting the marrow of the larger book, and ought to be at rest.

And in a subsequent letter to Georgina Hogarth, he still despaired over his inability to accumulate words satisfyingly: "So far from having 'got through my agonies,' as you benevolently hope, I have not yet begun them. No, on this *ninth of the month* I have not yet written a single slip. . . . My wretchedness, just now, is inconceivable." Even after he completed *Dombey*, he was convinced he felt unable to speak: "I am rather nervous after my hard work and go about perpetually persuading myself that I am choking even though I know there is nothing the matter with me."[17] Dickens's anguish about writing *Dombey*, his own need to satisfy his increasingly stringent standards of expression in fiction, is reflected in the novel's preoccupation with the problem of expressing things clearly, of getting out the word. This work conceives of expression in manifold senses: as verbal communication, primarily, but also as interchange between different parties, the moving forth of people and goods, the passing of legacies, and the spread of language and ideas. Communicative attempts such as these permeate *Dombey*, the novel in which characters struggle to hear and through which Dickens struggles to be heard. Within the plot, symbolism, and structure of the novel, Dickens examines the complications involved in trafficking bodies, transferring capital, and establishing contact. Others have written of the tendencies of *Dombey*, and Dickens's work more generally, to be consumed with "metaphors of circulation."[18] Yet, in the case of *Dombey*, the novel itself is implicated in Dickens's contemporaneous concerns with authorial expression and audience receptivity. Out of his own struggle to produce an innovative narrative, Dickens creates a work that has as a theme as well as context the risks and distortions of transmission and acquisition, of nothing less than the acts of voicing and receiving themselves.

"AWAY, WITH A SHRIEK, AND A ROAR, AND A RATTLE"

W ITH ITS telling conjunction, the title of the novel ushers in a dramatic change. No longer merely the "life and adventures" of a single protagonist, *Dombey and Son* puts special emphasis upon the filial bond.[19] The birth and death of the *Son* of the title, the younger Paul Dombey, frame the novel's first quarter and are responsible for much of the work's fame. But the title is a red herring, of course; as Mrs. Tox predicts upon Little Paul's premature demise, "To think that Dombey and Son should be a Daughter after all!" (225). Referring at once to the House, firm, and family of Dombey and Son, the title is commonly considered a sleight of hand practiced by a confident author upon his willing audience, but more to the point, the ambiguity of it allows for an intentional misrepresentation of the novel it names, a distorted broadcast of the subject of its story. Dickens keeps silent on the dominant role Florence will play in the narrative, just as he had in the manuscript's early stages expressed the desire to hush up even the word Dombey: "the very name getting out, would be ruinous," he told Forster.[20]

As the ambiguity of the title raises the question of distorted communication, so the son it refers to shoulders the burden of the anxieties within the novel toward obstructed reception. Frail, unearthly, and, as Dickens put it in the number plans, "*born, to die*," Little Paul himself leads to the disruption of the Dombey legacy (835). The ironic distance between the title and the subject of the novel is echoed in the rift between Little Dombey's name and his identity. Even the diminutive is purposely misleading, for "Little Paul Dombey" is one of the most generously drawn characters in all of Dickens—an "old-fashioned" changeling and benign victim with a rich inner life and a ready likeness to the young David Copperfield.[21] In other words, he is not exactly his cold father in miniature:

> They were the strangest pair at such a time that ever firelight shone
> upon. Mr. Dombey so erect and solemn, gazing at the blaze; his little
> image, with an old, old, face, peering into the red perspective with the
> fixed and rapt attention of a sage. Mr. Dombey entertaining compli-
> cated worldly schemes and plans; the little image entertaining Heaven
> knows what wild fancies, half-formed thoughts, and wandering specu-
> lations. Mr. Dombey stiff with starch and arrogance; the little image by
> inheritance, and in unconscious imitation. The two so very much alike,
> and yet so monstrously contrasted. (93)

The son represents a contrast terrifying to his father because, among other things, he lacks the basic capitalist sense that comes from experience. Little Paul famously asks, "Papa! what's money?", then proposes to "give" away over £300 to help Solomon Gills out of debt rather than, as his father corrects him, "lend" it (93, 134). And Paul's piercing question "Why didn't money save me my Mama?" operates as evidence of his naivete but also as a critique, if not an outright rejection, of his father's materialistic creed (94). In moments such as these, Little Paul's very innocence works to derail the transmission of worldly values from father to son.

Rather than join Dombey in his cold free-market calculations, Paul chooses to indulge a particular aspect of his fancy, his aural imagination. In a novel that roars with the tumult of rail and sea, Paul is an engaged listener, a receptive medium for the sound waves that flow beyond the reach of Dombey's hearing. Throughout *Dombey*, in fact, Dickens muses on the problems and impossibilities of hearing as well as of understanding voices. This extends from Paul's inattention to his father at Blimber's Academy—"Do you hear, Paul?"—to Mrs. Chick's questioning of Paul's dying mother, "What was it you said Fanny? I didn't hear you"; to Mr. Polly Toodle's failure to comprehend Mr. Dombey's command: "I heerd it, but I don't know as I understood it rightly Sir, 'account of being no scholar, and the words being—ask your pardon—rayther high"; to Dombey's offices, "within hearing of Bow Bells, when their clashing voices were not drowned by the uproar in the streets"; to Carker's taunting contempt for his humiliated sibling, "Why should I hear you, Brother John?" (145, 10, 19, 36, 293).[22] Paul's insistent questioning—"The sea, Floy, what is it that it keeps on saying?"—serves as a constant, if abbreviated, struggle to interpret the natural force that attracts him and is implicitly juxtaposed with his father's emotional insensibility: "He would hear nothing but his pride" (111; 539). Scholars have debated whether the ocean in *Dombey* might represent the mystery of life, or a transcendent voice of both death and communal reconciliation, or a force for human feeling, or (as one critic has proposed) merely a gross sentimentalism.[23] Even when the novel first appeared, in a popular duet that capitalized on Paul's aural inclinations ("What Are the Wild Waves Saying?"), one Victorian songwriter attempted to interpret the obscure sounds, with predictably tedious results, as Paul and Florence together sing, "The voice of the great Creator / Dwells in that mighty tone!"[24] Yet the central point, it seems, is that despite what critics, or for that matter songwriters, would have readers think, the waves never precisely disclose or clarify themselves: they never *say* what they mean. Within the novel itself, whatever the waves are whispering remains for readers muffled, distorted: for Dombey, even lost in transmission.[25] Babbage had written, as Dickens reminds readers in *Dombey*, that the air constitutes a permanent record of "all that man has ever said or woman whispered." For Babbage, not only the air but also the ocean waves keep records of all that passes over them: "The track of every canoe, of every vessel which has yet disturbed the surface of the ocean . . . remains for ever registered in the future movement of all succeeding particles which may occupy its place. . . . the waters, and the more solid materials of the globe, bear equally enduring testimony of the acts we have committed" (37–38). In the context of these earnest scientific speculations, Little Paul's wonder at what the waves were always saying makes more sense. According to Babbage, they would have been able to say quite a lot, even if their sound remained indecipherable.[26] Dickens's incorporation of "speaking waves" as a central trope of his latest fiction demonstrated his ongoing engagement with a scientific culture that, in the 1840s, still retained an air of educated amateurism and populism. I return later to the way in which, for Dickens writing *Dombey*, Babbage's chapter and the "speaking waves" had a more profound, personal appeal. But for now, it is sufficient to say that along with Babbage's *Treatise*, *Dombey* demonstrates similar interest not only in the transmission of sound but also in the struggle to make sense of it, which would take hold of acousticians with new fervor in the 1850s.[27] It is not too much to claim that Paul's questioning of the sounds of waves anticipates in general terms the fascination with wave theories of acoustics that, as Gillian Beer has shown, permeated literary as well as scientific production in later nineteenth-century Britain, where the formative work of Hermann von Helmholtz in his monumental *Die Lehre von den Tonempfindungen* (*On the Sensations of Tone*, 1863), and John Tyndall's popularization of it in *Sound* (1867), had such impact that it went on to inform modernist writing, most notably that of Woolf in *The Waves*.[28]

Such a struggle to understand the waves is indeed what Little Paul attempts, and his brief life ultimately represents a junction for two opposing forms of transmission: he possesses the animating force of the artist, who imaginatively receives and attempts to convey the sensory details of sound and sight, yet he bears the crushing weight of the son, who is obliged to fulfill the Dombey mercantile birthright. At Dr. Blimber's Academy, Paul's hearing seizes on "the loud clock in the hall," whose ticks only reiterate the schoolmaster's question to the new student:

> and then he heard the loud clock in the hall still gravely inquiring "how, is, my, lit, tle, friend, how, is, my, lit, tle, friend," as it had done before.
> He sat, with folded hands, upon his pedestal, silently listening. But he might have answered "weary, weary! very lonely, very sad!" (149)

Forlorn and resigned, Paul's tentative response evokes Mariana's, who, abandoned by her lover, wished for death in Tennyson's poem, one of Dickens's favorites ("I am aweary, aweary, / I would that I were dead!"). Paul too feels abandoned, in a role his father has thrust upon him, and the somber questioning of the clock underscores the shadow of Time, that augury of death that has loomed over him since his birth. In a novel dominated by rail travel, time represents a new threat because it has come to regulate movement and life as never before. When the end finally does come for Paul in the chapter titled "What the Waves Were Always Saying," it occurs, significantly, not at school but while Paul is "home for the holidays," surrounded by his father, Susan Nipper, Walter, his former surrogate mothers Richards and Pipchin, and of course, Florence. Paul's death in the house is emblematic, finally, of the failure of virtually all parent-child relationships in *Dombey*, from the Toodles with the incorrigible Rob the Grinder, to "Good" Mrs. Brown with her brazen daughter Alice Marwood, and to Cleopatra Skewton and the defiant Edith Granger.

If Little Paul embodies the trope of failed reception in the novel, James Carker, who seeks to rival Paul for Dombey's financial legacy, embodies the figure of duplicitous communicator, or false transmitter. When, as manager of Dombey's firm, Carker makes his debut appearance in the novel shortly before Paul's death, his considerate question to Dombey about the son and presumed heir masks a characteristic trace of self-interested sarcasm: "'Any news of the young gentleman who is so important to us all?'" (172). Confident of his own power over his fawning, grinning assistant, Dombey readily grasps, even identifies with Carker's egotism but woefully underestimates his force: "'You respect nobody, Carker, I think,' said Mr. Dombey. 'No?' inquired Carker, with another wide and most feline show of his teeth. 'Well! Not many people I believe. I wouldn't answer perhaps . . . for more than one'" — that "one" Dombey takes to mean Dombey, but readers recognize Carker means himself (173). Carker is in one sense, as Julian Moynahan has written, a "dark analogy of Dombey himself," though it is important to remember that Dombey appears formidably dark quite on his own.[29] The Dombey-Carker dyad has been passed over by readers who claim Dombey's estranged relationship with Florence as one of the many debts in the novel to *King Lear*. Yet in her *Shakespeare and Dickens* Valerie Gager demonstrates that such arguments are "insupportable" because they lack evidence of quotations and allusions and allege unremarkable plot parallels.[30] Rather, if critics insist on finding Shakespearean parallels with *Dombey*, then it should be granted that at least one of the other tragedies appears to have influenced the relationship Dombey shares with his manager. In his stagy Machiavellian plotting, Carker is more like an Iago to Dombey's proud Othello, the subordinate using the hero's unwitting trust to bring about his ultimate downfall.[31]

At Dombey's command, Carker becomes his "trusty agent," the emissary to the proud hero's estranged wife Edith, a decision around which the climax of the novel turns. The manager's question to his master at this point is slyly suggestive: "'Mrs. Dombey is aware of the probability of your making me the organ of your displeasure?'" (574). Carker's phallic pun on "organ" plays up his duplicity: he will communicate Dombey's "displeasure" to Edith even as he, a type of male sexuality unleashed, lustily pursues her in her husband's absence.[32] One look from Edith reveals to her the hypocrisy that Carker barely suppresses, the very hypocrisy that covers up his earlier seduction and ruin of Alice Marwood: "She raised her eyes no higher than his mouth, but she saw the means of mischief vaunted in every tooth it contained" (505). Dombey notes that "Carker plays at all games . . . and plays them well," but Carker's skill with cards and chess, with letters and ledger-books, with knowing glances and penetrating stares — what one scholar calls his "hyperliteracy" — is not enough to entrap Edith, who finally trumps the dealer at his own game (367).[33] The celebrated scene of his undoing, which no less a critic than Edmund Wilson, put off by its theatricality, labeled "one of the worst in Dickens,"[34] is on the contrary surprisingly effective, an energetic repulse by Edith of both the scheming messenger and the dubious correspondence he bears:

Her flashing eyes, uplifted for a moment, lighted again on Carker, and she held some letters out, in her left hand.

"See these!" she said, contemptuously. "You have addressed these to me in the false name you go by; one here, some elsewhere on my road. The seals are unbroken. Take them back!"

She crunched them in her hand, and tossed them to his feet. (728)

By neither retaining nor even reading the manager's false letters, Edith thwarts his attempts at deceitful communication. As she crushes Carker's missives, she reduces him to little more than a twisted snake "muttering and menacing, and scowling round as if for something that would help him to conquer her" (728). The indomitable Edith gets the last word: "I single out in you the meanest man I know, the parasite and tool of the proud tyrant, that his wound may go the deeper, and may rankle more" (729). With Dombey on his heels, the once-trusted emissary flees in desperation. Carker's corrupt communiqués, sycophantic agency, and botched adultery are revealed as nothing more than the abuses of a false go-between.

As Edith dramatically discards Carker's love letters unread, so the transmission of the written word in *Dombey* remains tenuous, secretive, and often highly charged, a situation reflected in Dickens's life as he worked on the novel. "I am working very slowly," he wrote to Forster in January 1847, "You will see in the first two or three lines of the enclosed subject with what idea I am ploughing along. It is difficult, but a new way of doing it, it strikes me, and likely to be pretty." His letters suggest a perpetual mix of excitement and exhaustion over writing: "I have taken the most prodigious pains with it; the difficulty, immediately following Paul's death, being very great. May you like it! My head aches over it now (I write at one o'clock in the morning), and I am strange to it." Meanwhile, his "occupation" of writing trapped him in his study, which he referred to as "My Cell": "I am always a prisoner, more or less, at this time of the month." Panicking, he told Forster, "I am horrified to find that the first chapter makes *at least* two pages less than I had supposed, and I have a terrible apprehension that there will not be copy enough for the number!" "I write in the grip of Dombey," he began one letter, and ended another, "at present, just recovered from convulsions of Dombey, after which I can never write legibly." To George Henry Lewes, he admitted, "between my Dombey and my managerial responsibilities, I am invisible and lost in abysses of work." His confessions to Forster capture the sense of highly charged anxiety he confronted daily when he turned to and from writing: "I am so floored: wanting sleep, and never having had my head free from it [*The Battle of Life*] this month past," he wrote in October 1846, and in April of the next year, he ended a letter, "Deepest of despondency (as usual in commencing Nos.)."[35]

Consumed himself by the struggle to work through new methods and means of composing the novel, Dickens emphasized how his fictional characters falter or collapse at various stages of reading and writing. There is Cleopatra Skewton, whose unintended howlers on sympathy, nature, and "impulsive throbbings" serve as skewed, ironic misreadings of Wordsworth. At the other end of the spectrum, there is Toots, whose distinction as head boy at Blimber's earns him the right to spend his time pointlessly writing "long letters to himself from persons of distinction, addressed 'P. Toots, Esquire, Brighton, Sussex'" and carefully preserving them in his desk (152). In Toots's aborted acrostic to Florence, he gets only as far as "For when I gaze," at which point "the flow of imagination in which he had previously written down the initial letters of the other seven lines, desert[ed] him" (306). In his clownish romance and writerly awkwardness, Toots anticipates the likes of John Chivery, who will busy himself composing and revising tombstone epitaphs in his head in response to Little Dorrit. Skewton and Toots are, however, the comic extremes. For Dombey, who tears his dead wife's letter into "fragments" and "put[s] them in his pocket, as if unwilling to trust them even to the chances of being re-united and deciphered," reading is associated with suppression, and writing with denial: his inscription on Paul's tomb marker originally reads "beloved and only child," as if to deny that Florence exists (49, 237).

Between the writing that is never received—Sol Gills's letters to Captain Cuttle—and the writing that is received all too well—Edith's damning separation note to Dombey ("He read that she was gone. He read that he was dishonoured. He read that she had fled" [636])—the question arises if any good at all can come from literacy in this novel. Not, it would seem, from the newspaper, which misreports that "every soul on board [the Son and Heir] perished" and sends Cuttle into mourning for the still very much alive Walter (447). And not for the unregenerate Rob the Grinder, who though "required to read out of some book to the Captain, for one hour every evening," is nevertheless destined to "lose his place" (as the heading to chapter 55, "Rob the Grinder Loses His Place," indicates) in both the book and the world when his master Carker dies (522). As if to emblematize the act of struggling literacy, the vignette on the title page of the first edition shows neither Dombey, nor Son, but Cuttle, eyes shut in concentration, listening as Rob haltingly reads aloud from a large volume, his finger pointing to the words (figure 1.1). In an added twist, the very literacy Rob has acquired at Dombey's bidding serves only to betray Carker's and Edith's rendezvous, in the stagy scene when Rob chalks "D.I.J.O.N." on Mrs. Brown's table as Dombey spies on him from behind a door.[36] There is also Edith's guilty acknowledgment of the church's golden letters of the Ten Commandments on her wedding day, as she realizes she has dishonored her mother: "which is it that appears to leave the wall, and print itself, in glowing letters, on her book!" (427). (Since Edith also appears to be destined for an adulterous affair with Carker, the scene seems more than slightly prophetic of *The Scarlet Letter*, published two years later.) And in a final case of important writing that goes unread, there is Edith's written confession to Dombey after they have separated, which she gives to Florence for her father. An interesting question to consider is why Dickens does not show Florence handing this note over to Dombey, or Dombey ever reading it. Whether Dickens is dependent

FIGURE 1.1. READING ALOUD: THE VIGNETTE TITLE-PAGE TO THE FIRST
EDITION OF *Dombey and Son* (1848), BY H. K. BROWNE ("PHIZ"), WHO
MISTAKENLY PUT CAPTAIN CUTTLE'S HOOK ON THE WRONG ARM. BY
PERMISSION OF THE HOUGHTON LIBRARY, HARVARD UNIVERSITY.

on readers to assume the letter arrives, or whether he is suggesting that Florence, by *not* giving it to him as the ending seems to indicate, is trying to withhold any upsetting reminder of Edith's existence, there is a certain appropriateness in Dickens's leaving Edith, through her writing, beyond Dombey's grasp, as she had been all along.

In *Dombey*, then, Dickens remains ambivalent, even pessimistic, about the transmission of the written word between characters. More renowned is his ambivalence toward another character in the novel, though technically it is not a character at all. Written during the "railway boom" of the 1840s, *Dombey* revels in the arrival of the train "with a shriek, and a roar, and a rattle" (276). Though the railway only features four times in the novel, these appearances have the cumulative effect of making the engines dominate the soundscape, with their tracks joining disparate sections of the narrative, much as they were made to connect London to distant parts of the English countryside. Critical attention to *Dombey* has typically centered upon these scenes, and many readers have debated whether the train symbolizes a destructive, ruthless force of change or a sign of welcome progress.[37] But it is more relevant to my argument here, and better reflects the limited space the railway takes up relative to the rest of *Dombey*, to consider the images of the railway as part of Dickens's greater concern, both throughout the novel and as he worked upon it, with finding an effective, satisfying means of verbal expression, of being heard, of *getting through*.

In certain respects, the train represents an expressive ideal. Its furious speed, sound, and power allow for an immediacy and dynamism that Dickens the author longs to possess in language. Dickens's language as he writes about the train acquires just such a tone as it rises to meet the challenge of its subject. Here he is, exuberantly, in "A Flight":

> Bang! We have let another Station off, and fly away regardless. Everything is flying. The hop-gardens turn gracefully towards me, presenting regular avenues of hops in rapid flight, then whirl away. So do the pools and rushes, haystacks, sheep, clover in full bloom delicious to the sight and smell, corn-sheaves, cherry-orchards, apple-orchards, reapers, gleaners, hedges, gates, fields that taper off into little angular corners, cottages, gardens, now and then a church. Bang, bang! A double-barrelled Station! Now a wood, now a bridge, now a landscape, now a cutting, now a—Bang! a single-barrelled Station—there was a cricket match somewhere with two white tents, and then four flying cows, then turnips—now, the wires of the electric telegraph are all alive, and spin, and blurr their edges, and go up and down, and make their intervals between each other most irregular: contracting and expanding in the strangest manner. Now we slacken. With a screwing, and a grinding, and a smell of water thrown on ashes, now we stop![38]

As Humphry House once lamented, "It is painful to stop quoting," and one can understand why.[39] With its breathlessness and its dizzying catalogue of noises, sights, and smells, this style of writing comes close to representing a pure rush of speed. Even with a brief mention, the Wheatstonian electric telegraph, the mechanical transmitter of coded communication, seems to jump to life in a pulsing twitch. Sheer verbal expression, the outward projection of subjective responses, does not often occur more dynamically in Dickens than in this marvel of a description of an express train ride.

But it is precisely this expressive power that makes the railway such a source of ambiguity in *Dombey*, for both the train and the language Dickens uses to describe it threaten to overrun the novel, much as they have the criticism about it. In an informative appraisal of this aspect of *Dombey*, Murray Baumgarten shows how the novel "articulates the transition from the stage-coach world to the railway civilization," and the transformation that Staggs's Gardens undergoes in two key railway scenes in *Dombey* succinctly demonstrates his point.[40] I am inclined, however, toward a more balanced view than other readers, who consider what happens to Staggs's Gardens "a change for the worse, to be seen as the death of something, not a birth."[41] In fact, it is both a death and a birth, though I am not sure Dickens either mourns the former or celebrates the latter. Rather, what really seems to matter in these scenes is the unique impact of their particular combination of image and text, that is, the close parallel Dickens sees and articulates between the forces of the railway and those of his rhetoric, or to put it another way, between the power of the express and that of his expression.[42]

The parallels that I am arguing for, between reading and writing *Dombey* on the one hand, and riding the rails on the other, had their basis in a fundamental change in the behavior of Victorian readerships as a result of railway development. As Wolfgang Schivelbusch points out, with the advent of trains, "Reading while traveling became almost obligatory."[43] In fact, the railway boom of the 1840s was accompanied by the rapid expansion of railway bookstalls, with the first one opening in 1841 at Fenchurch Street Station, followed by several others in the next few years. In 1848, the year *Dombey* was published in book form, the railway bookstall business offered such promise that W. H. Smith purchased exclusive rights to sell books to passengers along over one thousand miles of track; by 1851, he had 35 bookstalls in stations, by 1880, 450, and by 1902, 777.[44] It was not only that the spread of the railway at the time *Dombey* was published allowed more of Dickens's rural audience to acquire firsthand knowledge of the metropolis as they journeyed to and from it.[45] It was also that they were very likely, due to the commercial prospecting of Smith and others, acquiring this knowledge while riding *in the train itself*, as they read installments of *Dombey* and any other inexpensive London publications that they could find.

Not only were railway bookstalls on the rise as *Dombey* emerged from Dickens's pen, but cheap literature published exclusively for British train travelers also had begun to appear. In 1846 and 1847, the firm of Simms and McIntyre published one-volume, 2s. novels in their "Parlour Novelist" series, followed by novels in the "Parlour Library" series selling for the unprecedented low price of 1s. each. "The success of this daring venture was immediate and overwhelming," Richard Altick writes; within two years, Routledge had introduced their shilling-novel "Railway Library," followed by Bentley's railway series two years later, and Smith's own not long after that, alongside his own innovation, a circulating railway library that would fuel the mass demand for so-called yellowbacks starting in the 1850s.[46] Dickens had, in a sense, been a pioneer of cheap reprints for travelers; he was from early on associated with the Tauchnitz "Collection of British Authors," published beginning in 1841 for circulation exclusively on the Continent and banned from importation into England (*Pickwick* had been the second volume in the series); and he began reprinting, in 1847, his own works in his carefully considered Cheap Edition, a curious phenomenon to which I shortly will return.[47] But the advent of the railway bookstall and the inexpensive literary wares sold there was something wholly unprecedented and explosive in Britain, a development that would alter the way books were published, marketed, and read. It soon would become clear that the railway bookstalls had helped bring about "the decline and fall of the empire of expensive Fiction."[48] In the wake of these changes, even the typically skeptical *Punch* concluded that the North Western Railway "promises, if the plan succeeds, to become one of the greatest engines of literature," and that a train seemed "decidedly the best vehicle going for circulating a library."[49] Under these new pressures, the opportunities for Dickens were remarkable, but so too were the responsibilities great, particularly when there were those who blamed him for the initially salacious and crude quality of most railway reading: "Much of the mischief caused by this species of literature, we fear, may be traced to the influence on the public mind of the great writers of the day, and among the number, Mr. Charles Dickens," whose works, the journalist went on to say, "have not been without a certain amount of evil."[50]

Within this context it becomes clearer that *Dombey* was not only a novel about the railway, but also one in all likelihood read in its parts, *on* the railway. In writing *of* the train, Dickens would have been understandably concerned that he now was also, perhaps not wholly willingly, writing *for* the train, specifically, for rail-riders wanting to fill the time, perhaps during their commute into or trip out of the city. Not only did he have to keep in mind the probability of writing for the train traveler, but what was more important, he was also facing the imminent prospect of having to write *against* the competition of new hoards of cheap literature, entire popular novels selling for the same price as just one of his part numbers. These, then, are the principal anxieties that underlie the sounds of *Dombey*: the uneasy sensation that the roar of authorial expression might not be heard above the shriek of the express train but could be consumed within it; that the voice of the Inimitable's fiction might be drowned out by the cries of heaps of cheaper imitators' works; that the train, even as it created a massive new market for cheap reading matter, could, in effect, contain and drive the novel rather than the other way round.

Is it any surprise, then, that the railway winds through *Dombey* with such foreboding? The train in *Dombey* is pure force, embodying the noisy thrust of the novel, propelling the characters as well as the plot. In the first appearance the railway makes in the novel, it hits like the "shock of a great earthquake" (65). This famous section on the fragmentation that construction brings focuses upon "the hundred thousand shapes and substances of incompleteness, wildly mingled out of their places, upside down, burrowing in the earth, aspiring in the air, mouldering in the water, and unintelligible as any dream," like a surreal vision of "dire disorder," a chaotic spectacle worthy of Hieronymus Bosch (65). While this scene leaves readers somewhat taken aback, the residents of Staggs's Gardens have been left altogether behind, "uncommonly incredulous" (66). And of the impact of the railway on businesses at this point, there are only the most tentative signs—exactly three of them, placards advertising "The Railway Arms," "Excavators' House of Call," and "Railway Eating House." While the train ultimately will change the way business, including the book trade, is carried out, Dickens is particularly sensitive to the way such changes occur first at the level of language, quite literally, on the signs themselves, storefront signifiers that help initiate a new signified: the railway commerce that will have as central components railway bookstalls and "Railway Libraries." Entering *Dombey* with rhetorical force, then, the train similarly leaves hints that it will soon dominate the scene.

By the next appearance of the neighborhood in the novel, the engines have taken over. The inhabitants, consumed with all aspects of railway culture and marketing, are at the mercy of the train: "There was no such place as Staggs's Gardens. It had vanished from the earth" (217). The new order of engines swallows up the old order of hackney-coaches. Having done so, they rest like so many sleeping monsters:

> Night and day the conquering engines rumbled at their distant work, or, advancing smoothly to their journey's end, and gliding like tame dragons into the allotted corners grooved out to the inch for their reception, stood bubbling and trembling there, making the walls quake, as if they were dilating with the secret knowledge of great powers yet unsuspected in them, and strong purposes not yet achieved. (218–19)

Like these young engines pulsing with secrets and withholding their purposes, the novel is still new, the plot and conception shrouded in secrecy— "the very name getting out, would be ruinous." It is tempting here to draw the parallel between the dilations of the railway cars and the voice of the author, as powerful, unpredictable forces, with something to prove to both their riders and readers. In their very ambiguity, the dormant trains serve as an important symbol of the watershed novel, not yet a third over, but about to take a dramatic turn. As Staggs's Gardens has fallen to the railway world, so Dickens is about to tear down his bildungsroman with the death of Paul and, shifting gears to Dombey and daughter, lay the tracks for a quite different and unexpected exposition in its place.

When, "louder and louder yet," the train bursts forth upon the landscape in the chapters to come, Dickens's ensuing descriptions of the rails very nearly leap from the page, as the novel's most vividly expressive, and most often quoted, lines (276). But even here, expression—the power of the train as conveyed in the writing—brings a mingled measure of good and bad, a jolt of speed tinged by the specter of death. Although some critics have taken the scene of Dombey's train ride to Leamington as an explicit gauge of Dickens's attitudes toward the railway, it is important to clarify that from the outset, the scene is internalized as Dombey's heavily colored perspective on his own experience; thus, the train's force, so celebrated by Dickens in "A Flight," is twisted by Dombey into a vehicle for his own angst.[51] As Dombey rides the train in the wake of Paul's demise, "he carrie[s] monotony with him, through the rushing landscape, and hurrie[s] headlong, not through a rich and varied country, but a wilderness of blighted plans and gnawing jealousies" (275). Dombey's hopeless focus on Paul's death leads to a somber inversion of Wordsworth's joyous celebration of "all the mighty world / Of eye, and ear,—both what they half create, / And half perceive" ("Tintern Abbey," ll. 105–6). While the young poet had found his joy reflected all around him in the landscape near Tintern, Dombey rather "found a likeness to his misfortune everywhere" (277). The railway, precisely in its ability to carry him away, becomes another reminder of his failures to listen, respond, and fulfill his perceived patriarchal obligations to transmit his legacy through a son, failures that transform the ride forward into an apparent regression: "Away, with a shriek, and a roar, and a rattle, plunging down into the earth again, and working on in such a storm of energy and perseverance, that amidst the darkness and whirlwind the motion seems reversed, and to tend furiously backwards, until a ray of light upon the wet wall shows its surface flying past like a fierce stream" (276). The journey through the countryside elicits a crisis that culminates in a vision of Florence, whose reviled image only adds to Dombey's despair: "Her patience, goodness, youth, devotion, love, were as so many atoms in the ashes upon which he set his heel. He saw her image in the blight and blackening all around him, not irradiating but deepening the gloom" (278). Even as, with such linguistic force, the railway ride conveys Dombey out toward Leamington, it paradoxically provides a means for him to articulate his own egotism, regress further inside himself, and deny interpersonal expression.

To clarify that this is Dombey's subjective experience of the railway, as opposed to Dickens's objective depiction of the menace of it, I want to turn to a description of an express train ride from "The Lazy Tour of Two Idle Apprentices" (1857), the travelogue Dickens co-wrote with Wilkie Collins while taking a hiatus from his wife, Catherine, and attempting a rendezvous with his mistress, Ellen Ternan. The passage is astonishing, not least in the way it is by degrees repulsive and revealing:

Now, the engine shrieked in hysterics of such intensity, that it seemed desirable that the men who had her in charge should hold her feet, slap her hands, and bring her to; now, burrowed into tunnels with a stubborn and undemonstrative energy so confusing that the train seemed to be flying back into leagues of darkness. Here, were station after station, swallowed up by the express without stopping; here, stations where it fired itself in like a volley of cannon-balls, swooped away four country-people with nosegays, and three men of business with portmanteaus, and fired itself off again, bang, bang, bang!

In one of Dickens's uglier metaphors, the express is feminized as a violent hysteric with a voluminous appetite. One does not need to know the biographical details to recognize the misogyny that taints the more benign depiction from "A Flight" six years earlier. But as the narrator peers outside the window, his perspective shifts:

The pastoral country darkened, became coaly, became smoky, became infernal, got better, got worse, improved again, grew rugged, turned romantic; was a wood, a stream, a chain of hills, a gorge, a moor, a cathedral town, a fortified place, a waste. Now, miserable black dwellings, a black canal, and sick black towers of chimneys; now, a trim garden, where the flowers were bright and fair; now, a wilderness of hideous altars all ablaze; now, the water meadows with their fairy rings; now, the mangy patch of unlet building ground outside the stagnant town, with the larger ring where the Circus was last week.[52]

I quote at such length to show the way Dickens is driven to describe the panorama outside the train window in phrases that bear a striking similarity to the kind of shorthand one might supply not only for certain of his novels—the "pastoral country" of *Pickwick Papers* (1836–1837), the coaly, smoky inferno of *Oliver Twist* (1837–1838), the "moor" and "water meadows" of *David Copperfield* (1849–1850) and *Great Expectations* (1860–1861), the blackened landscape of *Bleak House* (1852–1853), the circus of *Hard Times* (1854), the "fortified place" that is the Marshalsea prison of *Little Dorrit* (1855–1857) and, in the book he would write soon after "The Lazy Tour," the Bastille of *A Tale of Two Cities* (1859), and, as if to foreshadow the books that were still years away, the "waste" of *Our Mutual Friend* (1864–1865), and the "cathedral town" of his childhood Rochester transformed into the Cloisterham of *Edwin Drood* (1870)—that is, not only for these novels but also for his personal life to this point: "got better, got worse, improved again, grew rugged, turned romantic." The express train ride elicits in him, not unlike the way it does for Dombey, an all but conscious recognition of the connection between his professional and private life and the engine, speed, roar, and progress (or regress) of the trip itself.

In the final appearance of the train in *Dombey*, the remarkable scene of Carker's death on the rails, the locomotive, the novel's dynamic express, brings retribution but at the same time corporeal and rhetorical fragmentation. Carker's flight through France echoes Dombey's somber train ride in its monotonous merging of mental states with the landscape: "The clatter and commotion echoed to the hurry and discordance of the fugitive's ideas" (735). Unlike Dombey's ride, however, the classic chase sends Carker like lightning through a capsule history of Dickens's featured forms of transport from *Pickwick* to *Chuzzlewit* to *Dombey*, from an old horse-drawn carriage across France, to a boat trip over the Channel, to a railway ride ending at a remote English junction, as if to suggest that the ensuing finale represents a pivotal movement for both train and career. And indeed it does. There is in each a ferocious determination that destroys even as it articulates, as Carker's violent end demonstrates:

> He heard a shout—another—saw the face change from its vindictive passion to a faint sickness and terror—felt the earth tremble—knew in a moment that the rush was come—uttered a shriek—looked round— saw the red eyes, bleared and dim, in the daylight, close upon him— was beaten down, caught up, and whirled away upon a jagged mill, that spun him round and round, and struck him limb from limb, and licked his stream of life up with its fiery heat, and cast his mutilated fragments in the air. (743)

This brutal passage unites action and diction. At the same time that the train tears Carker's body to shreds, Dickens shatters his prose, splicing a sentence into telegraphic phrases held together by dashes and commas, like so many tendons and ligaments of syntax.[53] The express train that once possessed the secret of the plot twists of the novel now fuels Dickens's expression as an unstoppable force to bring forth this denouement. The authorial voice and the train act in tandem: as the station man says to Carker, "Express comes through at four, Sir.—Don't stop" (742).[54]

After Carker's death by what Marcus refers to as "ritual dismemberment," Dickens uses the rest of *Dombey* to pick up the pieces.[55] The final act of the novel brings together not only Florence and Walter but also Mr. Morfin and Harriet Carker, Mr. Feeder and Cornelia Blimber, Toots and Susan Nipper, and Jack Bunsby and Mrs. Mac Stinger, for a total of five marriages in seven chapters. Such couplings are more than just a means to tie up loose ends, for through them Dickens seeks to counteract Carker's violent fragmentation, itself conveyed with such jolting language. The unusually high rate of marriages promises continuity in the face of disintegration and disruption. Of equal importance, it ensures, through the legacy of children, multiple opportunities for communal survival and transmission. With such marital abundance, closure would seem at last forthcoming in this darkly comic novel. Yet at least two crucial strands remain unresolved: Dombey's tyrannical relationship with Florence, and the status of estranged, outspoken Edith. It is through them that Dickens develops his lasting word in *Dombey* on the difficulties of expression and possibilities for satisfying reception.

FOREVER AND FOREVER THROUGH SPACE

KEEPING these considerations in mind, I want to turn to one aspect of the initial publication of the text that seems particularly relevant, despite the critical tendency to interpret this development as distinct and independent from the structure and workings of the novel. The sixth number of *Dombey* included a prospectus written entirely by Dickens, in which he announced, in a five-paragraph "Address," the imminent appearance of a "proposed Re-issue, unprecedented, it is believed, in the history of Cheap Literature."[56] This was, of course, the Cheap Edition, the first sequential, authorized republication of Dickens's early works, at the time a daring publishing move for a living novelist to make. Referring to the prospectus, he wrote to Emile De la Rue in 1847: "Have you seen anything of the enclosed? I believe it is the greatest venture—indeed, I have no doubt of it—ever made in books."[57] The initial series of the Cheap Edition began in 1847 with *Pickwick* and continued through the Christmas stories into 1852, by which time, after a slow start, it was turning the substantial profits that Dickens originally had expected of it. The "Address" that introduced it is a manifesto that reveals an author subtly in conflict with himself, trying at once to distance himself from his earlier books and to embrace them:

> It is not for an author to describe his own books. If they cannot speak for themselves, he is likely to do little service by speaking for them. It is enough to observe of these, that eleven years have strengthened in their writer's mind every purpose and sympathy he has endeavoured to express in them; and that their re-production in a shape which shall render them easily accessible as a possession by all classes of society, is at least consistent with the spirit in which they have been written, and is the fulfilment of a desire long entertained.

Dickens tells his audience that he resists venturing expression about his previous works, for they must "speak for themselves," and this they can do best only once they have undergone a long-desired "re-production" in a new form. The old editions, he writes, "continue to circulate at five times the proposed price," which he claims justifies "the belief that the living Author may enjoy the pride and honour of their widest diffusion" in a cheaper version.

In the prospectus Dickens promises that the Cheap Edition will be "carefully revised and corrected throughout," and he would go on to incorporate revisions and new prefaces, as well as new frontispiece illustrations by his familiar artists, into each novel in the series. Dickens is at special pains in the "Address" to emphasize the distinctiveness of the Cheap versions:

> The CHEAP EDITION will in no way clash or interfere with that already existing. The existing edition will always contain the original illustrations, which, it is hardly necessary to add, will constitute no part of the CHEAP EDITION; and its form is perfectly distinct and differ-

ent. Neither will any of the more recent writings of the Author; those now in progress of publication, or yet to come; appear in the CHEAP EDITION, until after the lapse of A VERY CONSIDERABLE PERIOD, and when their circulation in the original form shall, by degrees, and in the course of years, have placed them on a level with their predecessors.

The capitals highlight the publishing innovation Dickens was anxiously banking on: that texts that once were old, could become new again—yet retain some essence of their former identities as literary milestones and productions of the Inimitable. As Dickens puts it at the close of the "Address":

> To become, in his new guise, a permanent inmate of many English homes, where, in his old shape, he was only known as a guest, or hardly known at all: to be well thumbed and soiled in a plain suit that will bear a great deal, by children and grown people, at the fireside and on the journey: to be hoarded on the humble shelf where there are few books, and to lie about in libraries like any familiar piece of household stuff that is easy of replacement: and to see and feel this—not to die first, or grow old and passionless: must obviously be among the hopes of a living author, venturing on such an enterprise. Without such hopes it never could be set on foot. I have no fear of being mistaken in acknowledging that they are mine; that they are built, in simple earnestness and grateful faith, on my experience, past and present, of the cheering-on of very many thousands of my countrymen and countrywomen, never more numerous or true to me than now;—and that hence this CHEAP EDITION is projected.

In the midst of the railway boom, Dickens promises to release a traveler's library of his own works, parts and volumes specifically intended to fill the time spent by the lower middle classes in front of the fire and "on the journey," one now taken, no doubt, by rail.[58] The Cheap Edition is part of Dickens's ongoing attempt, furthered by his founding of *Household Words* in 1850, to identify his project as central to English middle-class domestic life, to reshape his works into, as he puts it, "any familiar piece of household stuff."[59] It is the closeness and intimacy of having his works coveted by readers at home or on the train that Dickens values and craves, and that will allow his voice to reach a newly enlarged audience across a wider class spectrum: in fact, his (unused) dedication of the Cheap Edition is to "the English People," and his initial preferred title for his journal will be "The Household Voice."[60] Yet underneath this monumentally public of addresses lies a paradox. Dickens wishes to refashion old shapes into beloved new guises, to resurrect the past as the lucrative present, in short, to make the Cheap, dear.[61]

It is perhaps then not a coincidence that this notice first appeared in part 6 of *Dombey*, the one immediately following Paul's death, when, as Dickens stated in his number plan, the "Great point of the No [was] to throw the interest of Paul, *at once on Florence*." This number is the critical moment at which Dickens revises the focus of his novel, from *Dombey and Son* to "Dombey and Daughter." The child who had been devalued since the opening of the story, and "was merely a piece of base coin' that couldn't be invested—a bad Boy—nothing more," now must fill the vacuum left by her dead brother and perpetuate the Dombey legacy (3). Much as the Cheap Edition did of its readers, Florence's final return and appreciation require "a lapse of A VERY CONSIDERABLE PERIOD" from her last appearance: "He [Dombey] did not know how much she loved him. However long the time in coming, and however slow the interval, she must try to bring that knowledge to her father's heart one day or other" (337). When the day at last arrives, Dombey's house has come down, "his riches [have] melted away," and he sees "her true self" through the mists of his imaginings. Penniless and despairing, Dombey now grasps the value of submissive love, as many critics have claimed, and falls weeping into Florence's embrace. His afflictions "have taught him that his daughter is very dear to him" (827). The prospectus that appeared after Little Dombey's death promised that Dickens's imminent Cheap Edition would "become a permanent inmate of many English homes, where . . . he was [once] hardly known at all." Similarly, Dickens's post-Paul narrative in *Dombey* enables Florence to fulfill the prophecy of valued "permanency" from that of the once forgotten older child (27). It is thus possible to turn the often repeated claim that with the death of Paul, Dickens effectively buries the earlier childish spontaneity of "Boz" quite on its head and, rather than see in Paul's death a severe break with the past, to see in Florence's endurance and triumph the hopeful possibility for continuity with the textual life that has come before.

Of course, I do not mean to argue that there exists a simple one-to-one correspondence between Dombey's children and Dickens's editions. But I do want to suggest that the analogy between the Cheap Edition and developments in *Dombey* broadens when considering the role of revision in each. For both the reprints and the novel, revision gives the lowly substance and bestows value upon the cheap. The importance of revision in the Cheap Edition was crucial for the success of it: the additions, changes, and illustrations gave the edition freshness and novelty. Within *Dombey*, meanwhile, Dickens revises the conception of his characters to shape Edith from a potential adulteress into perhaps the most compelling example in the novel of the figure cheapened by others who nonetheless knows and acts upon her real worth: "You know he has bought me . . . Or that he will to-morrow," she says of Dombey, "He has considered of his bargain; he has shown it to his friend; he is even rather proud of it; he thinks that it will suit him, and *may be had sufficiently cheap*; and he will buy to-morrow. God, that I have lived for this, and that I feel it!" (381, emphasis added). Edith's revisionary status is of a piece with the ways in which the novel "channels its critique of capitalism through the commercialization of the female body."[62] Dombey perceives Edith, as he does Florence, as a commodity, an inexpensive item he can choose to hoard or ignore. In Edith's case, his error costs him dearly. Her flight to Dijon would have tarnished her image had it come off the way Dickens originally planned, but revisions of plot and character allowed her to remain independent and cutting in the face of Carker and the prospect of permanent exile: "'I am a woman,' she said, confronting him steadfastly, 'who, from her very childhood, has been shamed and steeled. I have been offered and rejected, put up and appraised, until my very soul has sickened. . . . I suffered myself to be sold, as infamously as any woman with a halter round her neck is sold in any market-place. . . . Do you think . . . that I am to be stayed?'" (724, 729). The once-planned affair gives way to a woman's declaration of defiance, a scene of which Dickens provides many in later works, but perhaps none as powerful or satisfying as this.[63]

The often frustrated dynamics of expression that fill the novel and that have been examined in this chapter—the obstructed reception of sounds, language, and legacies—are encompassed by the greater motion the novel makes. The end of *Dombey* initiates the cycle the Cheap Edition perpetuated, of repeated transmissions through reproduction. In the final chapter the previously degraded, now dear daughter re-creates the novel's initial premise with subtle variations. Florence becomes more than Dombey's beloved bedside companion, who nurses him back to health from thoughts of suicide. Dickens's number-plan indicates that Florence brings Dombey a grandchild "*as if it were another Paul*, acting on his better nature" (emphasis added). More than that, she bears him two grandchildren propitiously named Paul and Florence and permits him in effect to relive the narrative a changed man.[64] Like Scrooge before him, Dombey awakens to revise his life, to seize another chance at communal generosity after nearly ruining himself in the pursuit of wealth. The closing sentence echoes a similar moment in the opening chapter, but now the focus is on the living granddaughter, not the dead mother: as Doctor Peps had "gently brushed the scattered ringlets of the child, aside from the face and mouth of the mother" as she "drifted out upon the dark and unknown sea that rolls round all the world," now Dombey walks by the sea with his granddaughter and "smooths away the curls that shade her earnest eyes" (10–11, 833). As it began with the final vision of the first Mrs. Dombey, so the book ends gazing on the youthful eyes of the second Florence. The narrator hints about the novel's cyclical structure in a passage that occurs midway through but importantly bears on its close: "In this round world of many circles within circles, do we make a weary journey from the high grade to the low, to find at last that they lie close together, that the two extremes touch, and that our journey's end is but our starting-place?" (477). Riders on the round-trip journey of rail travel found in *Dombey* a circular journey of Dickensian narrative. The work that muses for so long on the problem of transmission ultimately doubles back, repeats with a difference, like the trains that mysteriously roll in and out of Staggs's Gardens, and the waves that Little Paul struggles to decipher on the shore.

Dombey embraces a comic closure premised upon a recycling that prophesies reproduction not only of children but also of narrative, Dombey's narrative, as revised tale and text. This is at one with, although more than merely a novelistic manifestation of, the "massive return of the past" Marcus claims dominates this period of Dickens's life.[65] In reenvisioning itself, the novel attempts to integrate the past with the present, or put another way, moves forward by going backward. This arc not only parallels what Dickens himself initiated with respect to the three reprint series he oversaw, the systematic appearance of the Cheap, Library (1859), and Charles Dickens (1867) Editions of his works. Such circular motion also persists in Dickens's writings, most immediately and notably in *David Copperfield*, where he goes on to forge the ore of his remotest memories into the lore of a fictional present. So too does it underlie the activity that occupied much of Dickens's time over the last dozen years of his life, the public reading tours in which he performed, not selections from his later novels, but nearly exclusively those from his early works through *Copperfield*, tours that would send him around England on express trains and back once again to the United States.

It would make sense, then, that the idea for these readings appeared to have struck Dickens as he worked on *Dombey*. In October 1846, as he was writing the second number of *Dombey*, Dickens wrote to Forster: "I was thinking the other day that in these days of lecturings and readings, a great deal of money might possibly be made (if it were not infra dig) by one's having Readings of one's own books. It would be an *odd* thing. I think it would take immensely."[66] The desire of Dickens, "the most vigorous of voice-projectors," to broadcast loudly and widely his authorial voice was never greater than when he composed this novel, the most "ear-orientated" of his works.[67] Years later, when he first turned to his novels to create a public reading, is it any wonder he selected *Dombey*, or that he extracted "The Story of Little Dombey" from its first quarter? For his recurrent dramatic readings he sought out the work that rereads itself; he voiced and revoiced the prelude that is reclaimed by its coda.[68] Viewed anew, the title-page vignette of the novel is emblematic not only of the struggle for literacy, but also of close listening to a public reading (figure 1.1). *Dombey and Son* thus points ahead to the perpetual transmission and revision of his canon in print and performance. But such frequent repetition does not necessarily promise clear reception. Like the conquering engines roaring and trembling with their mystery, or the waves always indistinctly saying, the novel hints at meaning but keeps secrets, challenging readers to track the enigmatic persistence of its evolving reproduction.

Consider, finally, this passage from the ninth chapter of *The Ninth Bridgewater Treatise*:

> No motion impressed by natural causes, or by human agency, is ever obliterated. The ripple on the ocean's surface caused by a gentle breeze, or the still water which marks the more immediate track of a ponderous vessel gliding with scarcely expanded sails over its bosom, are equally indelible. The momentary waves raised by the passing

breeze, apparently born but to die on the spot which saw their birth, leave behind them an endless progeny, which, reviving with diminished energy in other seas, visiting a thousand shores, reflected from each and perhaps again partially concentrated, will pursue their ceaseless course till ocean be itself annihilated. (37)

As with those of the earlier passages from Babbage's book, the echoes of this passage in *Dombey* are subtle yet significant: Little Paul, like the momentary waves, is "*born, to die*," and the waves themselves ceaselessly bear to shore their "vast library" of "testimonies." But for Dickens the author, even more than for *Dombey* the novel, the images from Babbage's chapter engender a fantasy of endless transmission, in which a literary voice, the "motion of human agency" that is fictional narrative, crosses land as well as sea, "visiting a thousand shores" for eternity in the paperback covers of "endless progeny." In the address to the Cheap Edition, Dickens's stated forecast of "widest diffusion" for his works had an implicit model in Babbage's theory of vocal diffusion. If he could only publish and republish—and perform and re-perform—enough, Dickens would create, or so he perhaps hoped, a "vast library" of his ever-present voices. Forty years later, Thomas Edison's agent George Gouraud would set out in London to acquire phonograph recordings of Tennyson, Browning, and other famous Victorians as the basis for what he called a "Library of Voices." But Dickens already had started to build such an archive, in the spirit of Babbage's "vast library" etched on air, when he began to tour and, in the spirit of Sloppy in *Our Mutual Friend*, to "do the Police" and all his other characters "in different voices."[69] Without realizing it, Babbage the modern philosopher had tapped into the desire that Dickens the struggling writer began to play out with and alongside the noisy soundscape of *Dombey*: the desire to achieve authorial perpetuity at home and overseas—the desire, simply put, never to go out of circulation.

T HIS FANTASY of literary immortality culminated in the event that threatened not the Dickens phenomenon (which goes on, of course), but the life of the author who began it. Seventeen years after turning Carker into grist for the "jagged mill" of the express train in *Dombey*, Dickens narrowly escaped his own death in a railway accident on the same line. On 9 June 1865, the Tidal Express, which was carrying Dickens from Folkestone to London, jumped a stretch of absent track at a viaduct at Staplehurst, sending the engine across the riverbank and seven first-class carriages down into the riverbed. Dickens was seated in the only first-class car that did not go over, but remained dangling off the rails at an angle, still attached to the second-class car in front, with the rear touching the field below. Ten passengers were killed, and fourteen seriously injured.[70] Physically unhurt, he escaped through a window and took part in "the hard work afterwards in getting out the dying and the dead," bringing brandy and water to survivors as well as to two others who perished in his presence.[71]

In the immediate aftermath, Dickens experienced what would now be considered a type of post-traumatic stress disorder: "I am curiously weak—weak as if I were recovering from a long illness. I begin to feel it more in my head. I sleep well and eat well; but I write a half dozen notes, and turn faint and sick," he told Forster.[72] He was unable to write his own letters and lost his voice for over two weeks: "I most unaccountably brought someone else's out of that terrible scene," he claimed.[73] For months, he could not tolerate the sound of train traveling and refused to ride the express: "The noise of the wheels of my Hansom, and of the London streets, was as much as I could bear. So I made all speed back here [to Kent] again—by a slow train though, for I felt that I was not up to the Express."[74]

Shunning the express, he curtailed written expression. In August he managed to bring the final book of *Our Mutual Friend*, the manuscript of which he was carrying with him on the day of the accident, to a close. This was his last completed novel. While he continued his reading tours, the volume of writing after *Our Mutual Friend* dropped from a roar to a murmur. He instead propelled himself into reading aloud, where it seemed to him, like the waves always saying, "that a mere spoken word—a mere syllable thrown into the air—may go on reverberating through illimitable space for ever and for ever, seeing that there is no rim against which it can strike: no boundary at which it can possibly arrive." When he returned to Babbage's *Treatise* to cite this flight of fancy for his audience in 1869, he did so not in a novel or sketch, but in a speech. His death on the fifth anniversary of the day of the accident cut short the serial publication of *The Mystery of Edwin Drood*. He left his story, as he had found himself when the Tidal Express crashed and his car derailed, "suspended . . . at last."[75]

2

THE SOUNDPROOF STUDY
Victorian Professional Identity
and Urban Noise

I remember a funny dinner at my brother's, where, amongst a few others,

were Babbage and Lyell, both of whom liked to talk. Carlyle, however,

silenced every one by haranguing during the whole dinner on the advantages

of silence. After dinner, Babbage, in his grimmest manner, thanked Carlyle

for his very interesting Lecture on Silence.

— CHARLES DARWIN, *Autobiography*

SCATTERBRAIN LONDON

LATE in October 1864, during a dinner with family and friends, Charles Dickens received a telegram that read simply "LEECH DEAD." Marcus Stone, a guest at the dinner, later recalled, "silence fell upon us. . . . No one said a word. What was there to say?"[1] In the following weeks, as Dickens struggled to complete another monthly installment of *Our Mutual Friend* (1864–1865), he made an unusual confession to John Forster: "I have not done my number. This death of poor Leech (I suppose) has put me out woefully. Yesterday and the day before I could do nothing; seemed for the time to have quite lost the power; and am only by slow degrees getting back into the track to-day."[2] Dickens's biographers have described these lines as a "cry of personal lamentation," a sign that Dickens felt "desiccated, unable to work" after the death of John Leech, his close friend and, more famously, his illustrator for *A Christmas Carol* (1843) and other Christmas stories.[3] As the words of the novelist and Stone indicate, however, Leech's death caused Dickens more than "personal" pain. It brought on a professional crisis, for it reduced the characteristically prolific author to an unfamiliar state of nonproductivity. Leech's death, if only temporarily, stopped Dickens's hand and silenced him.

41

That the passing of Leech brought such silence is ironic, since what precipitated his death was noise. Clanging bells, cracking whips, clattering carriages, clamoring hawkers and cabmen, roaring crowds, barking dogs — these sounds regularly accosted Leech and other Londoners, but scattered about the streets stood the worst offenders of all: the itinerant musicians, in Dickens's words, those "brazen performers on brazen instruments, beaters of drums, grinders of organs, bangers of banjos, clashers of cymbals, worriers of fiddles, and bellowers of ballads."[4] Driven nearly mad by street music over his final years, Leech allowed this to exacerbate what already was for him a serious heart condition and nervous temperament. His final words to his fellow artist and future biographer William Powell Frith indicate the depth of his misery: "'Rather, Frith,'" Leech bitterly commented the month of his death, "'than continue to be tormented in this way, I would prefer to go to the grave where there is no noise.'"[5] Days later, he got his wish, bringing him the quiet he felt he had been unjustly denied in life.

In his antipathy toward street music in Victorian London, Leech had plentiful company. Throughout the city, artisans, academics, musicians, clergy, and doctors and their patients shared Leech's suffering and railed against what an author of a leading article from a May 1856 *Times* called "the noisy, dizzy, scatterbrain atmosphere of London."[6] As tempers flared, the fight against the oppression of street noises mounted in print and Parliament. With predictable indignation, another *Times* leader emphatically declared for the exasperated many, "there is no London nuisance equal to that of out-door music! . . . O for a little quiet in London!"[7] Anger and disgust among the middle classes soon found its outlet and target. The prolonged war of words and images that ensued not only resulted in new legal restrictions upon music-makers but also accelerated what Peter Bailey has identified as "a continuing struggle between refinement and vulgarity."[8] For the battle revealed a midsection of later Victorian society in the process of making one of its more elaborate, fierce efforts toward collective action and self-definition.

What can loosely be considered the anti–street music movement represents a critical aspect of the context in which much if not most of the major artwork and literature of the period developed. The influential urban historian H. J. Dyos was among the first to suggest the specifically acoustic nature of this context. He observed that in cities of the modern era, silence had become a commodity of precious value, while the impact of sensory overstimulation remained unclear: "What is less certain [than the modern value put upon silence]," Dyos wrote, "is whether the combined assault on the senses of a profusion of sights, smells, noises, crowds, moving objects, changing levels, constraints, commands, is an important source of disturbance to people."[9] Without doubt — with urgency, in fact — the excessiveness of one of the urban qualities Dyos mentioned, noise, evolved into "an important source of disturbance" during the latter half of the Victorian age. On a larger scale than before, noise began in this period to alter the agents, subjects, and conditions of artistic and intellectual occupations as well as much other professional employment.

Beginning at midcentury, advocates for silence on the streets waged a battle to impose the quiet tenor of interior middle-class domesticity upon the rowdy terrain outside. Thomas Carlyle's renowned attack on noise served as a kind of overture to those that followed. Carlyle's long-standing aversion to noises of all kinds, ranging from piano-playing neighbors to crowing roosters and chickens, is legendary; Thea Holme, among others, relates the facts in amusing detail.[10] By 1853, nearly two decades after moving to Cheyne Row in Chelsea, the "UNPROTECTED MALE," as Carlyle referred to himself, had had enough of "Demon Fowls" and other disturbances to issue bloodthirsty responses in defense of his territory: "Those Cocks must either withdraw or die. That is a fixed point; — and I must do it myself if no one will help: it is really too bad the 'celebrated man,' or any *man*, or even a well-conditioned animal (of any size) should be submitted to such scandalous paltrinesses."[11] He reserved special venom for his nemesis, a "vile yellow Italian" organ grinder. "The question arises, Whether to go out and, if not assassinate him, call the Police upon him, or to take myself away to the bath-tub and the other side of the house? Of course, I *ought* to chuse the latter alternative, — and do, for the wretch's organ is a *horse* one, I hear; drawn by a horse; and, one w[oul]d think, played by one!"[12] "All summer I have been more or less annoyed with *noises*, even accidental ones, which get free access thro' my open windows ... henceforth I hope to be independent of all men and all dogs, cocks and household or street noises," he wrote later that year, as his limited patience reached its end.[13] For Carlyle, to rest, but more important to *work*, depended upon denying outdoor commotion "free access" to interior professional space.

Carlyle's solution to the problem made spatially evident the complications that many Victorian intellectuals in London faced as they struggled for both professional differentiation and quiet. Carlyle sought to create a personal space that outside sounds could not infiltrate, a sanctum in which he would go on to write *Frederick the Great* (1858–1865). Although the idea of a soundproof attic study had occurred to him at least a decade earlier, events of 1853 revived his hope in it: "Masons (who have already *killed* a year of my life, in a too sad manner), are again upon the roof of the house, — after a dreadful bout of resolution on my part, — building me a SOUNDLESS ROOM! 'The world, which can do me no good, shall at least not torment me with its street and backyard *noises*.'"[14] The construction of Carlyle's study provided an intriguing juncture for a number of Victorian concerns. With new double walls, skylights, and slated roof with muffling air chambers beneath, the room signified what Carlyle referred to as his "glorious conquest": a professional seizure of urban space, and an architectural tactic by which to expel the threat of the noisy rabble and thereby preserve an authorial career.[15] Yet it was also a tactic that encapsulated the oddly positioned existence of silence-seeking professionals whose living and working spaces overlapped.

In her formative study of the Victorian home, Jenni Calder writes of the drive of the middle classes to escape urban realities and attain a degree of separateness and self-definition within the home: "Society itself was ugly. The aspect of the urban world was not nice to look upon. There was dirt, there was noise, there was human excrement, there was starvation, there was crime, there was violence, all on the surface, all very close to the senses of all who ventured beyond their front doors. . . . To have an interior environment that enabled such things to be forgotten was a priority of middle-class aspiration."[16] In one sense, then, Carlyle's plan for the soundproof study was another—even the definitive—step toward self-identification with members of the professional class, whose emerging sense of group identity directly conflicted with the problem of street noise. Carlyle's construction of a room specifically designed to keep out city noises provided a spatial reinforcement of a vocational identity, even as it kept the threats of the base distractions of society at bay. At a cost of some £200 to construct, however, the silent space did not come cheaply. Such a price lends support to Dyos's observation about the gradual commodification of silence in urban areas. At the same time, Carlyle's soundless room demonstrates how that shift could manifest itself domestically, or, in more general terms, territorially, as a phenomenon particular to an emerging stratum of professionals who sought through silence to localize, even spatially contain, noise.

Changing productions and conceptions of noise have tended to be overlooked or, more precisely, underheard in standard social and literary histories, but there are signs this is starting to change, as scholars have begun reconstructing "auditory landscapes" of the past to discern "the elaboration of collective and territorial identities."[17] Along similar lines, Jacques Attali's politicized history of music remains a provocative study of the relations between sound and power, and it offers a theoretical perspective from which to consider the street music problem. Attali writes that "all music, any organization of sounds is then a tool for the creation or consolidation of a commodity, of a totality . . . [and] any theory of power today must include a theory of the localization of noise and its endowment with form."[18] Noise, Attali goes on to claim, "indicates the limits of a territory and the way to make oneself heard within it, how to survive by drawing one's sustenance from it" (6). If Attali is correct to see throughout history an ongoing conflict between makers of music and those of noise, then the events under scrutiny in this chapter provide an especially suitable opportunity for testing the resonance of his claims. It follows that the anti–street music movement can be considered an urban territorial campaign, a conflict for control between regions of harmony and those of dissonance. That conflict often manifests itself in legal action, for "the institutionalization of the silence of others assure[s] the durability of power" (8). Noise, then, in a definition quite relevant to this discussion, "*is violence*: it disturbs. To make noise is to interrupt a transmission, to disconnect, to kill. It is a simulacrum of murder" (26). Attali's claim captures the underlying message in Leech's final words to Frith, in which the ailing artist expressed his belief that he was being violently driven to the only quiet place left him. And in Attali's terms, Carlyle's soundproof chamber institutionalized silence to "assure the durability" of the author's literary ability and power.[19]

While Attali offers a compelling theory of the relationship between sound and silence, that theory only represents a starting point for what follows. Later nineteenth-century Londoners' deliberations over street music served as a gauge of an urban community's explicit demands and entrenched biases. During the period under discussion, fights for silence repeatedly emerged as regional struggles against street music, insofar as they attempted not only to protect literal neighborhoods and city blocks from intrusive noises but also to defend more abstract regions of identity, those critical domains of nationality, professionalism, and the body. Hence, these ongoing battles over sounds were concretely as well as conceptually territorial. Even as those opposed proclaimed as their principal goal the removal of music from the streets throughout the City and West London, including Belgravia, Kensington, and Chelsea, they endeavored to maintain clear boundaries in three principal areas that necessarily interrelated and at times overlapped: first, defending the purity of English national identity and culture against the taint of foreign infiltration; second, upholding economic and social divisions between the lower classes and middle-class professionals; and third, protecting the frail, afflicted bodies of (English, middle-class) invalids from the invasive, debilitating effects of (foreign, lower-class) street music. What might have seemed a harmless entertainment thus came to represent a rallying point for the large numbers of Londoners, including Carlyle, Leech, and ultimately even Dickens himself, who heard in street music the strains of a powerful threat.

"BLACKGUARD SAVOYARDS AND HERDS OF GERMAN SWINE"

Seedy Savoyard, wherefore art thou grinding?
Rough blows the wind, thy pipes are out of order,
Old is thy tune, thy monkey is a nuisance,
So is thy organ.

"FRIEND OF TRANQUILLITY," in *The Owl*

TO REFER to the anti–street music attacks as such is perhaps misleading, for generally speaking, they were directed less against all outdoor music and performers than at certain types of music and particular players. Isolated published indictments of London street musicians appeared as early as the first decade of the nineteenth century, but the frequency of the reports rose significantly in the 1840s, when the *Times* began to print complaints against street noise on a regular basis. Scholars have noted that "the decibel count seemed to have increased from mid-century on" in London streets, in part from higher rates of immigration and commercial growth, and that street trading in the middle decades of the century was "augmented by a rare audibility."[20] In *London Labour and the London Poor* (1861), Henry Mayhew described the array of nationalities of what he estimated were upward of one thousand street musicians in London during the period, including English violin-players, street bands, and a harpist, Irish and Scotch pipers, a German brass-bandsman, a French hurdy-gurdy player, a host of Italian street entertainers, and numerous percussionists and minstrel-singers from England, India, and the United States.[21] The increasing number and variety of musicians throughout the 1850s brought an escalation of published letters of attack and one of the first appearances, in an 1851 *Times* headline, of the phrase "organ nuisance" to designate the larger problem of noisy street music.[22] This move by the *Times* allowed the press and public to simplify a larger problem by singling out a particular type of performer upon which to place blame for the interruptions of daily life. As a consequence, the street music nuisance of the 1840s resolved itself, through synecdoche, into the "organ-grinding nuisance" of the 1850s and 1860s. The Italian organ grinders came to be seen as the repulsive source of virtually all noise in the city, and their eradication the task of every "Friend of Tranquillity."[23]

This development was complicated by the fact that a number of the outraged had legitimate grievances against those street musicians who in essence used extortion to make their living. To get certain organ grinders to stop playing or go elsewhere, a noticeable segment of the complainants regularly had to pay them off, and this understandably only fueled the anger against them. Street music had few defenders, and these could do little to offset the quantity of outbursts of the incensed majority. In his *London* (1841), Charles Knight published an early defense in response to the 1839 Metropolitan Police Act, which attempted to legislate street noise. Knight openly sympathized with the musicians; street music, he wrote, "ought now to be left alone, if it cannot be encouraged by the State." Over two decades later, during the 1864 street music debates in Parliament, aristocratic MPs spoke out on behalf of the working classes, paternalistically claiming that doing away with organ grinders would deprive the poor of one of their few forms of entertainment. Also that year, the journal *Good Words* published a short article and illustration sympathetic toward the organ grinders, claiming they were "discoursing the best music of the day, and educating the ear of hundreds for a few halfpence."[24] Minor and infrequent as defenses such as these were, they failed to counteract the prevailing hostility toward street music. Perhaps of greater significance, the grinders, many of whom had only a rudimentary command of English, were for the most part not able to speak, let alone publish, for themselves. With the possible exception of interviews by Mayhew and some scant police reports, the words and sentiments of the musicians, when noted at all, were presented by intermediaries whose antipathy, fear, and ignorance shaped their depictions.

The noise itself was a very real and potent concern to those who felt the force of it. An early article by Charles Manby Smith that analyzed the problem echoed Mayhew (or perhaps foreshadowed him) by imposing external order in the form of nine separate "classes" upon the seemingly jumbled collection of "Music-Grinders of the Metropolis." One of the first authors explicitly to single out the organ grinders for their particular brand of disturbance, Smith used terms that other critics soon adopted when he described them as "the incarnate nuisances who fill the air with discordant and fragmentary mutilations and distortions of heaven-born melody, to the distraction of educated ears and perversion of the popular taste."[25] Smith's groupings of the grinders included "hand organists," "monkey-organists," "blind bird-organists," "flageolet-organists," and "the horse-and-cart organists." Under this last heading, Smith provided one of the most colorful of the many descriptions of the jarring sounds of organs during the period:

> The piercing notes of a score of shrill fifes, the squall of as many clarions, the hoarse bray of a legion of tin trumpets, the angry and fitful snort of a brigade of rugged bassoons, the unintermitting rattle of a dozen or more deafening drums, the clang of bells firing in peals, the boom of gongs, with the sepulchral roar of some unknown contrivance for bass, so deep that you might almost count the vibrations of each note — these are a few of the components of the horse-and-cart organ, the sum total of which it is impossible to add up. (199)

While the performances of smaller organs did not approach the magnitude of these massive productions, they ranged from dulcet and charming to more often, in the words of one scholar, "loud and coarse . . . [like that] of a monstrously amplified ice-cream van."[26] Smith's relatively early attempt to convey the cacophony of the horse-and-cart organ focused on the difficulty of scouting the vast territory of the machinery of the organ itself, which seemed beyond the reach of rational observation, a mechanism "impossible" to grasp. Curiously, his description evokes the bewildering sound and effect of the "iron horse" of the locomotive, which, along with the street organ, was a significant component of early industrial urban noise. Smith provided a spirited sense of organ-induced confusion while hinting at the damning tone that came to dominate ensuing arguments about the street music problem.

Smith's article was most important because it drew attention to the performers as distinctly alien to London. Smith's classifications included the grinder who was "nearly always a foreigner," or "not uncommonly some lazy Irishman, if he be not a sickly Savoyard," as well as "little hopping, skipping, jumping, reeling Savoyard or Swiss urchins" (198–99). Smith concluded that "with respect to all these grinders, one thing is remarkable: they are all, with the exception of a small savour of Irishmen, foreigners. . . . Scarcely one Englishman, not one Scot, will be found among the whole tribe" (201). Mayhew's comments on an "Italian with Monkey" who was formerly an organ grinder reiterated Smith's emphasis on foreignness in more insidious ways: "He wore the Savoy and broad-brimmed felt hat, and with it on his head had a very picturesque appearance, and the shadow of the brim falling on the upper part of the brown face gave him almost a Murillo-like look. There was, however, an odour about him, — half monkey, half dirt, — that was far from agreeable, and that pervaded the apartment in which he sat."[27] This pointed description of the stench of the man who might "almost" have emerged from a Spanish painting reveals a not-so-subtle contempt for an "uncivilized" foreigner, one of equal parts beast and earth.

As Smith's and Mayhew's comments suggest, those describing the "organ nuisance" repeatedly fell back on epithets such as the catch-all term "Savoyard," the use of which might easily be dismissed as a matter of convention. Yet in this case, such a convention is especially interesting and revealing. The *Oxford English Dictionary* traces the English adoption of the French word "Savoyard" back to the mid-eighteenth century and notes that it refers to "a native or inhabitant of Savoy. Well known in other countries as musicians itinerating with hurdy-gurdy and monkey." Although this latter meaning might appear to refer to the nineteenth-century influx of street musicians, it does not.[28] As the Italian musicians arriving in the nineteenth century were from the Duchy of Parma, not, as the earlier Savoyards had been, from the Duchy of Savoy, Victorians used an outdated term, one complicated even more by the events of 1860, in which France permanently annexed Savoy from the Italian kingdom of Piedmont-Sardinia, to delineate those who were in reality Parmesan immigrants. The distinction is a significant one: Parma went on to join Italy proper, while Savoy became part of France, and, as the "new Savoyards" used Savoy as a stopping-point on their way from Parma to London, it is likely that many Victorians in writing about the Parmesan musicians conflated the two places or just never knew the difference, unthinkingly applying an old term to a new phenomenon.[29] That they attributed the players' origins to Savoy, a province that alternated allegiance to Italy and France, is itself symptomatic of a heightened xenophobia, a fear of intrusion from those who are made to seem, in the wake of the events of 1860, doubly foreign.[30] Juggled as a political pawn between Cavour and Napoleon III, Savoy held a status that Cavour described to English visitors as the "Ireland of Italy."[31] The analogy resonated back home, for Victorian Londoners expressed toward the so-called Savoyards a degree of contempt similar to what they showed those others who provoked territorial and racial anxieties, those from the "Savoy of Britain," the loathed Irish.

A contemporary full-page *Punch* cartoon by John Tenniel fuses the political significance of the Savoy region with the "organ nuisance" of London in a provocative image. The illustration (figure 2.1) alludes both to the French acquisition of Savoy and to the growing sense that England was being overrun by itinerant musicians. In the cartoon, a respectably dressed Mr. Punch herds a group of organ grinders and hurdy-gurdy players to the edge of a cliff and bats at them forcefully with his umbrella, his top hat and spectacles flying off from the force of the swing. The foreigners, longhaired, unshaven, and wearing the "Savoy hat" noted by Mayhew, topple off the cliff and presumably into the sea below, their instruments still strapped to their backs and chests. The

PUNCH, OR THE LONDON CHARIVARI—March 17, 1860.

MR. PUNCH SURRENDERS THE SAVOYARDS.

FIGURE 2.1. JOHN TENNIEL'S VERSION OF A MUSICAL AND POLITICAL
DECONTAMINATION OF ENGLISH SOIL, FROM *Punch* 38 (1860): 111.

one organ grinder whose eyes are visible grimaces leeringly toward viewers
and his evictor, while Punch glares back at him in agitation, his eyes open
wide and hair on end; the caption reads "Mr. Punch Surrenders the Savoyards." Using these terms, the artist invokes the literal surrender of Savoy to
France even as he represents the expulsion of the "new Savoyards" (the
Parmesans) over the cliffs of Dover. Grafting a territorial fantasy onto a territorial reality, he transforms a controversy about offensive sounds into one of
invaded spaces. And his proposed solution is the purging of foreign performers from England, a musical decontamination.

Representations of the street music problem as a type of foreign infesta-
tion became commonplace in the 1850s, and few illustrations expressed more
malice than the work of the premier *Punch* artist and enemy of street sounds,
John Leech. A number of sketches particularly attested to his acute xenophobia. In the first (figure 2.2), while itinerant musicians wander in the background, "Field Marshall" Punch earnestly presents a recoiling organ grinder
with a bayonet, with the comment, "'Here's an instrument for you, go play
upon it in your own country!'" In the second (figure 2.3), an organ grinder occupies center stage in a double-page procession of "Some Foreign Produce
That Mr. Bull Can Very Well Spare." Both illustrations portrayed the street
musicians as haggard, shabbily dressed, dirty—as clearly foreign, even when
surrounded, as in the second image, by other foreigners. Further, both expressed the desire for the street musicians' deportation by capitalizing on
their status as aliens and suggested that itinerants ought to be turned away

49

F. M. PUNCH SYMPATHISES WITH THE POOR (!) ITALIAN ORGAN-GRINDER.

F. M. P. "THERE MY MAN, IT'S A PITY A GREAT HULKING FELLOW LIKE YOU SHOULD TURN A HANDLE TO MAKE SUCH A NASTY NOISE! HERE'S AN INSTRUMENT FOR YOU, GO AND PLAY UPON IT IN YOUR OWN COUNTRY!"

FIGURE 2.2. JOHN LEECH'S IDEA OF A MORE PROPER "INSTRUMENT" FOR ORGAN GRINDERS, FROM *Punch* 36 (1859): 204.

SOME FOREIGN PRODUCE THAT MR. BULL

FIGURE 2.3. LEECH'S XENOPHOBIA ON DISPLAY, IN A CARTOON THAT REFLECTS MORE WIDESPREAD ANXIETIES ABOUT RISING NUMBERS OF IMMIGRANTS IN LONDON, FROM *Punch* 34 (1858): 98–99.

and immigrants surrendered to their "own country" or simply refused. In his work, Leech used his subjects' foreignness against them, as a means to single them out as undesirables and advocate their expulsion.

As calls for the legislation of street noise increased during the late 1850s and into the 1860s, insults directed at the "organ nuisance" became more pointed and defensive, and many characterized the musicians as aliens who were less than human, indeed, bestial. A letter to the *Times* in January 1864 bemoaned the fact that "we consider ourselves compelled to endure the most deafening rows, conducted for the most part, if not universally, *by foreigners*," while editorials from the *Examiner* consistently represented the musicians as no better than degenerates and animals: they were "blackguard Savoyards and herds of German swine," "with sounds like those of a pig, to which they are so near akin"; their music recalled "the grunts and squeaks of a herd of filthy German swine."[32] Likewise, a writer for the *City Press* characterized the musicians as "filthy Germans—as filthy in speech as in looks . . . they howl like so many apes and baboons escaped from the Zoological Gardens, and looking much like these creatures too." The only way to deal with escaped wild animals, the author concluded, was to hunt them down: "no Londoner should sally forth to business without first spiking, or hanging, or shooting

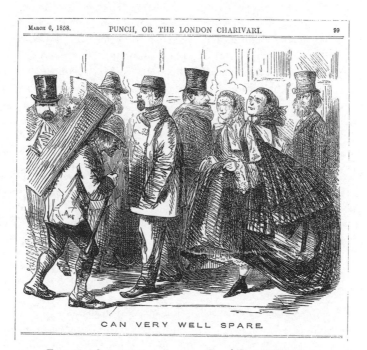

MARCH 6, 1858.   PUNCH, OR THE LONDON CHARIVARI.   99

CAN VERY WELL SPARE.

FIGURE 2.3. (CONTINUED), FROM *Punch* 34 (1858): 98–99.

one of the howlers of the streets."[33] Depicting the musicians as filthy animals, and ultimately urging urban self-defense, this position drew upon language of the hunt to demonstrate among other things the persistence of territorial concerns, of metaphors of invasion and containment, in the gathering opposition to street music. But it was for an emerging segment of middle-class professionals—authors, artists, and other "brain-workers"—that the notion of territory took on new meanings, and their attacks reflected the added strains of having simultaneously to define and defend their newfound socioeconomic turf.

WRITERS' BLOCK

I was once asked by an astute and sarcastic magistrate whether I seriously
believed that a man's brain would be injured by listening to an organ; my reply
was, "Certainly not"; for the obvious reason that no man having brain ever
listened to street musicians.

— CHARLES BABBAGE

ALONGSIDE these dismissals of street music as an invasive disturbance, conceptions of territory became increasingly charged for the class Dickens had his son-in-law Charles Collins describe in an article on the problem in *All The Year Round*: "The writer, the artist, the calculator, the comparative anatomist, the clergyman composing his sermon, the scientific man his treatise, surely the class of which such individuals as these form the component parts, is scarcely a small, and still less an unimportant one."[34] This group was just beginning to seek greater public respect and privileges as a professional class. Their attacks reflected the unusual difficulty of distinguishing their newfound socioeconomic turf from their homes. To understand what makes their allegations distinctive, consider for a moment this more conventional complaint from one Victor Baune, a City worker who lived on Philpot Lane:

> I go home from the City, the brain overwrought, feverish, and fatigued, and I require rest and change of occupation—reading, writing, music—and these are impossible with the horrible street music from all sides—the very atmosphere impregnated with that thrice-cursed droning noise—that abomination of London which makes me ill, which positively shortens my life from the nervous fever which it engenders.[35]

While engaging widespread Victorian notions of invalidism, Baune's horror at street music derives from a sense of entitlement and expectation in the domestic sphere. The "change of occupation" he describes plays on the dual sense of "occupation": as career and of space. For Baune, as for those in other established middle-class professions such as medicine and law, work and rest occupy different spaces. As Leonore Davidoff has noted, this was a period when most professional men divided their time between increasingly distinct arenas of home and office: "Men, especially middle-class men, had to leave the home for the struggles of the marketplace, or to take their part in the armed services, the Church, and politics."[36] After a day of tiring business in the City, the home became the place for leisure, the "reading, writing, music" necessary for maintaining one's domestic propriety, respectability, and identity. In assaulting the hearth, the "abomination" of organ grinding denied Baune and others like him the pursuit of "rest" so essential to the life of proper gentlemen. Yet for many families, "the separation of work from home was far from total."[37] The text accompanying an early Leech cartoon of an aggrieved writer at a window overlooking an organ grinder put it this way: "those houses which have the appearance of being devoted to *peaceful occupations*," occupations in both the professional and spatial sense, were being bombarded with the music of "Italian desperadoes" who left "business projects regularly knocked on the head, and nerves painfully attacked" (figure 2.4; emphasis added). For professionals lacking offices in the City, that is, the territorial distinctions so critical to the men Davidoff describes did not apply. The challenge street musicians presented to them was all the greater, since it put not just one but two principal components of their identities—labor and leisure—at risk, a double affront to their status.[38]

This loose federation of middle-class professionals, which included Dickens in its ranks, was just coming into its own at the middle of the century, increasing in numbers but still struggling for respect and recognition. The 1850s and 1860s were a transitional period for all the professions, as the growing size and wealth of society at large brought a corresponding need for professional services, which consequently underwent rapid expansion. Census reports indicate that the number of physicians grew by over half from 1861 to 1901, while the number of teachers more than doubled, of authors and editors more than tripled, and of actors more than quadrupled.[39] As W. J. Reader comments, the watershed Medical Act of 1858, which created a national registry of doctors, "went a long way towards establishing the approved pattern of a Victorian profession, whether in medicine or in any other occupation that aspired to equal dignity."[40] But medicine, like law, was an established field; it would require similar legal and bureaucratic developments across a wider spectrum before authors, artists, actors, and academics could enjoy similar stature. These developments included issuing royal charters, instituting field-specific examinations, and creating organizations designed "to raise status, financial rewards and occupational security by means of differentiation, regulation, and an emphasis on the gentlemanly virtues of education and middle-class morality."[41]

And yet this transitional period elicited heightened professional insecurity, as authors, artists, and the like attempted to form and protect their collective identity. They found it difficult to define their status objectively: "For none of them could you lay down exact qualifications: still less could you erect an examination ladder."[42] Further, they generally found themselves at the bot-

THE PEACE SOCIETY

WE understand that the attention of this excellent Society has lately been directed to a subject closely connected with the cause of peace, which is threatened by a regularly organised band of Italian adventurers. They seem to threaten us with all the horrors of the Battle of Prague, which caused the groans of the dying to be heard in every drawing-room, and there was not a seminary for young ladies into which the roaring of the cannon did not penetrate. A somewhat similar affliction now comes upon us in the very streets of the metropolis, below the very windows of our houses ; and the Peace Society will act properly in preserving as far as possible the public tranquillity. We understand that negotiations with this view are being carried on between the Peace Society and the Chief

THE DISTURBER OF THE PEACE OF PRIVATE FAMILIES.

of the Italians, with the view of ensuring peace to private families, and putting an end to the Polka war which is being waged through the medium of mere instruments in the hands of others. It is customary with the Italian desperadoes to commence hostilities in quiet localities, and particularly in front of those houses which have the appearance of being devoted to peaceful occupations. The list of victims would, if published, present a frightful catalogue of killed and wounded ; that is to say, of business projects regularly knocked on the head, and nerves painfully attacked by the dreadful discord of those organs of dissension which we have alluded to.

FIGURE 2.4. THE BRAIN WORKER AND HIS NEMESIS, IN A LEECH CARTOON
FROM *Punch* 8 (1845): 44.

tom of a hierarchy based on wealth and income, beneath the more financially secure practitioners of medicine and law. Thus, for many professionals in the 1850s and 1860s, access to privilege and status remained uncertain, if not unlikely. Those aspiring to respectability needed to fight aggressively to mark their territory as professionals, to define themselves as industrious intellectuals who ranked above manual laborers, who could stand alongside doctors, lawyers, and the military, and who were equally worthy of deference, legislative action, and, of course, quiet.[43] Street noise challenged this territorial concern at its problematic core: these workers defended their rights not from within distant offices, but from inside their homes.

More problematic still, the homes in which these male professionals tried to work had been newly feminized: now that the home "no longer had to serve as shop, workshop, or office it could be devoted to essentially female purposes—the care and nurture of children, the entertainment of friends and guests, the management of familial and matrimonial affairs."[44] In addition, Victorians also were beginning to endorse gendered conceptions of levels of sound. Women were increasingly "socialised as the quieter if not silent sex," while "bravura noise-making was an essential signal of masculine identity for much of this era."[45] The middle-class Victorian man who embarked on a home-based occupation requiring silence had, it would seem, quite an uphill battle if he were to convey the separateness and, indeed, noisiness of masculinity. Carlyle, for one, hoped his soundproof room would demarcate a newly masculinized space reserved for the sounding of his own writerly voices within his house, partly out of his acute fear of effeminacy. Norma Clarke has written perceptively of Carlyle's early anxieties over "the uncertainly gendered social identity which literature might bring with it," and his consequent need, in *On Heroes and Hero-Worship* (1841), to provide "a construction of the literary worker that excluded women from the definition." The "strenuous idleness" of the male writer is intrinsically unstable, and that instability manifests itself in the conception of Carlyle's soundproof study, built years after *On Heroes*.[46] Reinforcing a fragile masculine professionalism by enforcing (an allegedly) feminized silence within a feminized domestic space was an uncertain proposition at best, and it should come as little surprise that an architectural resolution of this messy problem turned out to be delusory: "The 'sound-proof room' was a flattering delusion of an ingenious needy builder, for which we afterwards paid dear," Carlyle later wrote. The room was "by far the noisiest in the house," "a kind of infernal 'miracle' to me then and ever since."[47]

At the very least, a consideration of Carlyle's responses to noisy disturbances complicates standard generalizations from this period about correspondences among space, sound, and gender. What is telling in this regard is his wife Jane's quite different response to the building of the soundproof study. While Thomas had gone abroad to escape the noise of the builders, Jane stayed behind to oversee their work. She wrote:

> The tumult has been even greater since Mr C went than it was before;
> for new floors are being put down in the top story and the noise of *that*
> is something terrific. But now that I feel the noise and dirt and discord
> with my own senses only and not thro *his* as well, it is amazing how little I care about it. Nay in superintending all these men I begin to find
> myself in the career open to my particular talents, and am infinitely

more satisfied than I was in talking *"wits"* in my white silk gown with white feathers in my head. . . . The fact is I am remarkably indifferent to *material* annoyances. . . . And when Mr C is not here recognising it with his overwhelming eloquence, I can regard the present earthquake as something almost *laughable*.[48]

Left to fend for herself in the genteel woman's traditional sphere of influence, Jane was, literally, at home in noise, albeit interior forms of noise. Or, rather, what Thomas insisted on attacking as noise, his wife came to perceive as the necessary and innocuous bustle of constructing and managing a home, the working sounds, so to speak, of one facet of her profession: "To see something *going on* and to help its going on fulfils a great want of my nature," Jane wrote to her husband.[49] While Jane was not cavalier about the nuisances that bothered Thomas, their contrary perceptions do indicate the difference between the socially defined labor of the homemaker, who oversaw the often noisy inhabitants and affairs of her house, and the hushed sound of the isolated author at work under her roof, who socialized within "the huge whirlpool of noise" made, as it were, by the silent voices inside his books and head.[50]

While Carlyle's struggle became well known in London, the task of swaying a professional scholarly community against a common enemy fell to Charles Babbage, the esteemed mathematician and inventor of the Difference Engine. Throughout the 1850s and 1860s, Babbage appeared before magistrates to lodge complaints against street musicians, but to no avail. Even when he succeeded in legally punishing the performers, as the first *Times* leader to publicize his plight indicated, there were those determined to undermine him: "A musical fanatic who was present in court, being touched with sympathy for the misfortune of the wandering musician, paid the fine, and CIRCEONI was discharged to the further annoyance of the human race."[51] Babbage became infamous for his outbursts against musicians, which resulted in perpetual harassment from neighbors, not to mention the musicians themselves. Babbage's "near mania" against organ grinders and the like not only "demonstrate[d], in a heightened form, the mental set of one type of urban reformer."[52] His notoriety also assured him an audience when he decided to publish, in likely consultation with Member of Parliament Michael Thomas Bass, a central text in the debates over the "organ nuisance."

Appearing in 1864, at the height of the street music controversy, Babbage's "Chapter on Street Nuisances" was a key tract in the development of class-based arguments against wandering musicians but spoke as well to the identification of the struggling urban intellectual with the ill city dweller. Throughout the piece, Babbage employs professional skills to attack musical disturbances as distinctly antiprofessional and presents the intellectual as an invalid professional, revealing the curious anxieties linking the bedridden and home-ridden during this period. Street music, he claims at the opening of his "Chapter," "robs the industrious man of his time; it annoys the musical man by its intolerable badness; it irritates the invalid; deprives the patient of that repose which, under such circumstances, is essential for his recovery; and it destroys the time and the energies of all the intellectual classes of society by its continual interruptions of their pursuits."[53] Babbage itemizes fourteen *"Instruments of torture"* in use on London streets, including *"The human voice in its various forms"* "shouting out objects for sale," in addition to the predictable musical suspects of organs, brass bands, and fiddles. He lists ten groups considered *"Encouragers of street music,"* which, he notes, are among "chiefly . . . the lower classes of society"; these include "Beer-houses," "Coffee-shops," "Servants," "Children," "Visitors from the country," "Ladies of doubtful virtue," and "Occasionally titled ladies" ("but these are almost invariably of recent elevation, and deficient in that taste which their sex usually possess," he is quick to add) (254). His third and final list pairs six nationalities with the aforementioned instruments: "Italians" with "Organs," for instance, "Natives of India" with "Tom-toms," and "The lowest class of clubs" with "Bands with double drum" (255). Babbage's acts of listing, of classifying the music and musicians in the tradition of Mayhew and earlier observers, are, of course, themselves a means to organize and discipline that which in reality defies order and control. But it is important in this respect that Babbage does so by linking the music to the lower classes—drunkards, household servants, prostitutes—and to "deficient" women and children. In all cases, Babbage suggests, the listeners and performers do not and cannot uphold the responsibility or status of the author himself, the professional (male) scholar deserving of peace.

Singling out for defense "those who possess an impaired bodily frame . . . [and are awoken] at all hours, in the midst of that temporary repose so necessary for confirmed invalids," Babbage seeks at the same time to confirm his own legitimacy as a laborer whose valuable calculations and time have been heedlessly interrupted (255). "I have witnessed much and suffered more," he writes as if from a sickbed, referring to "the great sacrifice of [his] own time" that street music has necessitated (255, 257). Along these lines, Babbage draws from his profession the tools, the ostensibly hard data of figures and computations, to use as his greatest weapon against the musicians. Although he claims that "it is difficult to estimate the misery inflicted upon thousands of persons, and the absolute pecuniary penalty imposed upon multitudes of intellectual workers by the loss of their time, destroyed by organ-grinders and other nuisances," this does not stop him from hazarding a guess based on his own experience: "On careful retrospect of the last dozen years of my life, I have arrived at the conclusion that I speak within limit when I state that one-fourth part of my working power has been destroyed by the nuisance against which I have protested" (257, 259). As for his evidence, Babbage writes: "I find by some notes, that during about eighty days, I registered one hundred and sixty-five instances [of interruptions], the greater part of which I went out myself to put a stop to the nuisance" (265). Elsewhere, Babbage, ever the orderly mathematician, itemizes and subtotals the disturbances according to date and type.[54] Armed with these incontrovertible facts of computation, he urges banning all unnecessary street noises and confiscating all offending instruments (269).

Babbage's perpetual quest for silence became a low comedy in which the entire neighborhood played a part. "A noisy mob . . . shouting out rather uncomplimentary epithets" followed him in his perpetual quest for policemen to banish street musicians, and when he turned to face his "illustrious tail, it stop[ped]" (262). His pursuers sometimes numbered over one hundred, and, he adds, "no week ever passe[d] without many instances" of such taunting (262). He has withstood the "smaller evils" of dead cats and broken windows, as well as threats against his life and house; some neighbors even "have gone to the expense of purchasing worn-out or damaged wind instruments, which they are incapable of playing, but on which they produced a discordant noise for the purposes of annoying me" (263–64). With indignation Babbage goes on to claim: "I have obtained, in my *own* country, an unenviable celebrity, not by anything I have done, but simply by a determined resistance to the tyranny of the lowest mob, whose love, not of music, but of the most discordant noises, is so great that it insists upon enjoying it at all hours and in every street" (259). Accordingly, he self-consciously takes it upon himself to represent and defend a beleaguered minority, those of frail professional status: "I am quite aware that I am fighting the battle of every one of my countrymen who gains his subsistence by his intellectual labour" — as well as those "4.72 persons per cent [who] are constantly ill" (259, 264). With no hint of irony, Babbage adopts in his "Chapter" as well as his public persona the role of the proud philosopher as invalid, one who must endure popular disdain and ridicule in order to protect his calling and time from those, richer as well as poorer, who failed to respect them.[55] In this regard, his tract expresses particular professional desires that constitute distinctly middle-class concerns of the period over aspects of rank and self-representation, as noted succinctly by F. M. L. Thompson: "The solid, industrious, and prudent middle classes understandably sought to differentiate themselves from the idle, dissolute, and thriftless, whether the extravagant undeserving rich or the rough undeserving poor."[56] It is nevertheless ironic that, of all London's brain-workers, it was Babbage who so aggressively acted out against organ grinders. In his philosophical work *The Ninth Bridgewater Treatise* (1837), after all, he had argued for the "permanent impression of our words and actions on the globe we inhabit." It was as if in perverse confirmation of this earlier professional claim that London street performers perpetually interrupted his work toward the end of his life.

MP Michael T. Bass, the political ally of London's anti–street music inhabitants, made the high point of his career the pursuit of legal restrictions for the "organ-grinding nuisance." A brewer at Burton, grandson of the founder of Bass Ale, and MP for Derby from 1848 to 1883, Bass succeeded, during his tenure, in endowing a church at Burton and establishing a recreation ground, public swimming pools, a library, and art gallery in Derby. But the measure that brought Bass greatest fame was his "Act for the Better Regulation of

Street Music in the Metropolis," which he first attempted to bring into Parliament in 1863. His bill proposed to repeal a section of the "Act for further improving the Police in and near the Metropolis" (2 and 3 Vict., c. 47 s. 57), which had required that a householder have "reasonable Cause" for demanding that police order street musicians to depart his neighborhood. Bass's act in its unemended form sought simply to replace this section with a new provision stipulating that the householder could make such a demand without any justification whatsoever, and moreover, that any musician who disobeyed could be fined a maximum of 40s. and taken into custody without a warrant. What Bass put at stake here was a particular type of cultural control critically necessary for those who worked at home: the power for householders to wield their privileges over an expanded urban environment, the ability to domesticate the streets.[57]

Published to coincide with parliamentary deliberations over a reconsideration of the bill the following year, Bass's *Street Music in the Metropolis* represented the most influential and substantial "organ nuisance" text. The 120-page volume is surprisingly informative and revealing, less a piece of vitriolic propaganda than an anthology of dozens of street music writings culled from letters, official reports, and the press. Its very organization into chapters on topics such as "Sufferers from Street Music," "Police Decisions on Street Music," "Opinions of the Press on Street Music," and "Parliamentary Proceedings" represents, like the bill it is meant to support, an attempt to impose order upon noise. In his preface, Bass indicates that a widely expressed need for orderly quiet led him to publish the book: "I have received letters from persons of all classes expressing their gratitude to me for taking up this question, and urging me to persevere. . . . Nothing but a careful perusal of their letters could convey the anxiety felt by so many persons for some effectual check to the daily increasing grievance of organ-grinders and street music" (v–vi). The "anxiety" Bass senses, however, as his preface goes on to demonstrate, is not that of "all classes" but of middle-class professionals, especially those laboring in their homes. He notes that members of "all the learned professions," as well as "the most distinguished literary and scientific men," and even a group of two hundred London composers and performers, have enthusiastically endorsed his stance in their correspondence with him. For the sake of their livelihoods and also to protect the ill, he maintains that the law must be emended. The letters, articles, and other evidence in his book, he writes, "will enable any Member of the Legislature and the public generally to form a correct opinion of the real state of the existing law, and will demonstrate what great obstacles are opposed by street music to the progress of art, science, and literature; and what torments are inflicted on the studious, the sensitive, and the afflicted" (vii). By collecting into a unified whole the angry voices of practitioners of the arts and sciences, Bass's book consolidates their power, even as it attempts to assuage the anxious among them with the construction of a telling statement of group identity and underscores the territorial anomalies of their working lives.

It follows that Bass and his supporters are most interested in observing and reinforcing differences between the industrious and the cacophonous, the respectable and the sordid. Efforts to draw territorial distinctions between middle- and lower-class lifestyles persist throughout the longest chapter in the book, the collection of protest letters titled "Sufferers from Street Music." In this section, letter-writers reiterate that street music must above all disturb neither their relaxation nor their occupations. Invoking whatever authority their professional identities can provide, the mounting chorus of their voices also evokes the pathos of their struggling work lives: "I am a clergyman in delicate health," writes "a sufferer"; "I have difficult law business, literary work, and am besides a musical composer," claims another; a third writes, "I am an artist . . . paying a large amount annually in local rates, and I do think it very hard that I cannot be allowed to pursue my calling in quiet" (10, 18, 32). An academic notes, "I am cruelly interrupted by grind-organs, in the midst of studies which demand the concentration of my whole attention"; the secretary of the London Mechanics' Institution bemoans the fact that their activities are disturbed by "nigger melodies"; "Much of my time is devoted to scientific pursuits," comments another complainant; and still another writes, "I am a clergyman, who . . . [has] to preach on a Sunday to a large congregation of 1,200 people, mostly of the upper and middle classes . . . [W]e are surely subjects of the Queen, more than the Italian organ-grinder, and I think it is not liberty but tyranny, if he is permitted to ply his vocation so as to make us desist from ours" (29, 34–37). "One engaged in literary pursuits" describes with disdain the "other class . . . of household servants, and others, whose wishes cannot surely be of any importance when weighed against those of . . . the scientific man, the author, the artist, and others who labour hard for the public benefit" (33–34). And a music teacher writing to Bass essentially speaks for all distressed Londoners "who live by their brains": "Why should a man, who has spent years in acquiring skill in his profession, who pays high rent and heavy taxes, be robbed of his time, while a vagabond, who pays neither one or the other, grinds two or three streets out of as many pence?" (31). The dominant themes of the letters, the aspects that unite these struggling teachers, artists, and writers in a collective identity, are an ardent defense of the home as workplace and an acute professional contempt for those less educated and fortunate.

The centerpiece of Bass's book, however, is a letter from none other than Dickens himself, cosigned by artists and writers who "cannot fail to have the greatest weight and authority," and it appears in larger print than the rest of the correspondence (40):

SIR, . . .
Your correspondents are, all, professors and practitioners of one or other of the arts or sciences. In their devotion to their pursuits—tending to the peace and comfort of mankind—they are daily interrupted, harassed, worried, wearied, driven nearly mad, by street musicians.

They are even made especial objects of persecution by brazen performers on brazen instruments . . . for, no sooner does it become known to those producers of horrible sounds that any of your correspondents have particular need of quiet in their own houses, than the said houses are beleaguered by discordant hosts seeking to be bought off.

Your correspondents represent to you that these pecuniary speculations in the misery they endure are far more destructive to their spirits than their pockets; and that some of them, not absolutely tied to London by their avocations, have actually fled into the country for refuge from this unmerited persecution—which is none the less grievous or hard to bear, because it is absurd.

Your grateful correspondents take the liberty to suggest to you that, although a Parliamentary debate undoubtedly requires great delicacy in the handling, their avocations require at least as much, and that it would highly conduce towards the success of your proposed enactment, if you prevail on its opponents to consent to state their objections to it, assailed on all sides by the frightful noises in despite of which your correspondents have to gain their bread.

(Signed) CHARLES DICKENS. (41–42)

The list of cosignatories reads like a roster of the Victorian cultural elite: Alfred Tennyson, John Everett Millais, Francis Grant, Forster, Leech, William Holman Hunt, Wilkie Collins, Frith, Richard Doyle, Carlyle, Alfred Wigan, Thomas Faed, E. M. Barry, Thomas Woolner, and so on—all told, twenty-eight representative authors, painters, engravers, illustrators, historians, actors, sculptors, architects, and scientists.[58] Most drew attention to their peculiar professional status by including their home addresses, many of which significantly were their places of work. Evidence suggests concern for Leech's health might have motivated Dickens to write the letter, if he did not in fact compose it at Leech's request.[59] But its message is one Dickens makes his own, with an unmistakable rhetorical forcefulness that would seem quite comic were his objections not so earnest.

While hardly on the scale of the vocational manifestos of, say, the Guild of Literature and Art or, later, the Society of Authors, Dickens's letter nonetheless unites an ad hoc professional collective in a petition to defeat street noise and reiterate the value of quiet. Kaplan's comment that the signers are "partly distinguished by their inability to sympathize with the inconvenient poor" points to the letter's implicit intention of reinforcing class distinctions.[60] But the most revealing aspect of the document is its emphasis, following Carlyle's lead, upon the home as a critical, if problematic, site of professional identity and therefore as a space to be defended at all costs. As Karen Chase and Michael Levenson suggest in their discussion of "the social force of the wall" in Victorian London, the petition, and Bass's book more generally, collected "the splenetic outcries of a cultural elite that saw the constant distractions in the thoroughfare as dangerously corrosive to privacy."[61] Alternatively, those "not absolutely tied to London by their avocations" could relocate to the country in desperation. Such early incidents of "write flight," so to speak, suggest the beginnings of the more widespread retreat artists were to make to suburban London in the 1870s.[62] This notion of territorial warfare underlies Dickens's final paragraph, in which he bitterly proposes that MPs who defend street music should try doing so surrounded, "assailed on all sides by the [musicians'] frightful noises" that would, ironically, interrupt their work. Dickens's defense of his territory did not end with the letter. The following April, while completing *Our Mutual Friend* at Somers Place in Hyde Park, he reiterated the conflicted dynamic of professional accomplishment, the space of home, and noise: "I am working like a dragon at my book, and am a terror to the household, likewise to all the organs and brass bands in this quarter."[63] For Dickens, nearing the end of his final completed novel, to write with such fervor was to demand private territory, that is, to terrify—both those inside who occupied the same domestic space and those itinerants outside who noisily threatened his professional endeavors.[64]

As the reference in the letter to street music as mere "horrible sounds" implies, the words "music" and "noise" became unstable terms throughout the debates. Peter Bailey has observed that, for Victorians, "leisure in particular represented an area where social distinctions were vulnerable."[65] As a result, many professionals who felt threatened by street organs considered it vitally important to maintain the semantic distinction between "music" as intended for those of refined tastes indoors and grinding noise as meant for the exterior masses. "Music, delightful as it is in season, is not desirable every hour from sunrise to midnight; but what torments us is not music, nor anything like music," a leader in the *Examiner* claimed. "The organ is an instrument of torture to human ears," which, it continued, produces not harmonious melodies but "hackneyed slang music." The author insisted that organ grinders were not musicians, since their technique solely consisted of "twirling round and round a handle like that of a small coffee-mill." A physician writing to Bass protested "the lawless noise which disgraces London," and a *Punch* parody offered up a "Programme for Quiet Street Musical Performance" replete with extensive and unsuccessful instrument tuning and appearances by a German band, a "Man with organ," a "Man, without organ, but with monkey," a "Combination of talent. Man with organ *and* monkey," an "organ with donkey," "Niggers, accompanied by an admiring crowd," a "Dancing Pony," and a "Grand Finale" of street minstrels, organ, and volunteer band playing simultaneously: "Such are the delights of the Great London Unmusical Season!" the author concluded.[66] The very title of an anonymous 1863 pamphlet attacked "the Itinerants Who Prowl About the Streets of London with Machines Assuming to be Music [*sic*] Played Mechanically by the Hand." "Who among the thousands who know what music is, will accept this definition?" the writer asked.[67] The most damning method of attacking street music, these aesthetic arbiters appeared to realize, was to deny its very musicality. "Lawless noise," "hackneyed slang," "unmusic"—all such epithets signified attempts to distinguish between an acceptable middle-class form of leisure and its less-refined manifestations on the streets.[68]

And yet the repertoire in the streets echoed middle-class tastes from the highbrow to the low, including "mostly popular middle-class and operatic songs, dances and marches, hymns, oratorio extracts (especially Handel), and light overtures."[69] Although some of the musicians were quite accomplished, what they performed depended in part on who would listen: as one of the organ grinders Mayhew interviewed commented, "'You must have some opera tunes for the gentlemen, and some for the poor people, and they like the dancing tune.'"[70] From "The Last Rose of Summer" to "Dixieland," from the prison song in *Il Trovatore* to "Rule Britannia," the music that circulated in the streets represented an unruly mix of the popular, the nationalistic, and the international, primarily geared to the substratum of the very poor, those in Clerkenwell and elsewhere who could not afford to attend even a third-rate music hall.[71]

In their rearrangement and widespread dispersal of musical works, organ grinders joined other street performers in presenting a challenge to central-ized class-based and political control. Edward Jacobs has described a London "street culture which practiced literacy as a festive disruption of and alterna-tive to rational schooling and industrial disciplines."[72] For Jacobs, costermon-gers' "slang submits industrial literacy to festive misrule," and the plagiarisms practiced by penny gaffs, bloods, and the like "did not simply reproduce mainstream literature. Rather, they engaged in a political struggle over the so-cial meaning of literature with the cultural fact of 'heteroglossia'" (97–98). Like street literacy, street music represented a festive disruption of disci-plines—in this case, those of middle-class work and leisure—and in its very status as "hackneyed slang," it presented a provocative other, an alternative to acceptable middle-class definitions of music. Just as the itinerant performer came to symbolize an invasive affront to professional labors, so his music be-came a "lawless" other, a threatening double to the respectable concert or drawing-room recital. It was in essence a Victorian variation on "rough music," "a latter-day charivari" that asserted populist unruliness against the "new standards of urban discipline" imposed by the moralizing force of the Metropolitan Police.[73]

Within this context, the need for Bass's act became that much more ur-gent. The publication of his book had its effect: in July 1864, his motion passed through to Royal Assent "without debate," although changes to the wording of the act partly moderated Bass's original extremist language.[74] "Babbage's [*sic*] Act has passed, and he *is* a public benefactor," the mathematician Augustus De Morgan wrote to the distinguished astronomer John Herschel, "A grinder went away from my house at the first word."[75] Leech captured the victory in a *Punch* cartoon that, in a sign of anticipation, actually appeared two months before the Assent was given (figure 2.5). In the cartoon, above the caption "Three Cheers for Bass and His Barrel of Beer, and Out with the Foreign Ruf-fian and His Barrel-Organ!" a burly Bass seems about to roll a barrel of his

222   PUNCH, OR THE LONDON CHARIVARI.   [MAY 28, 1864.

THREE CHEERS FOR BASS AND HIS BARREL OF BEER, AND OUT WITH THE FOREIGN
RUFFIAN AND HIS BARREL-ORGAN!

FIGURE 2.5. MP MICHAEL T. BASS EVICTS ONE OF LEECH'S
STEREOTYPICAL GRINDERS, FROM *Punch* 46 (1864): 222.

own ale into one of Leech's typically seedy organ grinders, presumably to
push him off the edge of the coast where he stands, still grinding away. In setting and purpose, the image is reminiscent of the Savoyard cartoon from four
years earlier (figure 2.1), yet in place of the comically irate Punch, Leech
championed the wealthy brewer Bass, his weapon not an umbrella but the
weight of his parliamentary power and, quite literally, his family name and
distinctly British business ("BASS & Co"). Leech rendered the purging of
organ grinders from England as an economic and occupational struggle as
well as a nationalistic one. This confrontation set barrel against barrel, the
English commercial success against his foreign foil. Yet even as Leech's poor
visual pun disturbingly pointed to the occupational echo between brewing
mogul and grinding mongrel, it expressed the anxious need to separate the
two. Propelled by Babbage, Dickens, and others, Bass's act sought through
legal means to establish such a distinction between professionals and intrusive outsiders, but only by facilitating professionals' greater meddling in those
outsiders' affairs. The act provided those members of the middle classes anxious about professional and territorial differentiation with a legal outlet, an
authorized means to control the sounds of the city streets. At the same time
that those protective impulses shifted outward, however, they turned even
further inward, marking the professional body as a vulnerable site where at

stake lay the most fundamental of all terms of identity: stability and nervous disorder, health and illness, life and death.

EMBODYING NOISE: THE LEECH CASE

The objection to street noises is not a matter of taste. It involves the progress
of honest labour, and the avoidance of great mental affliction.

—MARK LEMON, in a letter to Bass on Leech's behalf

THE COMMENT of the longtime *Punch* editor and friend of Leech un-wittingly draws attention to the physical effects of street music, for Lemon's word choice plays on a dual reference to aesthetic as well as sensory perception. The objection to street noises, after all, literally is not a matter of *taste* but of hearing. Street music generated xenophobic and aesthetic de-bates, to be sure, but it had damaging impact as a corporeal problem, an urban disease that disturbed not only the duties of middle-class professionals but also their well-being. That Victorians cast the street music problem as one re-lating to the body is not surprising, given the pervasiveness of illness during the period and the resulting cultural emphasis on the healthy body as indica-tor of moral and mental fortitude.[76] Critics have approached literary manifes-tations of illness from feminist perspectives to demonstrate "the persistent at-tempts by Victorian writers and physicians to define the terms of human physicality, to locate in the body the source of sexual and social divisions, to create a physiological blueprint that would explain the meaning of racial dif-ference and restore a sense of social and material order."[77] The "organ-grind-ing nuisance" in part appeared a threat to professional identity because it vio-lated "the terms of human physicality" and the "sense of social and material order." Barrel organs preyed on their middle-class victims through the invol-untary faculty of hearing.

Florence Nightingale made explicit the connection between hearing and health in her widely popular *Notes on Nursing*, published four years before the passage of the Street Music Act. Nightingale's text included an entire section devoted to "Noise," in which she discussed its tendency to disturb both the ill and healthy.[78] She wrote that "unnecessary noise is the most cruel absence of care which can be inflicted either on sick or well" (47). After denouncing nurses for whispering, moving slowly, even walking on tiptoe, she advocated a combination of "quickness, lightness, and gentleness" (45). Nightingale at-tacked women's fashions and accessories as noisome and debilitating, as ac-cessories to illness: "A nurse who rustles . . . is the horror of a patient, though perhaps he does not know why," she claimed, deploring "the fidget of silk and of crinoline, the rattling of keys, the creaking of stays and of shoes" and asking "what has become of a woman's light step?—the firm, light, quick step we have been asking for? . . . only a man can cross the floor of a sick-room with-out shaking it!" (47, 46). Unexpectedly, Nightingale gendered noise as female, even as she characterized patients as male invalids worthy of quiet reverence: "Never speak to an invalid from behind, nor from the door, nor from any distance from him, nor when he is doing anything" (49).

Nightingale sternly warned of the potential threat of noise to the body. She emphasized creating what amounted to a wall of silence surrounding the patient, within which sound would be minutely regimented: "It is inconceivable how much the sick suffer by having anybody overhead. . . . Remember that every noise a patient cannot *see* partakes of the character of suddenness to him" (57). The ill male and the intellectual were aligned in her work: "I have never known persons who exposed themselves for years to constant interruption who did not muddle away their intellects by it at last," she observed (50). For patients with "peculiarly irritable nerves" (such as Leech), she concluded, "any sacrifice to secure silence for [them] is worth while, because no air, however good, no attendance, however careful, will do anything for such cases without quiet" (57).[79] Nightingale's practical consideration of the relationship between bodily soundness and external sounds revealed the extent to which, by the 1860s, perceptions of the unhealthy effects of noise had acquired a new sense of urgency and caution amid a growing urban cacophony.

During a period, in fact, when complaints surged against the stink of the Thames and smoky London air, street sounds also came to be represented as threatening pollutants with noxious effects. A letter from "One of the Tormented" to Bass made such a point: "it [street music] is a nuisance in the most comprehensive sense of the term, and quite as destructive to health, comfort, and quiet, as *bad smells, bad drainage,* and the proximity of disorderly houses" (88). A leader from the *Morning Post* sarcastically insinuated that musicians themselves spread disease in the form of sound: "Italian organ-grinders, blind men with screeching clarionets, boys with droning hurdy-gurdies, sucking musicians in the first stage of trombones and ophicledes, have daily the power of creating a plague as bad as any in Egypt of old" (59). The same article concluded with an analogy that linked foul stench and filthy sight with repellent sound: "Smith is not permitted to annoy Jones by placing a manure-heap within reach of his nostrils; why should Jones be allowed to excruciate Smith's ears with Italian organ-boys?" (61). A *Times* leader grew even more visceral when discoursing on the vulnerability of the ear:

> There is no protection, we say, for the ear is the most helpless faculty we have. It is at once the weakest and most wonderful, the most ethereal and most persecuted of our senses. . . . A sense that deliberately constituted we subject day and night to a torture which is very nearly equivalent to cutting off a malefactor's eyelids and then crucifying him with his face to the sun.[80]

Without blinking, the author represented street music as a sort of aural crucifixion, a graphic bodily "torture" from which there was no escape but death. Street noise, this writer claimed, overpowered "the weakest and most wonderful" of the senses and denied corporeal soundness and integrity by repeatedly violating "the most helpless faculty" the body has.[81]

More than one Londoner classified street music as a kind of bodily infection by describing its toll on invalids. A physician from Mayfair commented in a letter to Bass "that sick persons and young children are constantly awakened, and kept awake, by street music at late hours" (14). A writer from Hyde Park noted, "what we want for children is sleep when they are well, and still worse when they are ailing. With street music this is impossible. In poor neighborhoods, no doubt, many a child has been killed by street music" (25). The actor Alfred Wigan agitatedly described his own invalid experience: *"Once, when I was lying dangerously ill, a neighbour of mine took a German band up into his balcony after they had been ordered off by the constable on duty, and kept them playing for about two hours"* (17). Babbage implied the connection between the homebound intellectual and the invalid in his "Chapter": "Those who possess an impaired bodily frame . . . are absolutely driven to distraction by the vile and discordant music of the streets waking them, at all hours, in the midst of that temporary repose so necessary for confirmed invalids." And amid its editorial hyperbole, the *City Press* would not even attempt to estimate the pestilent effects of street music: "How many of the sick and dying are daily harried by such abominations, it would be painful even to conjecture."[82] Invading ears, infesting bodies, the music of the streets, all these comments suggested, not only impaired the healthy but also worsened the condition of the already ailing.

John Leech embodied the metaphor of homebound artist as invalid, because indeed he was both. He spent his final years stricken with angina in his Kensington home, his physical distress intensified by street musicians, especially the grinders. Frith implies that Leech's "hyper-sensitiveness to noise" was closely linked to his professional anxieties: "I knew of his sufferings from himself; and the world must have guessed them from his attacks upon the organ-grinders, the bellowing street-hawkers, and the thousand and one noises that distress the London householder whose livelihood depends upon his brain."[83] Beyond such a threat to his professional identity, however, Leech in his drawings and to his close friends represented street sounds as what they fundamentally were to him: a bodily danger, a murderous menace. Frith notes Leech's "worn brain and the shattered nerves that throbbed with agony at noises which would scarcely have disturbed a healthy man," and another biographer writes that by June 1863, Leech "was confessing with desperation that street noises were killing him and they were 'driving him to suicide.'"[84] While it might seem feasible to explain Leech's response to the organ grinders as solely a case of "shattered nerves," or nervous breakdown — a malady common enough among Victorians — and leave it at that, the evidence within the artist's work indicates that his response was as much if not more so a register of corporeal anxiety, both a fear for his own bodily vulnerability and a disgust at the bodies of alien others.[85]

W'ANTED, by an aged Lady, of a very nervous temperament, a Professor, who will undertake to mesmerise all the organs in her Street.—Salary so much *per* Organ.

FIGURE 2.6. LEECH'S EARLIEST ORGAN-GRINDING CARTOON, PUBLISHED THE YEAR HE ILLUSTRATED DICKENS'S *A Christmas Carol*. FROM *Punch* 5 (1843): 246.

Appearing throughout his last two decades and about twice annually over his final six years, Leech's cartoons of the organ grinders revealed the vindictive side of an artist considered "before all else a *lovable* man," with, according to no less an eminent art critic than John Ruskin, a genius "capable in its brightness of finding pretty jest in everything, but capable in its tenderness also of rejoicing in the beauty of everything, softened and illumined with its loving wit the entire scope of [the] English social scene." Dickens wrote that Leech "almost always introduces into his graphic sketches some beautiful faces or agreeable forms," and that he "delights in pleasant things."[86] Leech's street music illustrations were hardly "loving" or "beautiful" but aggressively bitter, abandoning satire for malice. Even as Leech vented his frustration at street noises in the cartoons, however, he used them literally to embody those noises, to locate disturbing sounds in grotesque caricatures of foreign bodies—to make the audible not just visible but corporeal. His earliest cartoon on the subject (figure 2.6), in which a well-dressed grinder mesmerizes two entranced children with his playing, indicated the direction Leech's future representations were to take. With this inauspicious start, Leech launched his attack on noises of bodies by attacking noises *as* bodies. For example, a full-page cartoon from 1854 entitled "Foreign Enlistment" featured not just one but eight organ men hauling their instruments behind a notably erect regimental leader (figure 2.7). A xenophobic sight gag, the drawing's caustic joke lay in its contrast between bodies: that of the upright, crisply uniformed English soldier against those of his stooping, grinning, and disheveled Italian recruits, who are clearly unprepared for doing battle in the Crimean War. Readily aware of the incapacitating effect of street noise upon his own body, Leech depicted the street music problem as one of competing bodies, as in "One Good Turn Deserves Another," where a giant monkey grinds the organ while his former master stands by on a leash (figure 2.8). Such a role reversal and body switch represent Leech's blunt condemnation of organ grinders as overgrown monkeys—Darwinian primitives—and their organ-grinding itself as callous and deformed.

With his perception of street music as a series of "horrible noises that never seemed to cease in his neighborhood," it was a small step for Leech to

FOREIGN ENLISTMENT.

If we must have it—for Goodness Sake begin with the Organ Men.

FIGURE 2.7. LEECH'S SOLUTION TO THE STREET MUSIC NUISANCE: ENLIST ORGAN GRINDERS TO FIGHT IN THE CRIMEA. FROM *Punch* 27 (1854): 263.

ONE GOOD TURN DESERVES ANOTHER.

THE LAZY ORGAN GRINDERS HAVE HAD IT ALL THEIR OWN WAY WITH THE MONKEYS—NOW THEN—CHANGE ABOUT!

FIGURE 2.8. EVOLUTIONARY CONNECTIONS IMPLIED IN DARWIN'S *Origin of Species*, PUBLISHED THREE YEARS EARLIER, RESONATE IN THIS CARTOON BY LEECH, FROM *Punch's Almanack for 1862*.

portray the musicians as infested itinerants who with their proximity endangered healthy middle-class home life.[87] In a later, coarser style, Leech showed a householder dousing a haggard organ grinder with a carefully aimed hose, while a domestic and a child attack another with syringe and peashooter (figure 2.9). "The Cold Water Cure" indicated by the caption is a trite pun, a medical treatment for middle-class invalids here turned territorial defense against unshaven, unclean organ men—a defense discharged, significantly, from both within the home and outside the gates of it, upon the apparently filthy bodies of the streets. The borders of the home become fluid in this cartoon; in a visual indication of the interpenetration of public and

PUNCH'S ALMANACK FOR 1858.

THE PLEASANT LETTER-WRITER.

MARCH.

From a Lady to her Husband.

Ladybird Lodge, Kent.

DEAR EDWIN,

We got down safely, me, the children, nurse, and SUSAN, though I say again, as I said at parting, that your putting us all into a first-class compartment and telegraphing for a carriage to wait for us at the station and bring us here, was *nothing*, and *any other husband* would have escorted us down. *Business* is always ready to be in a wife's way when she requires the least attention. Dearest Mamma and Papa were rejoiced to see me, but think I look worn and troubled, and well I may, but it is pleasant at last to find *somebody* who cares to hear of one's grievances. Write by return of post, for I gave my purse with all my money in it to baby to play with, and darling Tootums must have dropped it out of window, which was your fault in not coming and taking care of such things yourself. Besides, I find the children all want new things to go about in. Don't forget.

Your affectionate wife,
ANGELINA.

EDWIN BROWN, ESQ.

P.S. I forgot to tell you I was obliged to give the coals and taxes money to MISS STICHLEY (dressmaker); she wanted it, poor thing.

ASYLUM FOR TRAGEDIANS.—The retired Hamlet.

PORTRAIT OF THE OLD PARTY WHO RATHER LIKES ORGAN-GRINDING.

RECREATIONS IN NATURAL HISTORY.

IT is interesting to know that the Dodo family, so long supposed to be extinct, has been again found, and will shortly be re-introduced into England, the Zoological Society having directed a vessel to be sent for some specimens. The Dodo has been found in the Isle of Retribution, one of the Canzellas group, about thirty-seven leagues from Ascension. The accuracy of JOHN SAVERY's celebrated drawing in the Ashmolean Museum is vindicated, but the animal does not eat cryptogamous plants, but fish, which it catches by means of the long feathers in its tail. It lies in ambush on a rock, dangling these feathers into the water, and letting the wind flirt them about like a fly. The fish, being attracted, snaps, and a small curve or hook, worked by muscular action secures him. The Dodo then sits upon him until he is thoroughly cooked by the warmth of the bird's body, and devours him. To save the imported specimens the trouble and exhaustion of this process, MR. MITCHELL, the indefatigable Secretary to the Zoological Gardens, has devised an imitation Dodo, to hold a heated iron within it, on the Italian iron principle, and this, placed on the fish, will ensure regular food for this interesting feature in the Regent's Park collection.

In the shadow of a small waist may be seen a large doctor's bill and the outline of a coffin.

HISTORICAL CHRONOLOGY

Compiled by M. P. COX.

B.C. 25. DETHRONEMENT of KING CANUTE upon the shore at Sandwich, after the Invasion of JULIUS AGRIPPA.
A.D. 800. Invasion of Great Britain by the Picts and Scalds, headed by SIR ROBERT WALLACE and the Man of Ross.

B.C. 19. LADY JOAN GREY burnt on Tower Hill for refusing to marry KING HENRY THE EIGHTH.
A.D. 357. Discovery by WAT TYLER of the Rye House Plot, resulting in the Banishment of TITUS OATES to JOHN OF ENDEN GROATS' house.
A.D. 166. CARDINAL WOLSEY proclaimed Regent during the absence in Ethiopia of EDWARD THE BLACK PRINCE.
A.D. 222. Death of GENERAL WOLFE upon the Field of the Cloth of Gold.

A.D. 99. OLIVER CROMWELL, the Pretender, beheaded for conspiracy with GUY FAWKES and LORD CHATHAM to blow up the House of Commons for the length of the Long Parliament.
A.D. 511. Ratification at Runnymede of the Bill of Rights.
A.D. 730. Defeat of the Austrians at the Battle of Bunker's Hill, and restoration of KING OTHO to the throne of Sweden.
A.D. 766. Marriage of EDWARD THE CONFESSOR with LADY JANE GODIVA.

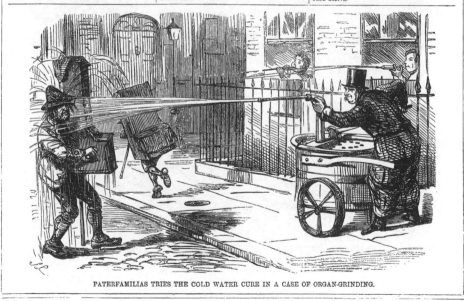

PATERFAMILIAS TRIES THE COLD WATER CURE IN A CASE OF ORGAN-GRINDING.

FIGURE 2.9. LEECH'S "COLD WATER CURE" FOR ORGAN-GRINDING, IN A CARTOON FROM *Punch's Almanack for 1858.*

SKETCH FROM A STUDY WINDOW.

FIGURE 2.10. A LANDSCAPE OF PROWLING ORGAN GRINDERS, AND A WINDOW
INTO LEECH'S HAUNTED MIND. FROM *Punch* 45 (1863): 53.

private spheres, the larger water blast that defends the home is itself on the street, the professional's pump turned on the itinerant's organ. Leech distilled, so to speak, an invalid's beneficial form of medical treatment into the grinders' soggy punishment, all the while maintaining a focus upon the threatening corporeal presence of the urban noisemakers. Nowhere was this focus clearer than in Leech's famous drawing, published shortly after the introduction of Bass's bill, of a suburban street as seen "from A Study Window" (figure 2.10). This image, which encapsulated Leech's intertwined professional and corporeal anxieties, shows hunched, ragged organ grinders haunting an otherwise empty street far into the distance, while near the center of the drawing crawls a large insect. This, Leech suggests, is a louse among lice, a key symbol of the embodied foreign pestilence that, organs in tow, disturbed his labors, corrupted his health, and infested his residential landscape.

As he neared death, Leech in his drawings and comments revealed a middle-class invalid's losing struggle to discipline obtrusive lower-class disturbances. Describing a lively confrontation between the artist and the grinders, Henry Silver shows how the musicians in their boldness exploited the limitations of Leech's condition as an invalid: "'J[ohn] L[eech] still nervous about himself, defied by 2 organ men yesterday who called him "You bl[ood]y sh[i]t" "You bl[ood]y b[u]g" etc. in the choicest Billingsgate. Said if he hadn't feared the excitement he would have knocked them down.'"[88] Thus, in "Italian Persecution (A Scene From Real Life)," when an organ grinder laughs at the threat of police intervention while refusing to move on from the house of a bedridden patient whose anguished face stares out from a panel above, the subtext presumably was Leech's own violated invalidism (figure 2.11, and see also the similar figure 2.12). The theme of bodily violation recurs in two late cartoons, in which a grinder's monkey leaps upon "a servant girl" and frightens her "into fits," and a "pony rears" upon hearing the organ, leaving its "young lady" rider "nearly frightened to death"; in neither case, the captions indicate, are the grinders arrested or punished (figures 2.13, 2.14).[89] These cartoons presented the musicians' effect on the social order and female body as a kind of animalistic chaos with no apparent penalty. Such fears of a disruptive challenge to the healthy and sickly body alike underscored Leech's entire campaign against the grinders. His illustrations of them represented persistent attempts to inflict a form of visual discipline upon aural disorder, to embody street music so as to expose it as alien and, ideally, to banish it. But for all the bluster of his illustrations, the frailty of Leech's own body did not let him fully realize his fantasy of distinction. Four months after the previous cartoon appeared, ground down by organs and coronary disease, Leech found final silence from the outsiders he so despised. Not one to resist hyperbole, Carlyle would go on to speak out against the freedoms that "'permitted Italian foreigners to invade London and kill John Leech, and no doubt hundreds of other nervous people who die and make no sign!'"[90]

176   PUNCH, OR THE LONDON CHARIVARI.   [MAY 1, 1858

ITALIAN PERSECUTION. (A SCENE FROM REAL LIFE.)

A QUIET STREET IN LONDON. TIME—NIGHT; HALF-PAST TEN.

In a Bed-room a Mother is tending a sick boy, who is suffering from nervous fever. At the door PATERFAMILIAS *is expostulating with an Organ-grinder, who is defying him with extreme insolence, alternated with performances on the instrument of torture.* POLICEMAN (*unseen*) *is in the kitchen considering whether* SUSAN'S *cooking, or* MARY'S *savings' bank-money would be the best investment.*

Pater. Go away, Sir. Be off, Sir. I have told you that there is a sick person here.

Organist. Eh! You sick yourself, I think, old fallah.

  ["*Poor Dog Tray.*"]

Pater. Be off, Sir!

Organist. Want to go to sleep, old boy, eh?

  ["*Keemo, Kimo.*"]

Pater. If you don't go, I'll call the police.

Organist (*grinning*). Pleece, eh! Pleece. I call 'em. Holla! I call 'em for you, old boy, Pleece.

  ["*Love Not.*"]

Pater. By Jove, you scoundrel, I'll serve you out.

Organist. Eh! (*grins.*) You no like music, old fellah! (*whistles at him.*) You no like music? Change for you, then.

  ["*Polka.*"]

Pater. I'll see for an officer, you rascal.

Organist. See for him, old fellah. Why not see for him, eh, old boy?

  ["*My Mary-Anne.*"]

[PATERFAMILIAS *rushes into the street, crying,* "Police," *and looks down every area but the right one, when, returning in despair, he encounters* Z 3985.

Policeman (*calmly*). What's up, Sir?

Pater. (*hurrying him up to* ORGANIST, *who is now playing* "Bobbing all around"). I have ordered this fellow off a dozen times—this is my house, and there's a sick person in it for whom the doctor prescribes quiet. He won't go. Move him.

Policem. (*to Organist*). Come, move on!

[ORGANIST *pretends not to understand him, and grinds on until the last moment, when the* POLICEMAN *lays hold of his hand. With a vicious glare he then goes to the next door but one, and strikes up* "Dog Tray."

Pater. (*in fury.*) Do you hear that?

[*They follow* ORGANIST, *and he is again stopped.*

FIGURE 2.11. LEECH'S "ITALIAN PERSECUTION," FROM *Punch* 34 (1858): 176.

FIGURE 2.12. ANOTHER VERSION OF "ITALIAN PERSECUTION," FROM *Punch's Almanack for 1864*.

ENTERTAINMENT FOR AN ORGAN-GRINDING RUFFIAN.

DISTURBING A STREET AND FRIGHTENING A SERVANT GIRL INTO FITS, FOR WHICH HE HAS
TO PAY 10s. ONLY.—(*See Police Report, Jan.* 1, 1862.)

FIGURE 2.13. LEECH'S "ENTERTAINMENT FOR AN ORGAN-GRINDING
RUFFIAN," *Punch* 42 (1862): 11.

242   PUNCH OR THE LONDON CHARIVARI.   [JUNE 11, 1864.

A SCENE IN BELGRAVIA—AND A FACT, TOO.

YOUNG LADY GOING OUT FOR A RIDE—ORGAN-GRINDER STRIKES UP—PONY REARS—CHILD NEARLY FRIGHTENED TO DEATH—NOT A CASE
OF ILLNESS!—CAN'T INTERFERE—DIRTY RUFFIAN PLAYS ON, WHILE POLICEMAN EATS ORANGE.

FIGURE 2.14. ONE OF THE LAST CARTOONS OF ORGAN GRINDERS LEECH
PUBLISHED BEFORE HIS DEATH. FROM *Punch* 46 (1864): 242.

"GREAT FACTS"

"Please remember the organ, sir,"
What? hasn't he left me yet?
I promise, good man; for its tedious burr
I never can forget.

—LEWIS CARROLL, *"Those Horrid Hurdy-Gurdies!"*

THE PASSAGE of the Street Music Act and the best efforts of Bass, Babbage, Dickens, Leech, and the rest, in the long and even short run, did little to displace street musicians. Hardly a friend to organ grinders, James Greenwood spoke for many when he wrote in 1867 that "there is no cure for the evil; organ-grinding has become a settled institution of the country, and as such must be endured."[91] H. R. Haweis, the inimitable author of *Music and Morals*, claimed in seeming utilitarian fashion that "the organ is a *great fact*, and perhaps, in a survey of street music in England, the most prominent fact."[92] (German bands constituted the *"second great fact* of street music" [461].) He went on to balance prevailing negative stereotypes of the grinders with a belated, romanticized reconsideration:

> I bless that organ-man—a very Orpheus in hell! I stand in the foul street where the blessed sun shines, and where the music is playing; I give the man a penny to prolong the happiness of those poor people, of those hungry, pale, and ragged children; and, as I retire, I am saluted as a public benefactor, and was ever pleasure bought so cheap and pure? (461)

A similarly positive portrait was provided by Adolphe Smith, who found the Italian street musicians "irresistible" and "fascinating," saluting them as those who had "nurtured in our courts and alleys echoes of purer music than could otherwise have reached these dismal abodes."[93] Richard Rowe concurred, writing that the organ grinders' "faces sometimes shed poetry on our prosaic thoroughfares."[94] Alongside these recastings of the organists as quaint objects of contemplation, complaints to the *Times* persisted, but with not nearly the force and focus of the period of the 1850s and early 1860s, partly because of the middle-class exodus to the suburbs that occurred throughout the closing decades of the century.[95] This suggests that the anti–street music movement was not only unsuccessful in banishing organists and their grinding but also, ultimately, provoked a backlash of romantic nostalgia that undermined the effectiveness of the act. With the passage of time, such nostalgia only deepened, as the remaining itinerant musicians became quaint curiosities, exotic reminders of the life that once animated metropolitan streets. The philosopher James Sully, for one, recognized that the real problem lay ahead, "with the natural unchecked tendencies of growing civilization," which were "but too plainly in the direction of an increase of noise."[96] Citing Babbage as one of those "endowed with more than the ordinary measure of sensibility,"

Sully appealed to Victorian notions of savagery and civility to silence the streets in the name of urban professionalism and went so far as to suggest that a future profession might arise to accomplish precisely this task (as, in a sense, one did, in the guise of the acoustical engineer): "Is it Utopian to anticipate a date when men of science will think it a profitable employment of their time to consider some means of diminishing the weird and terrible sounds which our railways have introduced into our nineteenth-century life?" (716, 715).[97]

Toward the end of the century, mid-Victorian aggressive attacks upon the intractable street music problem came to be regarded with a mingling of empathy and satire. Not long before embarking on his career as dramatist, George Bernard Shaw, considered England's first great modern music critic, wrote in one of his columns for the *Morning Leader* that the street musicians of his youth had all but disappeared: "I have been asked for my views on the barrel-organ question. I reply there is no barrel-organ question. . . . There are hundreds of thousands of children in London today who have never heard a barrel-organ. That is a tremendous fact."[98] Shaw reminisced fondly over his sightings of organists as a child but regretted that these had given way to street-piano players. He went on to propose fanciful legal action that mocked the Street Music Act:

> Let a short Act of Parliament be passed, placing all street musicians outside the protection of the law; so that any citizen may assail them with stones, sticks, knives, pistols, or bombs without incurring any penalties—except, of course, in the case of the instrument itself being injured; for Heaven forbid that I should advocate any disregard for the sacredness of property, especially in the form of industrial capital! (3:47)

Though he could readily do without the musicians' miserable dissonance, his ludicrously draconian measure only highlighted the impracticality of the then-current and ineffective law, Bass's act itself. Shaw reflected on his predecessors' attempts to regulate city streets with mixed feelings, sympathetic toward the desire for silence in which to think and work, but—this was the central shift—with a certain wistfulness for what had once been considered a nuisance, and a resignation to the inevitability of such noise, one of the facts of life, after all, for writers in urban modernity. Harry Furniss captures such a bemused mix of satire and resignation in his "A Quiet Sunday in London; or, The Day of Rest" from 1886 (figure 2.15). In this image, which pays homage to Leech's "The Quiet Street," Furniss presents a city scene absent organs, but so crawling with Salvation Army marchers and protestors yelling at anyone in their way that it verges on apocalyptic. The only restful figure in the picture is the unnoticed pickpocket lying in the corner, contentedly fingering his take of watches over Furniss's signature. Organ grinders, one almost is inclined to say, would be a relief, but Furniss indicates that the time when they were the predominant street nuisance has passed.

By the fin de siècle, the London professionals who worked out of their homes thought the noise of street music less an enemy to their labors than a resonant symbol of a piece with the sense of ennui and alienation that suffused the new era. Once repellent, street music now attracted those who might hear in its strains the sound of their own struggles or those of their age. In Germany, Theodor Lessing could claim that city noises both caused and revealed the degeneration and "cultural immaturity" of modern European urban life.[99] Yet at nearly the same time, in "The Barrel-Organ" (1897), Arthur Symons was mourning a frustrated romance by aligning his emotional state with that former target of Victorian scorn:

> Inarticulate voice of my heart,
> Rusty, a worn-out thing,
> Harsh with a broken string,
> Mended, and pulled apart,
> All the old tunes played through,
> Fretted by hands that have played,
> Tremulous voice that cries out to me out of the shade,
> The voice of my heart is crying in you.[100]

Several years later, describing the noise of prewar London, T. S. Eliot noted "many babies, pianos, street pianos, accordions, singers, hummers, whistlers," yet concluded: "I find it quite possible to work in this atmosphere. The noises of a city so large as London don't distract one much; they become attached to the city and depersonalize themselves."[101] Where it formerly had been singled out as an especial nuisance, street music became an impersonal fragment of the aural tapestry of the modernist city and a vanishing reminder of the past:

> I keep my countenance,
> I remain self-possessed
> Except when a street piano, mechanical and tired
> Reiterates some worn-out common song
> With the smell of hyacinths across the garden
> Recalling things that other people have desired.[102]

Artists and writers in vocations once opposed to and imperiled by street music ultimately appropriated and aestheticized it as a voice and symbol. So empowered, it offered new avenues for representation but also posed a new kind of threat, in the escapist sentiments of fatigued longing and disabling nostalgia it unexpectedly echoed and provoked. For Eliot and many of his contemporaries, city noise no longer worked against art, as Victorians had perceived it, but, ironically, within it.

THE DEPICTION of the street musician as an infectious, interruptive alien had allowed middle-class professionals to crystallize their own

A QUIET SUNDAY IN LONDON; OR, THE DAY OF REST.

FIGURE 2.15. HARRY FURNISS'S "QUIET SUNDAY" PAYS HOMAGE TO LEECH'S "QUIET
STREET" (SEE COVER ILLUSTRATION) AND INDICATES THE PERSISTENCE OF THE
"SCATTERBRAIN" SOUNDSCAPE OF LONDON, WITH PROTEST MARCHERS TAKING
THE PLACE OF ORGAN GRINDERS. FROM *Punch* 90 (1886): 142.

group identity and establish themselves as a formidable presence during the
mid-Victorian period. Calder's words serve as a reminder of what was at stake
for Eliot's predecessors: "If the Victorian period was the great age of middle-
class achievement, of middle-class energy and heroism, it was also the period
in which this aggravatingly undefinable class was trying hard, even desperately, to characterize and identify itself."[103] The texts and attitudes examined
here convey a sense of desperation that cuts deep: a growing need to consoli-
date a group identity, combined with an aggressive desire for separation along
lines of nation, class, and body. F. M. L. Thompson pinpoints an important development when he comments that accelerated arrests for "street offenses" in
the latter part of the century "made the streets, or at least the principal streets,
more and more into sterile territory on which the public had the right to passage but nothing else."[104] The concept of sterility concisely expresses the de-

sired outcome of the anti–street music activists, who sought to defer if not deny the realities of oncoming immigration and the inevitable expansion of the city. Such an antiseptic operation brought into conflict the *"great fact"* of the organ grinders with the other similarly great fact of the period, an emergent class of anxious artists and intellectuals whose anxieties stemmed in large part from their homebound status. Yet, if the ugly xenophobia and contempt of their response cannot be denied, then the tendency to judge these workers too harshly should also be resisted. Over a century later, with the oddly retrograde phenomenon of telecommuting in ascent, the territorial problems that plagued these home workers have renewed immediacy. Against the newer auditory challenges of accelerated technology—the bleeps and blare of cell phones, car alarms, and superhighways—battles continue for spaces to concentrate and to write.

GEORGE ELIOT'S EAR

New Acoustics in *Daniel Deronda*
and Beyond

And how should I begin?

—T. S. ELIOT, *"The Love Song of J. Alfred Prufrock"*

ON THE OTHER SIDE OF SILENCE

ALEXANDER Graham Bell and Thomas Edison disagreed about many things, not least on the correct way to answer the telephone. For his invention, Bell, with a nautical bent, favored "Ahoy!" Edison, more blunt and hard of hearing, yelled "Hello?" By the time T. S. Eliot wrote the line for Prufrock that forms the epigraph of this chapter, the interrogative roar had already routed the romance of the waves. Far-reaching and inquisitive, the phone call makes for spontaneous dialogue and instant narrative. But for this it demands, in the words of an earlier Eliot at the outset of her final novel, "the make-believe of a beginning."[1] When telephony bridges the distance of separation, it enacts the artifice that makes the intimate immediate. The phone conversation begins in a fiction that uncertainly probes, "Hello?"

George Eliot begins *Daniel Deronda* (1876) proper with a famous question. "Was she beautiful or not beautiful?" the narrator asks about Gwendolen Harleth, who is observed by Daniel Deronda in the act of gambling (3). The rest of the novel gives in place of a swift or definitive answer subtle developments in character and situation that provide small hope for an easy resolution. This opening, open-ended query introduces an element of indeterminacy that comes to signify what has been called the "radical uncertainty" of the narrative.[2] It is within this dynamic of instability that Eliot goes on to examine the risk that the two protagonists compulsively wager: the illicit need to establish contact across the divide of the self, engage another's sympathetic attention, and converse in confidence. Over the course of the novel, this desire becomes one as much of sound and voice, the ability to speak and listen, to hear and be heard, as of sight. Though at first it would seem that characters and readers of the novel are meant to struggle to resolve their mixed impressions of visual beauty—"Was she or wasn't she?"—Eliot ultimately places equal value on the challenge of close listening, on aurality alongside visuality, as a means to apprehend beauty as well as horror. The narrator of the earlier *Middlemarch* (1871–1872) grandly had proclaimed that with too acute sensibility "we should die of that roar which lies on the other side of silence," but it is instead on the other side of *Middlemarch*, in her final completed novel and later writings, that Eliot fully explores the components of that roar and the potential for it to unite or confound.[3]

As a late-nineteenth-century fictional representation of a proto-Zionism that, in its resonance with present-day Jewish nationalism, has come to seem strikingly modern, *Deronda* is a final novel like no other. Critics understandably have come to historicize it like no other as well, exposing both the narrow genealogy of Eliot's bold message of religious tolerance and the assumptions about racial identity upon which that message draws. In listening more closely to the sounds, voices, and silences of *Deronda*, however, I want to examine the place of interiority in Eliot's great novel of movement outward, the spaces in the text for the domestic and the personal as opposed to those of the nation and the world. While Eliot's use of music in *Deronda* has received considerable attention, these efforts often have served to clarify further the relation of the arts to the forms of Judaism the novel invokes. Such readings have tended to isolate the more recognizable musical moments of the novel from the rest of a rich soundscape, one whose depth depends as much on the powers of voice and silence as on music. Yet it is important to analyze these features of *Deronda* as parts of a whole, for doing so reveals the ways in which Eliot recognized the advent of an age defined by new emphases on and understandings of the capacity for listening, in which Victorian science at first gave substance and form to sounds that had once seemed indefinite and immaterial, and Victorian technology then fundamentally destabilized aural communication. Coming at the end of a series of works that in their breadth of perception still leave many readers in silent awe, the so-called post-realist *Deronda* confronts with singular tenacity the question of not only what the later Victorian novel might possibly have left to say, but also how it might say it.[4] Eliot finds a partial answer in thematizing the exchange of speech and sound itself. With the most contemporary setting of all her novels, her "story of English life but of *our own* day" acknowledges at once the frustrating challenges and newly charged power of contact in an age heralding amplified sounds, wired voices, and bottled talk.[5]

Although this chapter pivots around consideration of a single novel, my argument places in context Eliot's growing interest in epistemologies of sound, an interest that recurs throughout her writing but that takes on special meaning in the later stages of her work, as a result of concurrent cultural developments that I discuss later. In fact, one need not read far in *Deronda* before one mysteriously starts hearing things. The initial, celebrated querying gaze on Gwendolen is immediately followed—more accurately, accompanied—by telling, though typically ignored, noise: "There was a deep stillness, broken only by a light rattle, a light chink, a small sweeping sound, and an occasional monotone in French, such as might be expected to issue from an ingeniously constructed automaton" (3–4). These hollow echoes of the casino are consistent with the moral bankruptcy that Eliot attaches to gambling throughout the novel. However, this prominently placed reference to a sound machine also is a subtle clue to the sonic context and concerns of her later, more experimental writing. At the same time that Bell and Edison were embarking on careers as archetypal inventors by creating new marvels of sound transmission, Eliot at the end of her career as preeminent novelist-sage was reinterpreting the significance of sound and voice in British fiction. The metaphor of the speaking machine ultimately has significant but unexpected resonance not only for Gwendolen and Daniel, whose anguishing conversational scenes serve to drive forward their narrative as if with an electric charge, but also for Eliot herself, in the cultural context of her later years. The tense interplay between her two final main characters anticipates with uncanny artistry the threat and thrill of intimacy in a new era of mechanized communication.

HELMHOLTZ AND ELIOT: SYMPATHETIC VIBRATION

READERS have been so drawn to the significant impact of Charles Darwin's work upon Eliot's novels that the tendency has been to give less attention to the influence of other Victorian scientists on her writing.[6] This is understandable, if only because the names of many of these men and women have lacked the quality of perpetual controversy to keep them at the forefront of scholarly debate. One such individual was Hermann von Helmholtz (1821–1894), the last great nineteenth-century German "natural philosopher," whose impact on scientific culture was so profound at the time that it now seems taken for granted. While Helmholtz's contributions to the fields of physics, acoustics, optics, epistemology, and thermodynamics were less contentious than Darwin's to biology, they were similarly elemental and important for generations of thinkers ranging from Darwin himself to John Tyndall, Eliot, and Bell, on to Sigmund Freud and Albert Einstein, who wrote to his future wife in 1899: "I admire ever more the original, free thinker Helm[holtz]."[7] When scholars refer to Helmholtz now, it more often than not is in reference to his highly influential lecture "The Conservation of Force" (1847) or his foundational work on color vision: his invention of the opthalmoscope and his three-volume *Handbook of Physiological Optics* (1856–1867). But Helmholtz's research in acoustical physiology, which tends to get short shrift to his work in optics, constituted as much of a scientific and aesthetic breakthrough in this era.

When Helmholtz began his work on acoustics in 1856 (coincidentally, the year Eliot began writing fiction), he entered a field that was lacking a boldly comprehensive statement for the general reader, a *summa acoustica* that could simplify and connect the disparate areas of sound production, transmission, and what was most complex of all, perception. In one of his most important lectures, "The Physiological Causes of Harmony in Music," delivered in Bonn in 1857 (the year Eliot's fiction first appeared in *Blackwood's*), Helmholtz recapitulated the wave theory of sound motion on his way to theorizing nothing less than how the ear distinguishes different musical tones and how hearing works.[8] This lecture formed the basis of what is recognized as the modern masterwork on acoustics, his *Die Lehre von den Tonempfindungen* (1863), the third edition of which was translated into English by the philologist Alexander J. Ellis as *On the Sensations of Tone as a Physiological Basis for the Theory of Music* (1875). *Sensations of Tone* distinguished itself from previous writing on the process of hearing because it was, in the words of Russell Kahl, "the work of a physiologist-physicist-musician and may be interpreted as an attempt to deal scientifically and experimentally with problems, not only in physics and physiology, but also in aesthetics."[9] As such, while not inducing the kind of theological crisis brought on by that close predecessor in empirical inquiry *The Origin of Species* (1859), it still held out subtle significance for not only the development of Victorian science but also Victorian art. As Gillian Beer puts it, "in Helmholtz's view the ear was a much finer and more competent organ than the eye," and partly as a result of his work, "the ear became the chosen arbiter of refined discriminations."[10]

To present his theory of hearing, Helmholtz brought together several phenomena in acoustics that scientific advances earlier in the nineteenth century finally had made possible to explicate and connect more completely.[11] The first of these phenomena was the principle that all musical notes played on conventional instruments were composed of multiple tones sounded simultaneously, a fact long known to musicians trained to be able to discern the components of these sounds. Helmholtz wrote that layered on top of the fundamental, or simple, tone, the ear heard a "whole series of higher musical tones, which we will call the *harmonic upper partial tones*, and sometimes simply the *upper partials* of that musical tone, in contradistinction to that first tone, the *fundamental* or *prime partial tone* or simply the *prime*, which is the lowest and generally the loudest of all, and by whose pitch we judge of the pitch of the whole *compound musical tone*, or simply the *compound*."[12] Helmholtz stated, in other words, that all musical notes were complex in that they were composites of a fundamental and upper partial tones, or overtones, that ears typically could not distinguish except with proper training.

With practice, one could strain to hear these different tones within a single note, but the phenomenon of composite tones could be established as well using another feature of acoustics, that of sympathetic vibration or resonance. As experimenters since Galileo have known, sympathetic vibration occurs when sound waves at a particular pitch from one source cause distant materials—strings, bells, and glass are among the most receptive—to sound at that same pitch. The phenomenon is easily observed by singing into a piano, as Helmholtz explains: "Gently touch one of the keys of a pianoforte without striking the string, so as to raise the damper only, and then sing a note of the corresponding pitch forcibly directing the voice against the strings of the instrument. On ceasing to sing, the note will be echoed back from the piano" (61). So too, if the corresponding dampers are raised, will upper partials echo sympathetically on the other appropriate piano strings, though much more faintly. The familiar scenario of the opera singer's high note breaking a glass is another example of sympathetic vibration of sound waves, in this case, ones so strong that they shatter the resonant body. These types of display often had made for good parlor tricks, but, in experiments on the sympathetic vibration of fundamental and upper partial tones using devices of his own invention, specially tuned glass "resonators" (a word coined in the 1860s and taken from *Sensations of Tone*), Helmholtz recognized that the underlying principle held great significance for the problem of sound sensation.

Helmholtz was not the first to describe sympathetic vibration, but he was the first to place it so centrally and with such lucid precision in a broadly conceived theory of hearing. Helmholtz reasoned that if stringed instruments such as pianos could discern fundamental and partial tones through sympathetic resonance, and so could the ear (with training), then the ear too must be a resonant instrument. Rather, the ear, in one of Helmholtz's favorite analogies, is like the piano, in that it is an analytic organ, a resonator capable of separating compound notes into simple tones just as vibrating piano strings can. To elaborate on this point, Helmholtz described a kind of musical automaton, what might be considered a "Frankenstein's piano":

> Now suppose we were able to connect every string of a piano with a nervous fibre in such a manner that this fibre would be excited and experience a sensation every time the string vibrated. Then every musical tone which impinged on the instrument would excite, as we know to be really the case in the ear, a series of sensations exactly corresponding to the pendular vibrations into which the original motion of the air had to be resolved. By this means, then, the existence of each partial tone would be exactly so perceived, as it really is perceived by the ear. The sensations excited by the different higher partials would under the supposed conditions fall to the lot of different nervous fibres, and hence be produced perfectly, separately, and independently.

Now, as a matter of fact, later microscopic discoveries respecting the internal construction of the ear, lead to the hypothesis, that arrangements exist in the ear similar to those we have imagined. The end of every fibre of the auditory nerve is connected with small elastic parts, which we cannot but assume to be set in sympathetic vibration by the waves of sound. (190)

These paragraphs, which form the core of Helmholtz's resonance theory of hearing, offered up an image of the ear as a "nervous piano." Helmholtz claimed that the ear's "strings" are the rods of Corti, tiny hair-like receptors that are located in the cochlea (and had been first identified just over a decade earlier). Each of the approximately 3,000 receptors (modern claims put this number as closer to 20,000) in the ear is "tuned to vibrate maximally at a different frequency across the range of audible sounds."[13] Uniting established acoustical phenomena with recent breakthroughs in mathematics (Ohm's principle of wave analysis as derived from Fourier's theorem), physiology (Müller's doctrine of specific nervous energies), and anatomy (Corti's cochlea discoveries), Helmholtz set forth a resonance theory of hearing that was both revolutionary and elemental: it posited that hearing, a form of sensory excitation by the external stimuli of sound waves, is nothing less than a bodily form of sympathetic vibration, and the ear a kind of microscopic Aeolian harp wired to the brain.[14]

Drawn to Helmholtz's writings, in part for their characteristic blend of romantic imagery with encyclopedic knowledge and simplicity of exposition, George Eliot and George Henry Lewes owned six of his works, including the first French edition of *Sensations of Tone* (1868), which contains "some pencilled marginal linings," and the third German edition (1870), as well as his three-volume collected popular lectures (1865–1876), which included "The Physiological Causes of Harmony in Music," the 1857 lecture that formed the basis of *Sensations of Tone*.[15] Peter Allan Dale discusses the powerful influence of Helmholtz on Lewes, who ranked Helmholtz's greatness on a level with that of Shakespeare, Bacon, Newton, and Comte, and whose earliest published reference to him dates from 1855.[16] It is possible that Eliot discovered Helmholtz through her common-law husband's study of his research, though it is clear that she actively pursued her own interest in him independent of Lewes's work on physiology. In February 1869, not long before beginning *Middlemarch*, Eliot wrote in her journal: "I am reading about plants, and Helmholtz on music."[17] A curious entry in one of her notebooks from about this time reveals her fascination with the central activity of Helmholtzian acoustics:

If of two sonorous bodies tuned in unison or in octaves, one is made to sound, the other will also sound without being touched. Thus the pitch of the notes of a church bell may be ascertained by playing upon a flute under the bell. No sooner is the note blown than the bell will "begin to vibrate, emitting" softly the same note.[18]

This became the basis for the epigraph to chapter 31 of *Middlemarch*, in which Lydgate's flirtation with Rosamond evolves into love. Considering the ultimately disastrous mismatch of their relationship, however, the reference to sympathetic resonance seems ironic:

> How will you know the pitch of that great bell
> 'Too large for you to stir? Let but a flute
> Play 'neath the fine-mixed metal: listen close
> Till the right note flows forth, a silvery rill:
> Then shall the huge bell tremble—then the mass
> With myriad waves concurrent shall respond
> In low soft unison. (286)

These excerpts recapitulate one of the most important processes of *Sensations of Tone*, the one which, by the 1860s, widely had come to be considered the basis for the experience of hearing. Also by then, it had become a crucial sonic metaphor for the psychological and emotional tendencies and vulnerabilities of the heroes and heroines throughout Eliot's novels.

In fact, Helmholtz's new emphasis beginning in 1856–1857 on the importance of upper partial tones and sympathetic resonance or vibration for the basic sensory experience of the ear corresponded in singular ways, or perhaps it is more fitting to say sympathetically resonated, with aspects of Eliot's fiction from her first published stories of the same period onward. Victorian literature is replete with examples of the dramatic display, or absence, of sympathy, but in Eliot's work the notion of sympathetic resonance—the metaphor of sympathetic attention engaged through sounds, music, or voice—is central and pronounced. For Eliot, the ear is the most deeply receptive organ, and the sound wave the most penetrative and conjunctive to the individual held captive in the bounds of ego. "I wish to stir your sympathy with commonplace troubles," the narrator of "The Sad Fortunes of the Reverend Amos Barton" tells readers, urging them, in a sentiment that became the keynote of Eliot's fiction, to sense "some of the poetry and the pathos, the tragedy and the comedy, lying in the experience of a human soul that looks out through dull grey eyes, and that speaks in a voice of quite ordinary tones."[19] Tonal sensitivity is the quality shared by characters throughout *Scenes of Clerical Life* (1857–1858); the meaning of the music that dominates "Mr Gilfil's Love-Story" coalesces in the sound wave of the "deep bass note" of the harpsichord that revives Caterina Sastri, Maynard Gilfil's love interest, from her illness: "The vibration rushed through Caterina like an electric shock: it seemed as if at that instant a new soul were entering into her, and filling her with a deeper, more significant life" (183). And "Janet's Repentance" provides, in a metaphor of the sympathetic resonance of faint sounds, the credo Eliot came to write by: "Yet surely, surely the only true knowledge of our fellow-man is that which enables us to feel with him—which gives us a fine ear for the heart-pulses that are beating under the mere clothes of circumstance and opinion" (257).

This is not to claim a strictly Helmholtzian basis for the aural language and imagery through which Eliot most often invokes her doctrine of sympathy, but it is to trace a curious and meaningful parallel in the sensory investments and linguistic motifs of two contemporary if infrequently paired intellects. In her earlier works, Eliot's language of sound operates on two levels at once: most readily, as Alison Byerly and others have noted, in the Romantic tradition of Wordsworth's 1835 poem "On the Power of Sound," yet also on the level of a newly exploratory empiricism advanced by the likes of Helmholtz and his followers in England.[20] "All long-known objects, even a mere window fastening or a particular door-latch, have sounds which are a sort of recognized voice to us—a voice that will thrill and awaken, when it has been used to touch deep-lying fibres," Eliot writes in *The Mill on the Floss* (1860), one of her novels most greatly indebted to Romanticism, but one whose language at moments, as here, simultaneously evokes the Helmholtzian project to trace the arc of sound waves through to their distinct recognition by "deep-lying" nerve-fibers.[21] In *The Mill*, Maggie Tulliver is not only a doomed Romantic outsider but also a figure shaken in vibrations of sympathy by Stephen Guest's singing and music: "in spite of her resistance to the spirit of the song and to the singer, [she] was taken hold of and shaken by the invisible influence—was borne along by a wave too strong for her" (367). Maggie is a resonant listener, and Stephen's song generates a seductive sound wave, the effect of which aurally foreshadows that of the surging river current that ultimately engulfs her.[22]

While it thus is correct to claim that Eliot's fiction "frequently portrays the characters . . . as musical instruments, responsive to the invisible vibrations of the world in which they live," this statement does not go far enough to place her writing in the context of Victorian acoustics and contemporary research into what those "invisible vibrations" might mean.[23] Consider this evocative passage from *Romola* (1862–1863):

> When suddenly the great bell in the palace tower rang out a mighty peal: not the hammer-sound of alarm, but an agitated peal of triumph; and one after another every other bell in every other tower seemed to catch the vibration and join the chorus. And as the chorus swelled and swelled till the air seemed made of sound, little flames, vibrating too, as if the sound had caught fire, burst out between the turrets of the palace and on the girdling towers.[24]

Eliot's poetic imagery of Santa Croce pealing out the Great Council's success has tended to overshadow her remarkable description of the "science," so to speak, of sympathetic vibration at work, as the sound of one bell appears to throw others into euphoric ringing. What is more, the image of sound setting "little flames" afire evokes the "sounding flames" that John Tyndall, Helmholtz's great popularizer in England, made the centerpiece of his lectures on sound delivered at the Royal Institution in the 1850s and 1860s, and published in his *Sound* (1867). Scientists had experimented with sounding flames since the late eighteenth century, but Tyndall, a consummate showman, used them in new and magical ways: spectators marveled as his singing and sensitive flames, gas-generated jets of fire, produced "a kind of hurricane of sound," "powerful enough to shake the floor and seats, and the large audience" that occupied them; yet the flames remained sensitive enough to bow and nod to a verse he read aloud to them from Spenser.[25] In Eliot's hands, and ears, a description of a political triumph in fifteenth-century Florence unexpectedly reverberated with the acoustic explorations and displays of nineteenth-century Bonn and London that she likely read about in the press and perhaps also witnessed.

In the years after the publication of Tyndall's *Sound*, Eliot was certainly not alone among the English in developing an interest in Helmholtzian physiology. James Sully, future University College professor of the philosophy of mind, was a freelance writer who, as Kate Flint explains, had gone to Berlin in 1871–1872 to hear Helmholtz lecture and began publishing a series of articles from the early 1870s in such journals as the *Fortnightly Review* and *Westminster Review* that brought Helmholtz's work before the "British intelligentsia."[26] Several of his articles later were revised and collected in his 1874 *Sensation and Intuition*, which Eliot and Lewes read that year, although there is little doubt they already would have seen the essays as they first appeared in 1872–1873.[27] Whereas Eliot had encountered Helmholtz's work by the time Sully published his first essay about it, Sully's thoughtful responses to continental developments in physiology provide an important perspective on the Helmholtzian echoes in Eliot's fiction. In his "Recent Experiments with the Senses," a long essay published in the *Westminster Review* in 1872 and ostensibly about progress in optics but also addressing new developments in the understanding of hearing, Sully celebrated Helmholtz as "the naturalist who has recently done most in [the] objective analysis of sensation," noting that "his now famous doctrine of upper tones is a signal instance of this method of research."[28] Whether of the eye or ear, however, the characteristic of all this analysis, and the import of it for the larger arena of psychology, Sully claimed, was that it put unprecedented emphasis on "the influence of attention on our mental life": "the presence and influence of a powerful inducement, by detaining attention, serves to draw, so to speak, . . . vague and indistinct impressions into the focus of distinct consciousness" (189–90). Sully concluded that "a purposed act of attention will frequently extend the borders of conscious life by discovering impressions heretofore obscure and unknown," with an explicit analogy to the resonance theory: "So, . . . according to Helmholtz, we may bring ourselves to notice the upper tones which blend indistinguishably to the ordinary ear in a rich vocal note" (190). Sully might as well have made a literary analogy, for Eliot's fictional project is precisely to "detain attention," to "extend the borders of conscious life by discovering impressions heretofore obscure and unknown," to encourage readers to look and listen attentively for hidden and silent lives of distress and solitude. Following Helmholtz, both Sully and Eliot put prime value on extending the operations of consciousness through the expansion and redirection of the reception of sensation. Theirs was an affinity of which Sully, at least, became well aware. In "George Eliot's Art," an essay in which he paid her posthumous tribute, Sully quotes *Deronda* ("Men like planets have both a visible and invisible history" [149]) and explains: "Our author lifts the invisible history to a prominent position, partly because the visible history as soon as it becomes intricate cannot be understood apart from it; partly, too, no doubt, because the inner history, the lyric flow of inaudible emotions, and the keen dramatic oppositions of invisible desires and aversions, beliefs and doubts, has a deep interest of its own for the sympathetic mind."[29] Note his mixture of visual and aural metaphors, the "inaudible emotions" and "invisible desires," to describe psychological narrative, the "inner history" that Eliot's narrators seek in sympathy to voice and show. As if in recognition of the value of the new physiology for his own work and hers, Sully at once responded to and invoked the language and metaphors common to Helmholtz and Eliot, ones that she had used to advance her own cause in fiction. No wonder that Sully, in his tribute, believed her to be "touched by the scientific spirit of her age," and claimed for her the position of "the writer of stories who has moved furthest onward in the direction of contemporary ideas" (393)

The passages from Eliot's earlier fictions suggest that by the late 1860s, at which point Eliot explicitly stated she was reading Helmholtz, she was in a position to be particularly receptive to his acoustic theory, if she had not already encountered his ideas in the works of Tyndall, or, as was quite likely, directly. Indeed, following *Middlemarch* in the early 1870s, Sully would draw attention, in distinctly Eliotic fashion, to the implications of these ideas for psychology and aesthetics. Helmholtz's research had created a climate in which "sound began to assume the status as ideal function that sight had earlier held."[30] This shift had been apparent throughout Eliot's earlier fiction, but it was in *Deronda* that she fully demonstrated the new power of the acoustic. Even so, those critics who write about the prominent place of music in *Deronda* tend to slight or ignore the emphasis upon speech, silence, and other sounds in the novel.[31] At the same time, Peter Brooks's argument that *Deronda* prefigures psychoanalysis because it captures the "paradigm shift, comparable to that worked by Freud, from seeing to listening" — specifically, listening to speech — only tells part of the story, because speech constitutes but one part of the soundscape of the novel, and, as we shall see, Freud's "talking cure" was but a part of the larger story of the rise of listening.[32] Viewed in light of the shift brought about by Helmholtz, however, it is possible to consider these positions complementary aspects of a single overarching argument: that the world of *Deronda*, from Julius Klesmer's virtuoso piano-playing to Henleigh Grandcourt's intimidating silences and on to Gwendolen's and Daniel's fraught dialogues, is a sonic one, in which Eliot takes sounding and hearing to their Victorian limits, ultimately to reward the close listeners who sense and respond to the sounds others miss:

> Fairy folk a-listening
> Hear the seed sprout in the spring,
> And for music to their dance

Hear the hedgerows wake from trance,
Sap that trembles into buds
Sending little rhythmic floods
Of fairy sound in fairy ears.
Thus all beauty that appears
Has birth as sound to finer sense
And lighter-clad intelligence. (5o8)

This deceptively innocuous epigraph to chapter 44 returns to the principal metaphor Eliot had maintained all along in her fiction, that of the primacy of sound waves, "little rhythmic floods," to be heard in Wordsworthian nature for those finely tuned enough to sense them. Yet in moving beyond fairies and the pastoral to a "story of English life but of *our own* day," she shows in *Deronda* how this "roar on the other side of silence" becomes humanized and urbanized, how sound waves, in effect, resonate with and reshape the modern self.

The prominent musical scenes in *Deronda* support Eliot's intention to place the problem of hearing at the center of the novel. These scenes tend to feature piano with or without song and most often involve the actress and singer Mirah Lapidoth, whom Deronda rescues as she is about to commit suicide on the banks of the Thames, or the pianist-teacher-composer Klesmer, "a felicitous combination of the German, the Sclave, and the Semite" (41). As critics often have noted, musical quality in *Deronda* is associated with Jewish outsiders, not the British middle class, and as such, it is used by Eliot to critique what Emily Auerbach calls the "poverty of Victorian aesthetic standards," namely, the philistine or, in Klesmer's words, "mechanical-dramatic" musical tastes of the British bourgeoisie (1o5).[33] Jews in the novel are the more sensitive listeners as well as performers. On the one hand, Mirah possesses a "quick expectant ear" that is the origin of the bond between her and Deronda, for they meet after she hears him on the Thames singing the gondolier's song from Rossini's *Otello* (723). His music there resonates for her alone: "it was only to one ear that the low vocal sounds came with more significance than if they had been an insect murmur amidst the sum of current noises" (171). On the other hand, critics have argued that Klesmer, unlike Mirah, is more representative of a particular type of foreign musician: that he is modeled on a particular figure, such as Franz Liszt or Anton Rubinstein, and that his name is Polish-Yiddish for a Jewish itinerant musician.[34] There is, however, a potentially more interesting echo in Klesmer's name of that of Franz Mesmer, the Viennese physician who gained notoriety through that popular Victorian pseudoscience of sound and mind, mesmerism.[35] "Klesmer" is a Yiddishization of "Mesmer" that suggests foreign musical prowess as well as foreign mental domination. Mary Burgan claims that in *Deronda*, Eliot moves beyond portraying male virtuosi in "demonic" and mesmeric terms as, say, Wilkie Collins did in *The Woman in White* (186o) and George Du Maurier would do in *Trilby* (1894).[36] Yet the captivating Klesmer represents not so much a demonic as a domestic variation on such mesmeric characters. For Klesmer is the domesticated mesmerist, the performer brought inside the English home who commands unreal sounds from the Quetcham Hall piano to entrance or confuse his audiences.[37] When, in a galvanic episode that recalls Helmholtz's "nervous piano" and his resonators that appeared to "speak" vowel sounds, Klesmer plays his own (Wagnerian) composition *Freudvoll, Leidvoll, Gedankenvoll*, he has "an imperious magic in his fingers that seemed to send a nerve-thrill through ivory key and wooden hammer, and compel the strings to make a quivering lingering speech for him" (43). Just as Klesmer mockingly resists simplistic nationalist labeling—to Mr. Bult's charge that he is a "Panslavist," he answers, "No; my name is Elijah. I am the Wandering Jew"—so in his hands, the parlor piano and its music transgress the quaint and amateurish place they typically occupied in the Victorian home (224). He unwittingly uses sound to puncture smug bourgeois façades in one of the most anxious moments in the novel: the "dead face" scene. During Gwendolen's *tableau vivant* as Hermione from *The Winter's Tale*, Klesmer strikes the "thunderous chord" as if mesmerically to "awaken" her, which in turn jars open the panel that covers the picture of the mysterious dead face. Gwendolen's "piercing cry" upon seeing it and her glare "that was terrifying in its terror" leave her mute and fallen to her knees, violently awakened from her self-important play-acting by a vision, and sound, of death foretold. This climax, so at odds in its psychological import with the shallow theatrics that came before, does not preclude Klesmer from taking a final jab: "A magnificent bit of *plastik* that!" (54). In *Deronda* it is Klesmer who plays and speaks, using the words of young Clintock, to "the ears of the future," that is, to the likes of his student and future wife Catherine Arrowpoint, the kind of committed listener that, in one of the lingering open questions of the novel, it is unclear a character like Gwendolen could ever become (93).[38]

The forms of music that remain an expressive ideal are merely the most explicit dimension of a wider soundscape in *Deronda*. Gwendolen, for one, spends a large part of the novel under the weight of silence, muteness imposed from without and barely containing the anger within. Gwendolen's is an Eliotic silence, in that it masks a roar of pain, like that of the earlier fiction and as described in aural terms in the "Author's Introduction" to *Felix Holt* (1866):

> for there is much pain that is quite noiseless; and vibrations that make human agonies are often a mere whisper in the roar of hurrying existence. There are glances of hatred that stab and raise no cry of murder; robberies that leave man or woman for ever beggared of peace and joy, yet kept secret by the sufferer—committed to no sound except that of low moans in the night.... Many an inherited sorrow that has marred a life has been breathed into no human ear.[39]

Deronda not only traces the development of such a silence, as many have noted, but it also demonstrates what happens when the sufferer struggles to find both voice and sympathetic resonance, that is, a compassionate ear in which to break that silence through confession. Grandcourt, whom Gwendolen at first finds "adorably quiet," is actually maliciously so (121). His is the silence of the rake who hides his affair and illegitimate children from public knowledge, the false suitor who, in Alexander Welsh's words, "strains every ounce of power from concealment."[40] Even in their earliest encounters, Gwendolen senses the mesmeric force of Grandcourt's will to stifle opposing discourse: "she had begun to feel a wand over her that made her afraid of offending Grandcourt" (108). Already feeling crushed under "stifling layers of egoistic disappointment and expectation" by Klesmer's frank assessment of her musical mediocrity, Gwendolen is further oppressed by Grandcourt's immanent marriage proposal: "I am stifled," she says, after receiving his letter of intent that gives her "the expression of one who had been startled by a sound and was listening to know what would come of it" (243, 273, 270).

Gwendolen can listen, but she is not allowed to speak out. Even as Grandcourt prepares to propose marriage to her, she feels "compelled to silence" about her knowledge of his mistress Lydia Glasher, a secret disclosed to her at "the Whispering Stones" (278). The history of their marriage itself is dominated by what has been called "the refined torture of silence."[41] Living inside "her husband's empire of fear," Gwendolen remains "mute," filled with "the rage of dumbness" and "dumb repugnance," while Grandcourt "ke[pt] a silence which was formidable with omniscience," "retain[ed] a silence which served to shake the opinions of timid thinkers," and "held [Gwendolen's truthfulness and sense of justice] throttled into silence" (395, 552, 560, 568, 543, 623). On the rare occasions when he speaks, he does so using a "languid inarticulate sound" and an "inward voice," with what Garrett Stewart terms his "speech defects" (291, 632).[42] In portraying the villainy of Grandcourt's tyranny of silence, Eliot is attacking, in her words, "the high English breeding . . . [that] subdues all voices," surely, but more precisely, the repressive institution of Victorian marriage and the domestic expectations that often forced women to suppress or redirect their voices of protest or change (377). Deronda's adoptive father, Sir Hugo Mallinger, might as well be speaking about Gwendolen or any number of Victorian wives when he says of Deronda's birth mother the Alcharisi: "Those great singers marry themselves into silence" (408). Eliot suggests that the protocols of Victorian femininity encompassing marriage demanded of women an imprisoning silence, one such as Armgart, more uncompromising a figure of the woman singer than the Alcharisi, experiences in Eliot's 1870 closet drama when, having lost the voice that gave her her career, she feels "Prisoned now / Prisoned in all the petty mimicries / Called women's knowledge, that will fit the world / As doll-clothes fit a man."[43] Gillian Beer eloquently delineates how the spectrum of sound and silence in Eliot's work indicates the contradictory impulses of her own, in Beer's words, "muted life":

> Deafness and sound are two poles of a long and crucial continuum in her metaphoric life. The silent urgency of a style which implies

speech; the insistence on *voice*, dramatised in those recurrent women singers who form the type of the woman artist in her work; her reluctance to speak out directly on issues of the day lest her support do harm to causes she espoused; all these express the extent to which silent writing and reading gave dramatic expression to her particular psychic position.[44]

Working under cover of a male pseudonym, Eliot, or more explicitly, Mary Ann Evans, was uniquely sensitive to the muffled women's voices that often tried to speak behind the silent curtain of the Victorian institutions of femininity, domesticity, and marriage, and *Deronda* gives the lie to the hush of the silent wife, as, indeed, the earlier fiction betrayed the partial tones of the self clamoring to be heard on the other side of silence. An unlikely analogy puts this gendered point in different terms: Upon entering an anechoic chamber and hearing his heart beat and blood flow, John Cage, like an impish version of the idealized figure who hears the grass grow and the squirrel's heart beat in *Middlemarch*, proclaimed that "there is no such thing as silence," and went on to reorient his audiences' relation both to sound and performance in compositions such as *4'33"* (1952), also known as the "silent piece," which called for a pianist to stay silent onstage for three movements totaling four minutes and thirty-three seconds.[45] Three-quarters of a century before Cage aestheticized the concept of silence with respect to musical performer and audience, however, Eliot already had psychologized it in relation to the repressive roles of Victorian wife and husband.

For Gwendolen, the way out of the marital cage of silence depends upon her muffled voice finding a close listener. Critics, led by F. R. Leavis, who have found the novel a "good half" about a doomed marriage marred by a "bad Jewish half" have missed the way in which Eliot brings the two, quite literally, into conversation, breathing Gwendolen's terse speech into Daniel's open ears, and his speech into hers. It is significant in this respect that Henry James's well-known review of the novel is entitled "*Daniel Deronda*: A Conversation," because that is both what the book is about, and what ultimately holds its unconventional structure together.[46] Rather, *Deronda* is not only what one critic has identified as a "conversion story"; more fundamentally, it is also a *conversation* story.[47] Gwendolen, a married, self-absorbed Englishwoman, and Mordecai, Mirah's consumptive brother and a reclusive, visionary Jew, represent the two opposing extremes of characterization in *Deronda*, but they are united in their absolute need for a hearing and a hearer. Daniel himself is in Eliot's work among the figures most vulnerable to sympathetic vibration, and as a result, he becomes the resonant repository for both Gwendolen's confessions of guilt and selfishness, on the one hand, and Mordecai's fervently religio-nationalist reveries, on the other. The relationship among this triad ultimately overthrows the simpler dyadic division presumed by Leavis and other scholars.[48] Daniel is Gwendolen's and Mordecai's endlessly desired listener; his "exquisite quality" of a "keenly perceptive sympathetic emotiveness," his "subdued fervour of sympathy," make him particularly susceptible to their words and cries (462, 162). Put acoustically, Deronda's aural vulnerabilities mark him as a Helmholtzian resonator whose medium is the voice. The structural and interpersonal tensions of the novel partly derive from the fact that his responses to the voices he hears leave him torn between the opposing lures of romance and race, acting instinctively, yet at odds with himself and "in no sense free" (148).

The measure of Eliot's investment in the power of voice in *Deronda* is apparent in an epigraph that seemed scandalous and worth expunging to some when the novel first appeared, even (or so she claimed) to the author herself, and since largely has been overlooked in criticism of the work. In spite of its scandalous taint, or perhaps because of it, the epigraph alerts readers to the importance of the material voice as key to finding one's calling within the context of this novel of vocation: "Surely whoever speaks to me in the right voice, him or her I shall follow, / As the water follows the moon, silently, with fluid steps anywhere around the globe" (299). The lines are Whitman's, and they are taken from a poem titled "Voices."[49] In response to a journalist's attack that with such a reference Eliot appeared to condone "Whitman's nastiness," she wrote in a letter to Blackwood to have had "a sort of incipient intention to expunge [the] motto," yet added, "Of course the whole is irrevocable by this time," and proceeded to let the epigraph stand in all editions. Indeed, she claimed that "it was one of the finer things which had clung to me from among his writings," and it remains a powerful statement near the center of *Deronda*, pointing to the needs that Daniel, Mordecai, and Gwendolen develop for voiced transmission or counsel.[50]

At the same time, it allows the inference that such needs can have a physical or sexual component. Mordecai and Daniel's relationship, for one, is sexualized even as it is delineated in essentially aural and vocal terms. Solitary and wasting away when Daniel discovers him, Mordecai has sublimated his own physical needs into a predominating "yearning for transmission" of language and faith to "a companion and auditor": his "passionate desire had concentrated itself in the yearning for some young ear into which he could pour his mind as a testament" (440, 442, 440). When Mordecai and Daniel finally are alone together, they look each other over "with as intense a consciousness as if they had been two undeclared lovers" (462). Eliot derives Mordecai's self-absorbed desire for another like him, but more perfect, "his inward need for this expanded, prolonged self," at least in part from the works of Whitman, the nineteenth-century bard of expansive male selfhood (441). In *Deronda*, the particular instance of sympathetic vibration that involves the following of another's voice is a physical as well as spiritual experience, as when Daniel feels in the presence of Mordecai "a profound sensibility to a cry from the depths of another soul" (463). Eliot places special emphasis on the relation between sound and soul; Mordecai's "soul has an ear to hear the faults of its own speech," and he states to Daniel, "But our souls know each other. They gazed in silence as those who have long been parted and meet again, but when they found voice they were assured, and all their speech is understanding" (466, 533). This mingling of voice and soul, of the corporeal and the spiritual between men—summed up in Mordecai's dying words to Daniel, "Have I not breathed my soul into you?"—not only bears the mark of Whitman but also alludes back to later lines of Whitman's "Voices": "All waits for the right voices; / Where is the practis'd and perfect organ? where is the develop'd soul?"[51] In *Deronda*, Mordecai locates these in Daniel, whom he sees as "a Jew, intellectually cultured, morally fervid . . . beautiful and strong" and who has the "clear deep voice which was itself a cordial" but still remains "all ear for . . . hints of Mordecai's opinion"; as Daniel puts it, "I am ready to listen to whatever you may wish to disclose" (440, 466, 489, 463). All the better for the consumptive prophetic figure who, like one of "the great Transmitters" he admires, craves proper reception through the language of his ancestors and in the ears of his disciple: "I am only another prayer—which you will fulfill," he declares to the willing Deronda (484, 537). At once messianic and Whitmanesque, Mordecai's demands on Daniel evolve from the elder's fundamental need for what he knows is a rare sympathetic hearing.

Like Mordecai's, Gwendolen's desire for Daniel's willing ear is cast in religious terms but is sensually and psychically charged. Gwendolen, under the weight of a bad marriage that she knows hides the secret of Grandcourt's mistress, comes to see Daniel as a confessor: "Without the aid of sacred ceremony or costume, her feelings had turned this man, only a few years older than herself, into a priest" (401). Deronda later shuns this label: "he wished, and yet rebuked the wish as cowardly, that she could bury her secrets in her own bosom. He was not a priest" (642). Not a priest of any established religion, perhaps, but, unwittingly, of a nascent psychological practice that would become as widely followed: the faith in intimate vocalizing that, as Brooks suggests, would underscore Freud's "talking cure" in the treatment of hysteria by the turn of the century. Welsh writes that by the end of the novel, Daniel has stumbled into a relationship with Gwendolen "much as if he were inventing psychoanalysis in the Vienna of the eighteen-nineties." For Brooks, this process is inherently physical: "a large part of 'the talking cure' is learning to listen to and interpret the body."[52] What makes Gwendolen's scenes with Daniel stand out as much as they have in criticism of the novel is that they capture this process of listening to the body with a precision few fictions before it had attempted.

Evolving as it does through conversation, Gwendolen's and Daniel's attraction maintains a complicated relation to the issue of voice. She hears his voice as holding the key to her longings for escape from the repression of her marriage: "His voice, heard now for the first time, was to Grandcourt's toneless drawl, which had been in her ears every day, as the deep notes of a violoncello to the broken discourse of poultry and other lazy gentry in the afternoon sunshine" (303). In turn, Gwendolen's "clear soprano" attracts Daniel, who is described by the narrator as "fascinat[ed with] her womanhood" in the manner of "a delicate-eared bird," although ominously and unbeknownst to him, Gwendolen has had a bad history with musical birds: "there was a disagreeable silent remembrance of her having strangled her sister's canary-bird in a final fit of exasperation at its shrill singing which had again and again interrupted her own" (9, 298, 20). Brought together by a benevolent but intimate act—Daniel's redemption and return of the necklace Gwendolen secretly had pawned to continue gambling at Leubronn—the two negotiate for themselves a space within the novel that operates not on the level of plot or action but in glances and speech, a kind of private theatricality amid a work that, in the words of Rosemarie Bodenheimer, nevertheless "punishes and exorcises the will to perform."[53]

Gwendolen's and Daniel's conversations bridge the distance between the religious aura of Mordecai's ascetic lodgings and the stale comforts of Grandcourt's stifling estate. Their stolen moments of dialogue reveal the depth of strain beneath a genteel front, and the intensity of Gwendolen's roar on the other side of her marriage into silence. In only their third exchange, after her marriage and over the piano at Diplow, Gwendolen turns to Daniel with "such an appealing look of sadness" to speak "with a hard intensity unaccountable in incidental talk like this," which, in turn, prompts a "graver, deeper intonation" from him (382, 383). Gwendolen's conviction that "he was unique to her among men ... [and] becoming a part of her conscience" feeds her "hunger to speak to him," and what is more, her desire for a kind of telepathic communion with him: "I wish he could know everything about me without my telling him," she thinks to herself (386, 400). Daniel's quality of sympathetic resonance ensures that he, in essence, already does: "He could recall almost every word she had said to him, and in certain of these words he seemed to discern that she was conscious of having done some wrong—inflicted some injury. . . . He thought he had found a key now by which to interpret her more clearly" (404). Gwendolen later wraps the necklace he returned around her wrist as a sign of attachment to him and "looked up at him with pain in her long eyes, like a wounded animal asking for help" (410). Their intimacy advances another step by the window at the New Year's ball, when Gwendolen speaks "in a subdued voice" to him as she hints at the mistake of her marriage, and Daniel "was almost alarmed at Gwendolen's precipitancy of confidence towards him" (415). To watch such a seemingly brash woman plea for trust and absolute guidance understandably jars him. "You must tell me then what to think and what to do," she insists, and later, "What should you do—what should you feel, if you were in my place?" (415, 419). When Daniel encourages her to pursue activities outside the scope of her married life, Gwendolen looks "startled and thrilled as by an electric shock" in a moment that captures the overall tone of their conversations together:

> For the moment she felt like a shaken child—shaken out of its wailings into awe, and she said humbly—
> "I will try. I will think."

They both stood silent for a minute, as if some third presence had arrested them,—for Deronda, too, was under that sense of pressure which is apt to come when our own winged words seem to be hovering around us. (421)

Amid conversations rife with such silence and stifled language, it should come as no surprise that Daniel, among the most careful of listeners, invokes the analogy of hearing to amplify his most urgent advice to Gwendolen: "Take your fear as your safeguard. It is like quickness of hearing. It may make consequences passionately present to you" (422). But even as their talk brings them together here, there remains a wrenching distance between them that Daniel, for all his sympathy, cannot breach: "It was as if he saw her drowning while his limbs were bound" (422). Gwendolen's final utterance in this scene becomes a kind of incantation for her over the rest of the novel: "It may be—it shall be better with me because I have known you" (423). Her words convey not only a sense of the respect she has for Daniel's presence but also the fundamental and problematic distance between their lives and choices. This is a problem of distance that *Deronda* returns to with a solution that is both Eliotic and Helmholtzian: it is an appropriate summing-up of her fictional project that at the same time points ahead to one of the great technological breakthroughs of the age.

The solution that Eliot provides to address both Daniel's newfound religious identity and his increasingly problematic, confidential relationship with Gwendolen is revealed late in the novel by Kalonymos, the acquaintance of Daniel's natural grandfather: "What he used to insist on," Kalonymos tells the grandson, "was that the strength and wealth of mankind depended on the balance of separateness and communication, and he was bitterly against our people losing themselves among the Gentiles" (672). With the idea of "separateness with communication," Eliot very nearly captures the essence of *Deronda* in a single phrase, one that evokes the tenuous balance between self and other, individual and community, and home and world, that so often is the goal of her fictional project. "I think I can maintain my grandfather's notion of separateness with communication," Daniel pledges as he decides to travel east on his proto-Zionist quest (673). The resolution of "separateness with communication" is one that, on the one hand, forces him to make what would seem to be a more traditional kind of moralistic decision between adolescent infatuation or mature commitment to a racial and religious ideal. That is, it serves as a nationalist as well as a personal resolution to the "Jewish question" as well as the "Gwendolen question," and a religio-racial answer as well as one to the problem of the too intimate, too human voice. But, on the other hand, and more interesting for my purposes, the idea of "separateness with communication" can be considered an acoustic process, a distillation of the essence of sympathetic vibration. And such a Helmholtzian echo in the theme of this, Eliot's grand finale in fiction, was at the same time sounding in the telephone, the mechanism that made aurally possible the psychological and nationalist condition *Deronda* espoused.

"ON THE VERGE OF A GREAT DISCOVERY":
TALKING CURES

He'll hear no tone
Of the maiden he loves so well!
No telephone
Communicates with his cell!

— W. S. GILBERT, *H.M.S. Pinafore* (1878)

FROM 1874 to mid-1876, as Eliot, in London, sketched, then composed, and completed her experimental final novel that called for new kinds of "separateness with communication," a Scotsman in Boston, after botching his translation of a German edition of *Sensations of Tone*, ended up inventing the telephone. The same process in which Eliot engaged in her fiction had intrigued Alexander Graham Bell from a young age: one of his biographers recounts that "while playing the family piano, Aleck had noticed the effect of sympathetic vibration." As Bell put it, "I was familiar with the fact that when we sing a vowel-sound into a piano, while the pedal is depressed, the piano reproduces not only the pitch, but approximately the quality of the vowel uttered."[54] His fascination with this process heightened his interest in Helmholtz's book on acoustics, which he discovered in 1866. However, Bell could not understand the language of the original, and the English translation had not yet appeared. Undeterred, he proceeded to attempt to re-create an experiment that his poor knowledge of German had led him to believe Helmholtz had done years earlier. While Helmholtz had shown that vowel sounds could be produced by sounding electromagnetized tuning forks into his specially designed resonators, Bell was under the belief that Helmholtz had actually concluded, far more radically, that vowel sounds could be *electrically transmitted over wires*: in other words, that Helmholtz had used electricity to postulate the principle behind the telephone. This was, to put it mildly, a fortuitous misunderstanding, one that in the end became a triumph of ignorance. As Bell commented years later, "If I had been able to read German, I might never have begun my experiments in electricity."[55] In 1874, Bell combined electricity with the principle of sympathetic vibration initially to seek to create a "multiple" (originally, "musical") telegraph, a device capable of transmitting several messages at once on a single wire by utilizing a different pitch for each message, but what materialized was something at once more straightforward and revolutionary. On 2 June 1875, two weeks after Eliot had sent off the first eight manuscript chapters of *Deronda* for Blackwood's inspection, Bell listened over the wire as Thomas Watson plucked a reed into a receiver in another room: the note was transmitted, and "the telephone was born." In February 1876, just as the first monthly part of *Deronda* was published and went on sale, Bell filed one of the most valuable and understated patents in history, for an "Improvement in Telegraphy." Not until 10 March did he transmit those famous first intelligible words: "Mr Watson—

come here—I want to see you," followed by Watson's response, "Mr Bell do you understand what I say?"[56]

The major public debut of the telephone, as is well known, was at the Philadelphia Centennial Exposition in June 1876, which was also the month Eliot finished writing *Deronda*. The guests at the demonstration included not only Dom Pedro, the emperor of Brazil (whose famous comment, "My God! It talks!" was likely apocryphal), but also the president of the Philosophical Society, William Thomson, later Lord Kelvin, who brought news back to England with an announcement at the fall meeting of the British Association, which took place just as the final part of *Deronda* was published: "I heard 'To be or not to be, . . . there's the rub,' through an electric telegraph wire; but, scorning monosyllables, the electric articulation rose to higher flights, and gave me passages taken at random from the New York newspapers."[57] In the fall of 1877, by which time the first telephone line had been installed in Boston and phones were selling in the thousands in the United States, Bell gave a dozen lectures in Britain, where there had been increasing interest in what the papers were calling his "speaking telegraph." In his lectures, Bell made explicit that his telephone emerged from basic knowledge of both singing into a piano and Helmholtz's work and was nothing more nor less than an electrified mechanism for sympathetic vibration. Showing an illustration of his "first form of articulating telephone," Bell explained: "If you had a large number of steel rods to the octave, and were to speak in the neighborhood of such a harp, the rods would be thrown into vibration with different degrees of amplitude, producing currents of electricity, and would throw into vibration the rods at the other end with the same relative amplitude, and the *timbre* of the voice would be reproduced" (see figures 3.1a–b).[58] By far Bell's most notable event abroad was his January 1878 demonstration of the telephone to the queen on the Isle of Wight. The show, featuring famous callers strategically stationed across the country, lasted from 9:30 P.M. until midnight, and by the time it ended, well behind schedule, the orchestra that had assembled in Southampton to close the proceedings had already packed up and gone home, leaving William Preece, electrician to the Royal Post Office and chief engineer, to hum "God Save the Queen" into the mouthpiece. "It is the National Anthem! But it is very badly played!" Victoria reportedly said to Bell (see figure 3.2). With undiminished excitement, she offered to buy, and then received as a gift, a set of phones from Bell and had them installed at the palace and Windsor.[59]

Lewes and Eliot themselves soon became early converts to the new technology, over a year before the first British telephone exchange was operating in London. Lewes likely first had heard of the telephone from Thomson's 1876 speech at the British Association, and his diary from 21 March 1878 reads: "We went to the Telephone office to have the Telephone explained and demonstrated. Chat with Kate Field and Colonel Reynolds."[60] Field, the American singer, actress, journalist, telephone publicist in England, and featured performer in the January demonstration to the queen, wrote later of

FIGURES 3.1A–B. SEPARATENESS WITH COMMUNICATION I: BELL'S 12 FEBRUARY 1877
SALEM LECTURE ON THE TELEPHONE. WATSON IS IN BELL'S STUDY IN BOSTON,
LISTENING ON THE OTHER END OF THE LINE. FROM GEORGE B. PRESCOTT, *Bell's
Electric Speaking Telephone: Its Invention, Construction, Application, Modification, and
History* (NEW YORK: D. APPLETON, 1884), 437–38.

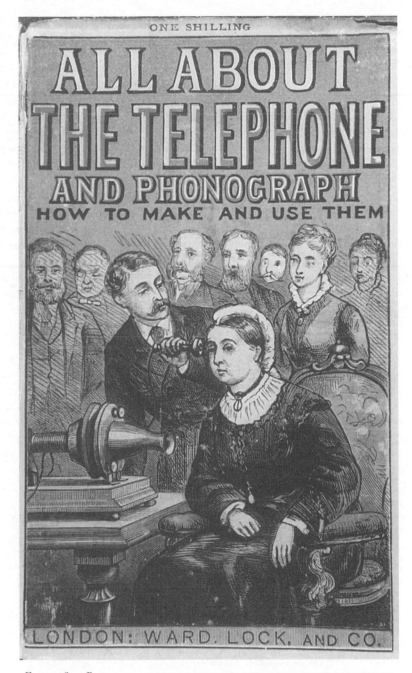

FIGURE 3.2. BELL DEMONSTRATES AN EARLY VERSION OF THE TELEPHONE TO
QUEEN VICTORIA ON THE COVER OF THIS "YELLOWBACK" INTENDED FOR
RAILWAY READING. THE BURNDY LIBRARY, DIBNER INSTITUTE FOR THE
HISTORY OF SCIENCE AND TECHNOLOGY, CAMBRIDGE, MASSACHUSETTS.

this experience with Eliot: "Only once did I succeed in luring her away from The Priory, and that was to see the telephone, about which she was very curious. Yes, she would be able to come with Mr. Lewes, provided no one else was present. So one afternoon George Eliot visited the office of Bell's Telephone in the city and for an hour tested its capacity—'It is very wonderful, very useful,' she said—'What marvellous inventions you Americans have!'"[61] William Baker notes that by April, possibly as a sixty-first birthday present for Lewes, "a telephone ha[d] been installed at the Priory."[62] And in May, Eliot was testing out the new technological terminology in her letters: "Thanks for letting me know that my friends M. and Mde. d'Albert-Durade are as well as usual. If telephonic converse were possible for us, we could say many things to each other."[63]

There are, of course, no telephones in *Deronda*, set as it is in the 1860s, a decade before its period of composition. But it is a novel that, like Eliot, dreams of the possibilities for "telephonic converse"; a book about which its author well might have said with Bell in 1875, "I feel that I am on the verge of a great discovery."[64] With the telephone, Bell engineered a vocal telegraph, an electric wire that would transmit not only a rhythmic click but also resonate with the range of tones in the human voice. It is the case that a half-dozen telegrams are sent in *Deronda*, and the telegraph is the form of distance-bridging communication technology that not only Eliot but also James, in a review of the first part, explicitly invokes: "The 'sense of the universal' is constant, omnipresent. It strikes us sometimes perhaps as rather conscious and over-cultivated; but it gives us the feeling that the threads of the narrative, as we gather them into our hands, are not of the usual commercial measurement, but long electric wires capable of transmitting messages from mysterious regions." For James, the electric telegraph serves as an important metaphor to suggest both the psychological depth and exotic internationalism of the novel, the "messages from mysterious regions" of the mind as well as the globe that circulate within it.[65] But within a work that emphasizes, and coincides with, a more confidential, visceral transmission of tone, music, and voice, the telegraph remains an underdeveloped trope. Moreover, the telegraph was a distinctly brusque, constrained public medium: the communications it transmitted necessarily were terse, business-like, and exposed.[66] As Welsh notes, Eliot's use of the telegraph heightens the more general sense within *Deronda* of the threat of damaging secrets and plots being revealed.[67] But, like Bell, Eliot seemed in 1876 on the verge of something that in its aural intimacies would leave the telegraph far behind. Put another way, the telegraphic communication that Eliot employs may help her to establish context in *Deronda*, but it does not fully satisfy the prescient dialogical demands of the novel, which are more akin to the imminent "erotic possibilities" provoked by the "flirtatious orality" of Bell's invention (see figure 3.3).[68]

Those demands are heightened in Gwendolen's and Daniel's final scenes together, which reiterate that what Gwendolen all along has been seeking is Daniel's perpetual presence through his speech and hearing. The two of them meet once more as the climactic moment of Grandcourt's drowning

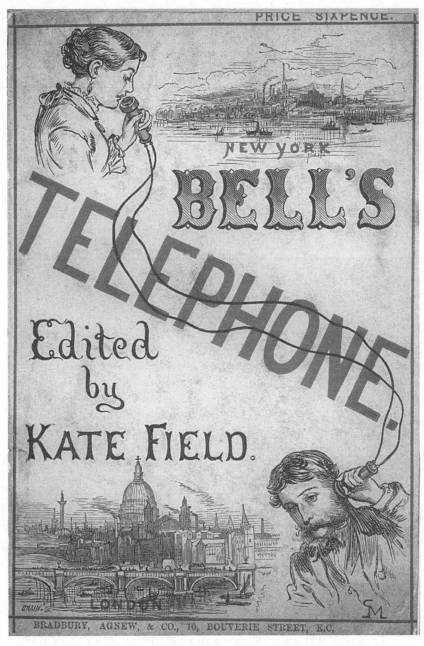

FIGURE 3.3. SEPARATENESS WITH COMMUNICATION II: THE FRONT COVER OF KATE
FIELD'S 1878 *History of Bell's Telephone* SUGGESTS THE KIND OF ROMANCE THE NEW
TECHNOLOGY MADE POSSIBLE—IN THIS CASE, A TRANSATLANTIC TRYST. COURTESY
OF SMITHSONIAN INSTITUTION LIBRARIES, WASHINGTON, D.C.

approaches. Gwendolen confesses her own terror in an episode that pushes the limits of speech:

> "I am afraid of everything. I am afraid of getting wicked. Tell me what I can do."
>
> She had forgotten everything but that image of her helpless misery which she was trying to make present to Deronda in broken allusive speech—wishing to convey but not express all her need. . . . there was a subdued sob in her voice which was more and more veiled, till it was hardly above a whisper. . . .
>
> The feeling Deronda endured in these moments he afterwards called horrible. Words seemed to have no more rescue in them than if he had been beholding a vessel in peril of wreck—the poor ship with its many-lived anguish beaten by the inescapable storm. How could he grasp the long-growing process of this young creature's wretchedness?—how arrest and change it with a sentence? He was afraid of his own voice. The words that rushed into his mind seemed in their feebleness nothing better than despair made audible. . . . He felt himself holding a crowd of words imprisoned within his lips, as if the letting of them escape would be a violation of awe before the mysteries of our human lot. (567)

The scene is a showdown between imprisoned voices. Yet even this tense silence contains a sympathetic echo, as Gwendolen's fear of herself brings Daniel to fear the sound and effect of his own voice. And no wonder: his is a voice that Gwendolen values inordinately and above all else, one whose words about hearing return to her just before Grandcourt's death: "She remembered Deronda's words: they were continually recurring in her thought—'Turn your fear into a safeguard. . . . It is like quickness of hearing. It may make consequences passionately present to you.' And so it was. . . . if she ever thought of definite help, it took the form of Deronda's presence and words, of the sympathy he might have for her, of the direction he might give her" (627–28). But Gwendolen's voice too lingers for Daniel: her "words of insistence that he 'must remain near her—must not forsake her'—continually recurred to him with the clearness of imagined sounds" (579). Gwendolen later tells Daniel of Grandcourt's death "in a muffled voice" and adds, "with an inward voice of desperate self-repression" and "in the lowest audible tone, 'You know I am a guilty woman?'" (639, 641). Even as Daniel is moving outward, placing his sympathies more and more fully with a nationalist cause, Gwendolen's distress turns her inward, as the drowning scene replays itself automatically in her mind's eye: "Things repeat themselves in me so. They come back—they will all come back" (716). Plagued by "the lava-lit track of her troubled conscience," Gwendolen risks turning into a victim who, automaton-like, relives her trauma and repeats, "I will try—try to live" and "it shall be better with me"; one who will become trapped in the cell of the self, and not develop into the outspoken, powerful woman she hoped to be (718, 750). If anything can pull her out of herself, it remains Daniel's "presence and words." She tells him, "I shall remember your words—every one of them," and he leaves her, amid a final conversation rife with silences, with a promise that, in the careful way he phrases it, allows them both their separate wants: "We shall not be quite parted. . . . I shall be more with you than I used to be. . . . If we had been much together before, we should have felt our differences more, and seemed to get farther apart. Now we can perhaps never see each other again. But our minds may get nearer" (717, 750). Within the triangular dynamics of the novel, Daniel chooses to follow Mordecai's voice abroad but also to remain an absent presence: he will, in Gwendolen's remembrance of his words, be more close to her aurally than he ever was physically. Though she will write him a final brief, restrained, and unsentimental note before he leaves, "the sense of [his going] was like a dreadful whisper in her ear, which dulled all other consciousness" (750). We do not know, and are not meant to, if they ever have contact with each other again. The tone at the close makes it seem unlikely. There nevertheless remains a certain appeal in the thought that, perhaps several years later, Helmholtz's resonance in Bell's technology might have brought their minds and voices together once more, allowing them the kind of separation with perpetual intimacy Eliot intended for them.

In Vienna in 1876, in the midst of his third year of medical school, Freud already had taken a course with Ernst Brücke, the man who would become his most important mentor, on "The Physiology of Voice and Speech."[69] Joining together in Berlin in the 1840s, Brücke, Helmholtz, and Emil Du Bois-Reymond had founded the positivist school of German science that denounced vitalism, "with its loose, poetic talk of mysterious innate powers," and advocated in its place a rigorous "physical-mathematical method."[70] In a letter to his future wife in 1883, Freud, echoing Lewes, wrote of Helmholtz: "he is one of my idols."[71] And at about the same time, he wrote to her in a separate letter that Eliot's "Daniel Deronda amazed him by its knowledge of Jewish intimate ways that 'we speak of only among ourselves.'"[72] It may indeed be, as one critic claims, "a commonplace that Eliot anticipates Freud, whose earliest publications began to appear only a decade after Daniel Deronda," but it is surprising, then, that scholarship that accepts this claim has neglected to notice Freud's comment on the novel and the more explicit links between the two it suggests.[73] It is highly significant to read, a decade before the emergence of psychoanalysis, of Freud's amazed admiration for Eliot's ambitious portrayal of the intimacy that exists within a closed circle of speech. Understood in conjunction with the knowledge of Freud's veneration of Helmholtz, of his early interest in the power of the confidential voice, and of his tellingly worded response to Deronda, the metaphor he later invokes for his professional role almost seems inevitable:

> To put it in a formula: he [the doctor] must turn his own unconscious like a receptive organ towards the transmitting unconscious of the patient. He must adjust himself to the patient as a telephone receiver is

adjusted to the transmitting microphone. Just as the receiver converts back into sound waves the electric oscillations in the telephone line which were set up by sound waves, so the doctor's unconscious is able, from the derivations of the unconscious which are communicated to him, to reconstruct that unconscious, which has determined the patient's free associations.[74]

In other, Helmholtzian, words, the Freudian psychoanalyst must, like the telephone, act as a sympathetic resonator, a device to reconstitute and clarify the unconscious that emerges in vocal communication with the patient.[75] As Kittler puts it, "Freud, determined to sacrifice his knowing subjectivity, produces a transposition of media onto himself: his ears become a telephone receiver."[76] Freud put into practice what Helmholtz, Eliot, and Bell had made possible with their physiological, literary, and technological experiments: a new depth and type of analysis of voice derived from principles of sympathetic reception and reconstruction but paradoxically premised on precisely the kind of clinical distance and separateness the telephone afforded. Indeed, after 1876, as Bernhard Seigert writes, "The media of sound transmission and recording not only revealed to physicists and physiologists that the existence of the voice [was] grounded in the parameters of frequency, amplitude, and phase; more dramatically, such media allowed these parameters to be individually manipulated, making possible an analysis of the very thing that, in the romantic era, had been thought to be the indivisible foundation of all syntheses."[77] In the end, then, it is not only that Eliot and then Freud "taught us, in different ways, to listen to the body" but also that their contributions represented, for the one, the more ambivalent, and for the other, the more aggressive components of a broader determination at the end of the century to deromanticize the voice and to anatomize the psyche at a proper distance, even while recognizing the individual's fragile positioning in the midst of modern sociopolitical and technological transformation.[78]

Deronda remained as close as Eliot was willing to get to her own time and place in her novels. Her final published work, the collection of essays entitled *Impressions of Theophrastus Such*, appeared in May 1879, but in it she assumed the voice of a crotchety bachelor commenting on the foibles of his acquaintances and surroundings.[79] Six months later, the twenty-three-year-old journalist and then-aspiring novelist George Bernard Shaw began work in the Way-Leave department of the London office of the Edison Telephone Company. "I was interested in physics and had read Tyndall and Helmholtz," Shaw later explained.[80] His job called for him to persuade Londoners to allow the company to put telephone poles on their rooftops. By the end of the year, he had received just one consent—but this was enough to get him a promotion once he threatened to quit, and when he finally did quit in June 1880, his volume of rejection letters from publishers only increased. Dramatic success was still years away and would be greatest, ironically enough, with *Pygmalion* (1914), the play that marks the intersection of voice and technology using the props of tuning forks, singing flames, phonograph cylinders, and, of course, a telephone.[81] Meanwhile, over the rest of 1880, Eliot began to write another novel, one set during the Napoleonic Wars. At the time of her death that December, she only had completed the opening section of the manuscript. It begins:

> This story will take you if you please into Central England and into what have been often called the Good old times. It is a telescope you may look through a telephone you may put your ear to: but there is no compulsion.[82]

"Every limit is a beginning as well as an ending," Eliot wrote in *Middlemarch* (818). So too, at the end of her own life, she crafted a tantalizing beginning that widened the arc of the "separateness with communication" of *Deronda* to include herself, as author and speaker, and her readers, as confidential listeners. With vanishing Victorian grace, Eliot in this fragment finally allied her fiction and the technology it augured. The novel that might have been became the telephone call that transcended time and place. Her gentle greeting left readers on the line, on willing hold, as it were, waiting for the sound of the storyteller's voice to return to their ears.

4

THE RECORDED VOICE
FROM VICTORIAN AURA TO
MODERNIST ECHO

Not in vain the distance beacons. Forward, forward let us range,

Let the great world spin forever down the ringing grooves of change.

— ALFRED TENNYSON, *"Locksley Hall"*

TENNYSON'S TALKING MACHINE

THROUGH his nameless speaker's voice in this celebrated couplet, Tennyson makes not only an ambiguous appeal to technological innovation at the dawn of the Victorian period but also, as readers ever since have observed, a conspicuous slip. The author later acknowledged his mistake in a note: "When I went by the first train from Liverpool to Manchester (1830) I thought that the wheels ran in a groove. It was a black night, and there was such a vast crowd round the train at the station that we could not see the wheels. Then I made this line."[1] Within the line itself, however, the fact that trains move on rails matters little. There, what registers are the rhythmic trochees that drive the lines forward and the resonant phrase "ringing grooves of change," which echoes the metallic clang of the steam engine, even if it does run the wheels in ruts. Thus, while that pivotal word "grooves" is Tennyson's aural solution, it still poses an empirical problem. Or does it? Though he could not have known it when writing the lines in the late 1830s, the poet saw his innocent error become in the 1870s a prescient truth. Over the last quarter of the nineteenth century, new "grooves of change" came into use, ones etched by the stylus of the phonograph, initially on tinfoil and then wax cylinders, early recording surfaces on which Victorians left the first tentative marks. As if in fulfillment of his prophetic but unintended claim, in 1890, the elderly poet laureate acquired a phonograph and recorded a selection of his works, delighting, over his final years, in the mysterious mechanism whose grooves spun forth the ringing tones of his own voice.

I begin this chapter on the phonograph with a reference to Tennyson, the poet who most embodies the Victorian age, because the critical focus on the widespread modernist response to voice-recording machines and other communications technologies has often obscured the fact that the phonograph was first and significantly a Victorian invention.[2] It is frequently observed that references to commercial rivals of the Edison phonograph, the Berliner gramophone and Bell-Tainter graphophone, appear throughout the modernist canon. They occur, for instance, in T. S. Eliot's *The Waste Land*, James Joyce's *Ulysses* (both 1922), Thomas Mann's *The Magic Mountain* (1924), William Faulkner's *As I Lay Dying* (1930), and most memorably perhaps in Virginia Woolf's *Between the Acts* (1941), where the machine presents the disembodied, nameless voice that speaks to and for the war-shattered generations of Woolf's characters: "To the valediction of the gramophone hid in the bushes the audience departed. *Dispersed*, it wailed, *Dispersed are we*."[3] Well before the gramophone lamented for dispersed modern audiences, however, the phonograph had summoned the Victorians. The first appearances, applications, and representations of voice recording on the phonograph in late Victorian England have been eclipsed by attention to the later manifestations of it. Yet these are important to consider not only to enable a fuller understanding of the cultural origins of a familiar modernist trope but also to apprehend the ambiguous power dynamics that lie at the heart of the Victorian twilight.

Victoria's reign had been marked by an increasing volume and an increased awareness of sound—from the shriek and roar of the railway to the jarring commotion of urban streets, and from the restrained tinkling of the drawing-room piano to the hushed propriety of the middle-class parlor. As the century came to an end, self-respecting English citizens who had spent decades struggling to process a new world of sounds took the opportunity to seize upon a new means of sound production. One of the advantages of the phonograph was that it allowed householders not only to make socially acceptable noise of their own but also to bring that noise inside, in ways that would drown out the distractions of the itinerants and poor beyond their doors. As a machine that repeated what was sounded into it in what seemed identical tones, the phonograph addressed a deeper escapist need on the part of users, a longing to hear perpetually the reproduced self rather than listen to the demanding din of others. And in this sense, it differed in two key respects from the sound-based communications technologies that evolved alongside it. Unlike the telegraph and telephone, the phonograph was explicitly designed for archival purposes and also ultimately to function without a specially trained and designated operator. Of the three forms, that is, only the phonograph offered a form of preservation through direct, immediate interaction with its audience. It is important to remember that the early phonograph was, unlike the more familiar playback-only gramophone that would come to dominate the market at the beginning of the twentieth century, a home recording device. As such, it encouraged active engagement from Victorians, who could readily make their own amateur records at home rather than purchase them. This condition should not be underestimated, for such interactive potential enabled intimate, revealing responses, both on records and in print.[4]

Writing of the Decadent movement of the 1890s, Arthur Symons famously described its ideal: "to be a disembodied voice, and yet the voice of a human soul."[5] In separating a voice from a body, yet preserving the unique sound of the self, the phonograph in a literal sense enacted the fundamental paradox of the Decadent tendencies that Symons identified. In an important work on phonograph technology, Evan Eisenberg has characterized listening to phonograph records as engaging in a mechanized "private ritual": "Record listening is a séance where we get to choose our ghosts."[6] As an etcher of voice, the phonograph presented Victorians with a means of inscription that brought into homes what amounted to a ritualized fulfillment of the essence of Decadence. Indeed, the phonograph, it might be said, indulged more staid, bourgeois listeners in a distilled and domesticated form of that Decadence. For late Victorians recorded and replayed their records fascinated by, if not always attuned to, the often disturbing rituals contained in these actions. The shift from a cylinder phonograph-dominated market to a disk gramophone-dominated one at the beginning of the twentieth century encapsulates my argument in technological terms: that Victorian responses to the phonograph, the machine that initially offered the possibility of home recording, were inherently more personal and interactive than modernist ones to the gramophone, by which time the market had come to be controlled by international companies that mass-produced playback-only machines and disks.

While moderns used the gramophone to depict their concerns over the disintegration of artistic "aura" in an age of mechanical reproduction (to echo the title of Walter Benjamin's formative essay on the work of art in the modern era), Victorians utilized the phonograph in ways that spoke to their own concerns over issues ranging from the domestic to the imperial. Criticism has identified a "phonographic logic" operating in Joseph Conrad's turn-of-the-century writing, and to claim, rightly, I think, that Conrad sees the "phonographic" process of disembodying voice into contextless synecdoche as ultimately destructive and inadequate, in ways that are distinct from later modernist attitudes. The value of such criticism lies in its focused illumination of the way technology can influence technique in the work of a pivotal literary figure.[7] My work, on the other hand, takes a broader approach, to present a cultural study attentive to the varied, often contradictory late Victorian manifestations of the phonograph, ones that predated and either directly or indirectly influenced Conrad's and twentieth-century authors' writings. The phonograph, with the power to record and replay, promised a special kind of communal integrity, even as it extended a troubling sense of fragmentation.

What made the phonograph both thrilling and terrifying was that it offered a salvation not apart from but alongside the morbidity of the fin de siècle. Seemingly able to flout death itself, the phonograph presented an alternative to Victorian ideologies of domination. Through its mechanical reproduction of voice, it offered forms of control and interaction that late Victorians initially found not impersonal and fearful as moderns often did, but, in a period of diminishing mastery over empire and the self, individualized, reassuring, and even desirable.

"SEND ME MR. GLADSTONE'S VOICE"

FROM THE DEBUT of the phonograph in London, the British literary establishment interacted with and felt the influence of it. The genesis of the device itself has passed into myth: in late 1877, the story goes, Thomas Edison, "the Wizard of Menlo Park," designed and had assistants assemble the machine he promptly christened with a crude tinfoil rendition of "Mary Had a Little Lamb." The phonograph went on to receive a warm reception in England. It was first mentioned in a January 1878 *Times* article based on the report of Henry Edmunds, electrician, inventor, businessman, and acquaintance of Edison, and was initially demonstrated at a February lecture that year at the Royal Institution by W. H. Preece, electrical consultant to the British Post Office, who had a phonograph constructed based on drawings of Edison's prototype.[8] The packed audience for Preece's lecture included Tennyson and the esteemed scientist of sound, John Tyndall. Though the subject of the talk ostensibly was the recently invented telephone, the author of an account from the *Graphic* reported that this consisted of a "very feeble" demonstration, making the phonograph "the crowning wonder" of the event. After Preece tested the device with "Hey Diddle Diddle, the Cat and the Fiddle," Tyndall took the stage "and gave the phonograph a well-known quotation from the pen of Mr. Tennyson, who was present, 'Come into the garden, Maud,' which was afterwards echoed to the satisfaction of the audience." While neither Tyndall's foil recording nor Tennyson's reaction to it have been preserved, the fact that at the end of the lecture "a crowd collected round the table to see, speak to, and hear the phonograph, and the theatre was not cleared until eleven o'clock, when the gas was turned out," invites speculation that the notoriously shy but curious poet may have lingered afterward to record himself even as early as this, a dozen years before he acquired a phonograph of his own.[9]

In two significant articles on the phonograph published a decade apart, Edison himself recognized that it would revolutionize the perception of the spoken and written word. Edison's position reflected the more widespread tendency in the period to couch technology in imperialist terms: the phonograph, he wrote in 1878, enabled "the captivity of all manner of sound-waves heretofore designated as 'fugitive,' and their permanent retention."[10] So enslaved, sound could be made to work for mankind, Edison presciently claimed, not only in business for letter-writing and dictation, but also for such wider applications as books, education, music, advertising, and as an enduring record: "for the purpose of preserving the sayings, the voices, and the *last words* of the dying member of the family—and of great men—the phonograph will undoubtedly outrank the photograph.... It will henceforce be possible to preserve for future generations the voices as well as the words of our Washingtons, our Lincolns, our Gladstones, etc., and to have them give their 'greatest effort' in every town and hamlet in the country."[11] The phonograph would be an equal opportunity sound master, capturing the voices not just of the masses but the elite, whose records would in turn constitute an uncanny oral congress, what Edison called a "Library of Voices." This remained impractical until 1888, when, spurred on by competitors such as Alexander Graham Bell, the inventor finally perfected the phonograph, replacing the flimsy sheet of foil with a more durable wax cylinder or "phonogram" as the recording surface. Suddenly the press, which had lost interest in the 1877 tin phonograph almost as quickly as it had seized upon it, was once again all ears. In typical fashion Edison issued claims equally reassuring and ludicrous for the potential of the improved machine: "On four cylinders eight inches long, with a diameter of five, I can put the whole of 'Nicholas Nickleby' in phonogram form," he boasted. Yet beyond such immediate (and exaggerated) literary uses, he added, "The phonograph, in one sense, knows more than we do ourselves. For it will retain a perfect mechanical memory of many things which we may forget, even though we have said them."[12] With powerful omniscience, the phonograph, then, could conquer mental failings by reasserting past speech in seemingly undistorted form.

The perfected phonograph of 1888 made the odd prospect of the Library of Voices at last possible but only through a deluge of international publicity. Edison achieved this with the help of Colonel George E. Gouraud, his principal overseas agent, who had played a major role in the European introduction of his telephone and lighting system, and who became the most vocal phonograph enthusiast in Britain, recording dozens of prominent and obscure Victorians for posterity.[13] The colorful influence of this theatrical showman too often has been relegated to a footnote in the life of his boss. A native New Yorker and decorated Civil War veteran, Gouraud received a *Vanity Fair* profile in 1889 that conveyed his energy and marketing savvy (see figure 4.1):

> He was imported from America, where he was born within sound of Niagara forty-eight years ago, as Dutch cheeses and Duchesses are imported in more recent years. An ardent, vigorous, and patriotic young man, he enlisted on the side of freedom when the slave war broke out, fought with distinction, rising to the rank of Colonel. But his most notable achievement was the invention of Edison, the inventor; though there is a story that he discovered that surprising genius in a New York coffeehouse in the middle of a night, where the future author of the

FIGURE 4.1. COLONEL GEORGE GOURAUD AS "LITTLE MENLO,"
FROM *Vanity Fair* 41 (13 APRIL 1889). THIS WAS ONE OF THE
LAST PORTRAITS MADE BY THE FIRST *Vanity Fair* CARICATURIST
CARLO PELLEGRINI ("APE") BEFORE HIS DEATH IN JANUARY
1889. AUTHOR'S COLLECTION.

phonograph, without a dime in his pocket, was waiting for something to turn up in the way of supper. Since then he has been closely associated with Edison, has crossed the Atlantic thirty-four times on his own and Edison's affairs—bringing to England on one occasion the telephone, and on other occasions other wonderful things; and he has been the means of placing more capital on the market, in connection with inventions, than any other man in either hemisphere.[14]

Gouraud called his Victorian house on Beulah Hill in Upper Norwood "Little Menlo" after Edison's home base. It was here that the colonel regularly threw "phonograph bacchanalia," for which he typically donned his cavalry uniform and corps badges and decorated the house with "photographs of Fort Sumter, portraits of Washington, Grant, Lincoln, Robert E. Lee, and 'Stonewall' Jackson—and Jefferson Davis, hung upside down"; further, "his war-stained accoutrements—the ears of the charger he rode at Ball's Bluff, the battered bugle of the First Squadron, and pistols belonging to Major Ball Waring, the notorious duelist—hung on the terra-cotta wall amid graphic sketches of Civil War incidents."[15] The bizarre juxtaposition of such visceral military memorabilia with displays of the latest American technological wonder served to underscore not only the nationalist pride behind the phonograph but also the symbolic violence that accompanied the mystery of the workings of it. Assembling a collection as strange as that of what Gouraud referred to as his "invisible company" on cylinder recordings demanded a kind of force in the seizure of such a vital component of an identity as the individual's voice.[16] With the advent of the phonograph, the dream of recording became, in Friedrich Kittler's words, "at once reality and nightmare": "Phonography means the death of the author; it stores a mortal voice rather than eternal thoughts and turns of phrase.... As a photograph of the soul, the talking machine put an end to the innocent doctrine of innocence."[17] Putting the paradox another way, even as the phonograph rendered a speaker's voice immortal and disembodied his or her speech, it seemed to preserve in the distinct tones, accents, and breath of that voice a fragile mortality, the very *corporeality* that words on a page or sentiments in a poem lacked. The communal fantasy of the phonograph, then, was perversely at the same time a dissevering "nightmare," one not entirely lost on Gouraud and his compatriots as they planned the London introduction of Edison's perfected machine.

From as early as the end of 1887, Gouraud urged Edison to follow his instructions when deciding to present the new machine abroad. Gouraud would "issue cards, in these terms: To meet Prof. Edison / Non presentem, sed alloquentem! (Not present but in the voice)." Gouraud suggested that the opening line for Edison's first transatlantic cylinder cloak the technology in Romantic terms: "Phonogram No. 1. 'Shall I call thee bird, or but a wandering voice?'—Wordsworth ["To The Cuckoo"] Then go on with your address . . . Nothing could be more appropriate than the words, 'But a wandering voice', and I have registered them in connection with the word 'Phonogram.'"[18] Attempting to ascribe middle-class respectability to the phonograph, the agent appropriated the poet of nature for the marketing of technology. But perhaps the most potent commentary on the cultural status of the new phonograph was provided in a poem Gouraud had his brother-in-law, clergyman and author Horatio Nelson Powers, write and then recite on the first phonogram Edison sent to London in June 1888 (figure 4.2, *bottom*). Powers's "The Phonograph's Salutation" attests to the macabre power of the "speaking writer":

> I seize the palpitating air. I hoard
> Music and Speech. All lips that breathe are mine.
> I speak, and the inviolable word
> Authenticates its origin and sign.
>
> I am a tomb, a Paradise, a throne;
> An angel, prophet, slave, immortal friend:
> My living records, in their native tone,
> Convict the knave, and disputations end.
>
> In me are souls embalmed. I am an ear
> Flawless as truth, and truth's own tongue am I.
> I am a resurrection; men may hear
> The quick and dead converse, as I reply.
>
> Hail English shores, and homes, and marts of peace!
> New trophies, Gouraud, yet are to be won.
> May "sweetness, light," and brotherhood increase!
> I am the latest-born of Edison.

After the mass of metaphorical associations makes the phonograph out to be a self-contained contradiction—it is at once the master who seizes and the slave who is seized, a tomb and a resurrection, the organ of hearing and that of speech—the final stanza takes a curious turn, with a dubious Arnoldian invocation, toward a call for cultural and economic conquest of the motherland.

This was certainly on the mind of Edison, who with typical concision recorded his own doggerel on a cylinder accompanying Powers's:

> Gouraud, agent of my choice
> Bid my balance sheets rejoice
> Send me Mr. Gladstone's voice[19]

"We have unbottled your voice, and its echo has resounded throughout Europe," Gouraud cabled back to New Jersey.[20] Edison's jingle combined New World profits with Old World plunder in a curiously novel relationship. If the phonograph made possible the commodification of sound, then, Edison reasoned, it followed that the most valuable sounds were the ones soonest to be lost. A cylinder of the aging prime minister would indicate for Edison the real promise of the fiscal success of the machine. Unsurprising, then, that many of Gouraud's early records seemed destined to evoke the deathly or the dying.

FIGURE 4.2. *Top*: GOURAUD AT THE HANDEL FESTIVAL IN THE CRYSTAL PALACE, RECORDING "OVER 4000 VOICES OVER 100 YARDS AWAY" WITH THE NEWLY ARRIVED PHONOGRAPH. *Bottom*: GOURAUD AND HIS FAMILY AT LITTLE MENLO LISTENING TO EDISON'S VOICE, WITH THE INVENTOR'S PICTURE ON THE STAND TO THE LEFT AND THE AMERICAN FLAG AND CIVIL WAR MEMORABILIA DECORATING THE MANTELPIECE. FROM THE *Illustrated London News* (14 JULY 1888): 29.

Within days of the arrival of the machine, he made the first ever recording of a public concert: this was *Israel in Egypt*, sung by thousands on 29 June at the annual Handel Festival in the Crystal Palace (figure 4.2, *top*). The cylinders of it that survive in the Edison archives give forth ghostly silences, broken by what seem mournful keens of some distant chorus.[21]

Enthusiastic to make more ghosts as a reliable form of advertising, Gouraud engineered the earliest surviving recording of literary significance made in England. On 30 August 1888, Henry Irving, the Shakespearean actor who, for his personal secretary and manager Bram Stoker, would become an inspiration for the count in *Dracula* (1897), visited Little Menlo and recorded an excerpt from Monk Lewis's *The Captive* (1803). In this gothic monodrama, which had so horrified the audience at the premiere that Lewis withdrew it after the opening night performance, a woman is driven insane after being imprisoned in an asylum by her "tyrant husband."[22] On the recording, Irving recited the first lines:

> Stay, gaoler, stay, and hear my woe!
>   [S]he is not mad who kneels to thee,
> For what I was, too well I know,
>   And what I am, and what should be,
> I'll rave no more in proud despair;
>   My language shall be mild, though sad:
> But yet I firmly, truly swear,
>   I am not mad! I am not mad!

In his choice of this scene for recitation, Irving intuitively gestured to the as yet unexplored ways the phonograph would become a prison-house for spoken language. The result of this encounter between Shakespearean and speech machine was the capture of an uncanny rendering of Irving's voice by the "gaoler" Gouraud. This was not lost on the writer Joseph Hatton, who observed the recording session and recollected: "It was very strange later in the day, when we stood upon the terrace of Colonel Gouraud's house watching the changing effects of a wonderful watery sunset, to hear coming from the house these words spoken in a weird voice — not Irving's voice, as it seemed to us, yet with its intonations and inflexions, but a voice that sounded as if it might be proceeding through the bars of a dungeon, deep in the basement of the beautiful chateau which Colonel Gouraud has built himself, overlooking one of the loveliest of the many fine landscapes round London."[23]

Hatton's description captures the ominous yet alluring dimension of Gouraud's spirited assembly of his Library of Voices. For middle-class users of the phonograph now could people a dungeon in the sheltered interiors of their suburban domestic idylls: the comfort of the listener's parlor would accommodate the fashionably gothic desire to host ghosts. An August 1888 *Pall Mall Budget* cartoon, entitled "Possibilities of the Phonograph," depicts the actions and deceptions the illustrator imagines the machine might enable. These include a futuristic scene in which Macaulay's New Zealander stumbles across a ruined London littered with boxes of Victorian voices on cylinders, with "Irving's Voice" visible on a label attached to one of these. Another panel features a vignette of the actor in the present day shivering in a nightcap. The caption reads, "Capital for tragedians suffering from cold. All you have to do is speak your part to the machine and let the call boy take it down to the theatre" (figure 4.3). "'Yours will be a haunted house, in truth,'" an interviewer asked Gouraud in 1888, to which he replied, "'Yes, but I shall not long monopolize the "ghosts," for every possessor of a phonograph will doubtless have his album in time.'"[24] For his first significant London recording, Gouraud had snatched segments of the Handel Festival oratorio that recounted the en-slavement of the Jews by the Pharoahs. With this, as if by strange coincidence, he initiated his plan to capture voices of a group of chosen people by phono-graph. As Edison's representative, the colonel was in a new kind of fin-de-siè-cle cultural business, selling the thrill of ghostly incarceration for domestic entertainment.[25]

It was fitting, then, that Gouraud's first major literary catch was to have been the preeminent Victorian sensation novelist and ghost story writer Wilkie Collins. Collins, who had made his name in 1860 with *The Woman in White*, had toured America in 1873–1874 with performances of several adapta-tions of his work, including "The Dream Woman," his 1855 story of a man haunted by the ghost of a murderous woman to whom he briefly is married. It is possible that Edison had sent a special request to get Collins's voice, for Gouraud evidently invited Collins to Little Menlo sometime in the late sum-mer of 1888. In an unpublished letter, Collins, who was ill with gout, chest pains, and shattered nerves, declined:

> I sincerely appreciate this compliment which is implied in the invita-tion with which you have honoured me. Mr Edison[']s fame has been nobly gained. His place in history is already secured, and his landmark set up on the territory of Science.
>
> But, in the present state of my health, I fear there is little hope of my being able to profit by this opportunity which you have been so good as to offer me of investigating the most wonderful invention of our time. I have been already away from London (which is my only ex-cuse for this late reply), trying what a purer air will do for me—and I shall probably be far away from Little Menlo next month.

This is dated 24 September 1888, a day short of a year from Collins's death.[26] The extent of disappointment in his reply becomes clearer when one consid-ers the preoccupation his fiction shows not only with the supernatural and ghostly but also with crime and contemporary developments in science and detection. As the presumed inventor, with *The Moonstone* (1868), of the English detective novel, he likely was fascinated both by Edison and the prospect of a machine that could serve to "convict the knave" in a "Criminal Voice Detec-tion Department," as Powers and the *Pall Mall Budget* cartoonist had specu-lated the phonograph well might (figure 4.3).

THE POSSIBILITIES OF THE PHONOGRAPH.— BY AN IMAGINATIVE ARTIST.

FIGURE 4.3. COMIC SPECULATIONS ABOUT THE PHONOGRAPH, FROM THE *Pall Mall Budget* 36 (16 AUGUST 1888): 19. REPRODUCED FROM THE COLLECTIONS OF THE LIBRARY OF CONGRESS.

In November and December of that year, Gouraud finally succeeded in obtaining his prized specimen in the voice of Gladstone himself. Edison's Gladstone cylinder (or perhaps a copy of it) plays back in barely a whisper the gruff sounds of the Grand Old Man: "I lament to say that the voice which I transmit to you is only the relic of an organ, the employment of which has been overstrained. Yet I offer to you as much as I possess and so much as old age has left me, with the utmost satisfaction as being, at least, a testimony to the instruction and delight that I have received from your marvellous invention." Gladstone, the relic of an imperial age, optimistically pointed to an imminent, very different sort of dominion, the ascendant American technology that was capturing his voice in grooves etched on wax: "All I see is that wonders upon wonders are opening before us. Your great country is leading the way in the important work of invention. Heartily do we wish it well; and to you, as one of its greatest celebrities, allow me to offer my hearty good wishes and earnest prayers that you may live long to witness its triumphs in all that appertains to the well-being of mankind."[27] Upon being invited by Gouraud to hear this recording in March 1890, James Russell Lowell, one of America's most distinguished men of letters, who was at this point the ailing president of the Modern Language Association and (so he put it in another letter to Henry James) "swimming" in opium, replied that it would be impossible for him to attend, but he went on to attest to Gladstone's eloquence and Edison's industriousness: "My own ears have happily often borne witness to the marvellous carrying-powers of the most eloquent voice of our time, but I never dreamed that it could ever make itself audible across the ocean with all its compass of persuasive intonation. Surely there is no greater wonder of human invention than this which we owe to the genius of Edison."[28]

One of the major accomplishments of the new machine, as Gladstone's words suggested, was that it created a new *kind* of relic, a hollow, grooved talisman of identity. Such was the outcome of the first interaction between a prominent poet and the phonograph from which a recording survives, involving not Tennyson but Robert Browning. This earliest record of a major literary figure is significant for its historical value, of course, as well for the ominous power it accrued in the period immediately following its making.[29] The rarely heard record originated during a 7 April 1889 dinner party hosted by the artist Rudolf Lehmann that Gouraud and Browning attended. At one point Gouraud, always on the hunt for personalities to add to his Library of Voices, directed Browning, who "had a most decided objection to public speaking," to talk into the phonograph.[30] The poet agreed—though whether enthusiastically or not is unclear—and Gouraud provided a brief introduction:

> [*Col. Gouraud:*] My dear Edison: [*pause*] My dear Edison: I have sent you by the means of the phonograph living, interesting souvenirs of my brief residence in London. Nothing that I have sent you will be more welcome to you than the words which will follow now— words that are none other than those of one of England's—I may say, of one of England and *America's* great descriptive poets: those of Robert Browning. Now listen to his voice.
> [*Browning:*] Ready?
>> I sprang to the saddle, and Joris, and he;
>> I galloped, Dirck galloped, we galloped all three;
>> "Speed!" echoed the wall to us galloping through;
>> "Speed!" echoed the —I forget it! er— [*followed by a few indistinct syllables then a pause*]
>> Then the gates shut behind us, the lights sank to rest
> [*pause*]

I'm most terribly sorry but I can't remember my own verses; but one
thing which I shall remember all my life is, the astonishing sensation produced upon me by your wonderful invention. [*pause*] Robert Browning!
[*Col. Gouraud*:] Bravo bravo bravo![31]

In what approximated a loud, high-pitched brogue ("my" is pronounced as
"me," for example), Browning began to recite his perennially popular "How
They Brought the Good News from Ghent to Aix," only immediately to flub
his lines and cut it short, perhaps from embarrassment, the effects of wine, or
senility. With a reassuring round of applause and cheers from Gouraud and
the other guests, the recording abruptly ended.

It was after Browning's death in December that year that the small white
wax cylinder, no longer merely a curiosity, acquired peculiar significance from
the use of it in an unprecedented form of poet worship. On 12 December 1890,
the first anniversary of the poet's death, F. J. Furnivall, president of the Lon
don Browning Society, brought together Gouraud, Lehmann, H. R. Haweis,
and a few others at Gouraud's offices for a playing of the record. Haweis described the event in a letter to the *Times* as "unique in the history of science
and of strange sympathetic significance . . . [and an] extraordinary *séance*." At
the next replaying, at Haweis's house a few weeks later on the anniversary of
the poet's funeral, a larger crowd was similarly entranced, as shown in an illustration of the huddled group "Listening to the Master's Voice" through
headsets (figure 4.4).[32] Not everyone was enthusiastic. Some were even re-
pulsed. Browning's sister Sarianna called it an "indecent seance" and indig-
nantly wrote to a friend: "Poor Robert's dead voice to be made interesting
amusement! God forgive them all. I find it difficult."[33] But whether enrap-
tured or unforgiving, no one seemed to realize the irony inherent in the com-
memoration ceremony. Mixing technology and spiritualism, faithful listeners
gave disproportionate validity to what was, after all, a false start. In listening
and relistening to just a lapse, they memorialized, of all things, their hero's
forgetfulness. The recording preserves not the transcendence of poetic genius
but the humanity of memory's imperfection. Benjamin, for one, might have
been surprised with the "aura" created by such a copy of an original voice. In
this instance, the phonograph enabled a new kind of intimacy by bringing listeners closer not only to "the sound of a voice that is still" but also to the public hesitation of a retiring mind.

Perhaps the greatest cache of literary recordings from this early period,
however, is the better known cylinders made by Tennyson, of which about two
dozen are still extant. These recordings are the first made by an author of substantial portions of his own work. Tennyson, who had watched Tyndall recite
lines from *Maud* into the phonograph at its London debut in 1878, was visited
at Farringford by Charles Steytler, an associate of Gouraud, in May 1890, for
the purposes of obtaining some specimens of the poet laureate reading
"Charge of the Light Brigade"; Gouraud planned to use these in a fund-rais-

LISTENING TO THE MASTER'S VOICE
A MEETING OF THE BROWNING SOCIETY AT THE HOUSE OF THE REV. H. R. HAWEIS, CHELSEA, FORMERLY THE HOME OF DANTE GABRIEL ROSSETTI

FIGURE 4.4. AN "INDECENT SEANCE" FOR THE LATE ROBERT BROWNING: POET-
WORSHIPPERS "LISTENING TO THE MASTER'S VOICE" ON PHONOGRAPH. GOURAUD IS
IN THE BACKGROUND JUST RIGHT OF CENTER, WITH HIS DISTINCTIVE MUSTACHE AND
PINCE-NEZ. FROM THE FIRST VOLUME OF *Black and White* (14 FEBRUARY 1891): 45.
ARMSTRONG BROWNING LIBRARY, BAYLOR UNIVERSITY, WACO, TEXAS.

ing event for survivors of the charge later that year.[34] Having obtained the recordings he came for, Steytler left the phonograph with Tennyson, perhaps at his request, also quite possibly because Steytler decided it was too bulky to haul back to London (153). In the ensuing weeks and months, Tennyson recorded all or part of about a dozen poems, including "'Ask me no more,'" "'Break, break, break,'" "Boädicea," "'Sweet is true love,'" "The Charge of the Heavy Brigade," additional versions of the "Light Brigade," "Northern Farmer: New Style," "Come into the Garden, Maud," "Kapiolani," and the Wellington Ode.[35] These cylinders fell into obscurity until about 1920, when Charles Tennyson found them, in his words, "standing in a brown paper parcel, with the old phonograph, against the fortunately not very effective hot-water pipes, in the room at Farringford which had been the poet's library" (3). A selection of these were released much later on a now hard-to-come-by record and cassette introduced by Sir Charles.[36]

What is surprising is not just that the cylinders survived, however, but that they have received so little attention. In his *Reading Aloud*, Philip Collins details how Tennyson was "one of the most memorable and powerful of readers-aloud," and Eric Griffiths devotes an entire chapter in *The Printed Voice of Victorian Poetry* to "Tennyson's Breath," yet both authors make no mention of the recordings that captured that reading voice and breathing.[37] It is as if textual critics simply have not known what to do with the poet's own readings and the sound of his voice. Only relatively recently has it been acknowledged that these literary firsts "mark a watershed in the history of poetry," and that the "ferocity" of Tennyson's voice indicates "that a limit is at hand, a frontier crossed."[38] Listening to them today "gives the reader a *frisson*," Robert Martin writes in his biography of Tennyson, as "it is still possible to fall under the hypnotic spell of his reading," delivered in a traditional oratory that demonstrates forceful rhythm, controlled breathing, and a determination that Jed Rasula terms "bardic resolve."[39] The records had equally powerful effects on those who heard them when they were first made. In the spring of 1890, while accompanying Henry Irving on a visit to the poet, Bram Stoker had occasion to listen to the recordings. He and Irving "went for a smoke to Hallam's study, where he produced his phonograph and adjusted a cylinder containing a reading of his father's."[40] Stoker continues:

> The reading was that of . . . *Charge of the Heavy Brigade*. It was strange to hear the mechanical repetition whilst the sound of the real voice, which we had so lately heard, was still ringing in our ears. It was hard to believe that we were not listening to the poet once again. . . . One seems to hear the thunder of the horses' hoofs as they ride to the attack. The ground seems to shake, and the virile voice of the reader conveys in added volume the desperate valour of the charge. (1:220)

Focusing on the "strange" element of hearing the artificial voice, Stoker's response epitomizes the nuanced relationship the phonograph held with the new community of listeners it created. (This experience appears to have lingered in Stoker's memory; he invoked his uncanny reaction several years later in *Dracula*, when Mina Harker responds with a similar *"frisson"* to the recorded voice of Dr. Seward.) But in his emphasis on collapsing the gap between the real voice of the poet and "mechanical repetition" of it, Stoker hits on, it seems to me, precisely what makes the phonograph such an attraction for Tennyson.

In Browning's case, the phonograph ironically had left speechless that master of the dramatic monologue, the poet whom A. S. Byatt called the "great ventriloquist." But for Tennyson, who was equally shy of public reading—Philip Collins notes he never gave public recitals and "would not even, as an undergraduate, give the customary public declamation of his Prize poem *Timbuctoo*"—it was the opposite: the new machine so intrigued him that he willingly committed many of his famous works to wax and, if Stoker's story can be taken as representative, had them replayed for himself and his guests.[41] Why would an eighty-year-old poet take (and talk) so enthusiastically to the machine that had alienated and confused his younger colleague? As if to protest Kittler's claim that "record grooves dig the grave of the author," Tennyson used audio technology to show that he would not go quietly.[42] The phonograph gave the great poet of divided mind the opportunity to perform a kind of self-fragmentation, literally to etch in an ostensibly permanent fashion different voices of the self. For the Tennyson of "The Two Voices," that defining earlier work in which an internal voice of faith narrowly defeated that of skepticism and turned the poet away from suicide, phonograph cylinders realized what paper never could: the creation of an unchanging, confident, emphatic, and most important, *audible* voice to combat the ever-present voice of doubt within. Tennyson's move to record himself may seem strikingly modern as an act of mechanical reproduction, yet it was in keeping with the aims of his poetic project: to express the plurality of selves that constitutes the self, to doubt the voice of faith yet crave it too. As he neared the end of his life in the 1880s and 1890s, Tennyson began to hear what his son referred to as "perpetual ghostly voices" (3:251). Did the father, in the echoed tones of his own recorded voice, seek to pose a material challenge to the "Silent Voices of the dead" that whispered to him in his last completed poems? ("The Silent Voices" [1892], 3:251, l. 4). For the elderly laureate, perhaps, the faithful tones of the phonograph articulated with enduring presence a message that might resist the ethereal, enigmatic voices he heard murmuring of death.

SINFUL SPEECH

IF THE phonograph offered a kind of humane salvation to some writers, it infuriated others who found it mercilessly mechanical. After "filling four dozen cylinders," Mark Twain confessed to William Dean Howells in April 1891 that he had given up trying to dictate his latest novel, *The American Claimant*, into a phonograph that Howells had rented for him. "You can't write literature with it," he wrote to Howells, "because it hasn't any ideas & it hasn't any gift for elaboration, or smartness of talk, or vigor of action, or felicity of expression, but is just matter-of-fact, compressive, unornamental, & as grave & unsmiling as the devil."[43] With a cynicism not unlike that of his modernist descendants, Twain found the phonograph an enemy to art and imagination. Three years earlier, in fact, after his English publisher Andrew Chatto had urged him to "tell the story of Smith [sic] of Camelot to Edison's phonograph & let us have it," Twain had planned to dictate *A Connecticut Yankee in King Arthur's Court* (1889) into one of the machines, but cancelled his order for two phonographs when the North American Phonograph Company proved unable to fill it.[44] He went on to blast the supposed practicality of the new invention within *The American Claimant* itself, when his hero Colonel Sellers proposes a "grand adaptation of the phonograph to the marine service": "You store up profanity in it for use at sea. . . . a ship can't afford a hundred mates; but she can afford a hundred Cursing Phonographs . . . Imagine a big storm, and a hundred of my machines all cursing away at once—splendid spectacle, splendid!—you couldn't hear yourself think. Ship goes through that storm perfectly serene—she's just as safe as she'd be on shore."[45]

The phonograph appeared for some, as suggested by one of the earliest images associated with it, a "recording angel," but for others like Twain, it was a cursing devil. It might delight and affirm those recording their voices, but it could also mock and betray them. Endless repetition of a disembodied voice had the potential to distort even the most benign speech into a monotonous rant that sounded diabolical, perhaps even terrifying: as an audience member at one of the early demonstrations of the machine famously put it, "It sounds more like the devil every time."[46] Although the art of ventriloquy historically had fostered the notion of a gap between speaker and voice, the phonograph mechanized this theatrical act, displacing it with a simple scientific process that had similar results.[47] Quite suddenly in the 1880s, throwing voices became easy but lost was the control that the ventriloquist had always had over placement and timing. With such fiendish possibilities, the phonograph carried inherent risk, for the playback process was open to manipulation by anyone with access to the controls. Having made a record, how would it be used, and when, where, and for whom would it be played? Those questions occupied fin-de-siècle authors as they explored the impact of the phonograph on the relations between voice and identity and the dynamics between mastery and degeneration.

In January 1891, just four months before Twain passed damning judgment on the new recording technology, the young doctor Arthur Conan Doyle, on the verge of his historic breakthrough, had his literary agent send out his first submission to the new *Strand Magazine*. The story, which was printed unsigned due to an editorial oversight, was entitled "The Voice of Science," and it appeared in the March issue, shortly before "A Scandal in Bohemia" ushered in the remarkable run of Conan Doyle's Sherlock Holmes stories in the same pages.[48] "The Voice of Science" not only introduced Conan Doyle to readers of the *Strand*, but it also introduced the trope of the "phonograph trick" that he would recycle in two of his later stories. In "The Voice of Science," the prospect of a bad marriage is foiled when a secretly made phonograph record publicly exposes the suitor's shadowy past. The central figure in "The Voice of Science" is one of Conan Doyle's typically up-to-date, independent-minded women, the widowed mother Mrs. Esdaile, "honorary secretary of the ladies' branch of the local Eclectic society" in Birchespool: "she supported Darwin, laughed at Mivart, doubted Haeckel, and shook her head at Weissman, with a familiarity which made her the admiration of University professors and the terror of the few students who ventured to cross her learned but hospitable threshold."[49] With her daughter Rose, "who was looked on as one of the beauties of Birchespool," she plans a "scientific conversazione" at her house, so cluttered with the latest inventions and experiments that it "had become a museum" (312). "In the post of honour on the central table" is a tinfoil phonograph, which Esdaile "hope[s] . . . will work without a hitch"; at the gathering she wants to play back a record she had made at a British Association meeting of a professor's remarks "on the life history of the Medusiform Gonophore" (313). Meanwhile, the pressure is on Rose, who has until the end of the evening to reply to a marriage proposal made by Captain Charles Beesly, who will be attending the gathering, and who is rumored to have moved in high circles back in India. Mrs. Esdaile, however, has not endorsed the match: "'Well, dear . . . ,'" she tells Rose, "'you are old enough to know your own mind. I shall not attempt to dictate to you. I own that my own hopes were set upon Professor Stares . . . think of his reputation, dear. Little more than thirty, and a member of the Royal Society'" (313). Also opposing the marriage is Rose's brother Rupert, who tries to disclose some of the rumors he has heard about the captain from one who knew him in India, but Rose refuses to listen. When alone with the phonograph, Rupert takes matters—rather, the tinfoil records—into his own hands: "Very carefully he drew forth the slips of metal which recorded the learned Professor's remarks, and laid them aside for future use. Into the slots he thrust virgin plates, all ready to receive an impression, and then, bearing the phonograph under his arm, he vanished into his own sanctum" (315). When the guests arrive, the machine is back in place, and Captain Beesly engages in small talk with Rose: "'don't call me Captain Beesly; call me Charles. Do, now!' 'Well, then, Charles.' 'How prettily it sounds from your lips!'" (315). The phonograph is finally called into service, and it speaks: "'How about Lucy Araminta Pennyfeather?' cried a squeaky little voice. . . . Rupert glanced across at Captain Beesly. He saw a drooping jaw, two protruding eyes, and a face the colour of cheese" (316). It continues—"'How about little Martha Hovedeen of the Kensal Choir Union? . . . Who was it who hid the ace in the artillery card-room at Penshawur? Who was it who was broke in consequence?'"—at which point the captain runs out of the house, never to be seen again. Rose marries Professor Stares as her mother had urged her to and lives happily, innocently ever after, even though "there are times when she still gives a thought to the blue-eyed Captain, and marvels at the strange and sudden manner in which he deserted her" (317).

As in many of Conan Doyle's other fin-de-siècle fictions, the lightness of touch in "The Voice of Science" is at odds with the darker insinuations that lurk beneath the surface. The phonograph in "The Voice of Science" is used to protect the purity of the Esdaile home, where, after all, a widowed mother reigns, from the sexual degeneracy that threatens it in the form of Captain Beesly. Specifically, the phonograph is feminized as a knowing, sinful strumpet, even as Rose, the "beauty of Birchespool," is antiseptically transformed into a docile accessory of science, the young bride who should be seen first—"looked on" by her husband, aptly named Professor *Stares*—and heard second. In language bristling with innuendo, the machine becomes both the passive participant in and speaker of illicit sexuality. Rupert, when "all ready" to make "an impression," secretly "thrust[s]" his "virgin plates" into the "slots" of the phonograph, carries it off to his "sanctum," and returns it only once it is ready to talk dirty like a kept woman—to broadcast in public the sexual escapades of the captain. Meanwhile, Rose mechanically utters in a "little tinkling voice" what the captain tells her to; like the early business phonograph Edison was beginning to market, she takes dictation, in the form of the marital command her mother disingenuously gives her: "'I shall not attempt to dictate to you.'" In her ultimate obedience to her mother's wishes and her rational marriage to the professor, "one of the most rising scientists in the provinces," Rose preserves the family's propriety, avoiding direct understanding of or contact with the insatiable sexuality of the captain, even as she commits to the sexualized professionalism of the "rising" professor (317). The phonograph metaphorically must become a devilish bawd to manipulate the young Rose into angelic and, so to speak, scientific conformity and to keep the gears of social machinery running smoothly. The fallen machine ends up just repeating gossip about sex and gambling, but the *real* "Voice of Science" in the story, finally, is the reasonable mother's, the practical view Rose defers to, the quiet, repressive drone of the mechanism of social convention.

For Conan Doyle, as this story suggests, and for other writers of the period, the phonograph seemed charged with a sexualized femininity.[50] This perception had emerged alongside the debut of the machine and was on display in a George Du Maurier *Punch* cartoon that offered "A Suggestion": replace "hirsute Italian organ-grinders" in the streets with "fair female phonographers playing our best poets in their own original voices!" (see figure 4.5). In the cartoon, Du Maurier's prominent street post rigidly rises toward the gaping mouth of a phonograph horn held by a "fair female" grinder. As might be suspected of the artist who would go on to write *Trilby* (1894), in which a painter's model is mesmerized into a diva, "a singing-machine—an

A SUGGESTION.

HOW MUCH BETTER IF, INSTEAD OF HIRSUTE ITALIAN ORGAN-GRINDERS
PARADING OUR STREETS, WE COULD HAVE FAIR FEMALE PHONOGRAPHERS
PLAYING OUR BEST POETS IN THEIR OWN ORIGINAL VOICES!

FIGURE 4.5. GEORGE DU MAURIER'S PHONOGRAPHIC
"SUGGESTION," FROM *Punch* 74 (1878): 179.

organ to play upon—an instrument of music—a Stradivarius—a flexible
flageolet of flesh and blood—a voice, and nothing more," Du Maurier in this
earlier illustration symbolically aligned the phonograph with an objectified
female "instrument." The massive machine at once presents a (male) poets'
vocal organs as well as represents the (female) phonographer's sex organs,
both of which are to be "played" by her on the streets.[51] A more manifest association of phonographs with women was reinforced over the 1890s by the
use of the first popular commercial phonographs in the workplace, as office
dictation machines, from which female amanuenses transcribed business
correspondence.

With a vibrating diaphragm of an ear and a horned mouth, the phonograph indeed seemed, as Charles Grivel writes, "a machine with a body," and
in the literary sphere, this also typically was a feminine body, as presented in
some of the earliest fictional treatments of the device, French writings from
the late 1880s and early 1890s. These included Villiers de L'Isle-Adam's sym-

bolist/sci-fi novel *L'Eve future* (1886), in which a brooding Thomas Edison creates the "Eve of the future," an android with two golden phonographs for lungs.[52] An English version of *L'Eve future* did not appear, however, for nearly a century. A more influential text was Jules Verne's novel *Le Château des Carpathes* (1892; English translation, 1893), a gothic parody set mostly in a Transylvanian castle owned by the evil Baron de Gortz. To the terror of the townspeople and the young Romanian count/hero Franz de Telek, the castle appears haunted by the ghost of a dead opera star (named "La Stilla"—"the silent one"), who had been engaged to Franz and whose final aria, cut short by her death from fright at seeing the baron in her audience, still can be heard every night echoing from the ramparts. In the end, all is exposed when Franz besieges the castle in mad pursuit of La Stilla's ghost, only to "[stumble] into the baron's private operatic fetish theater," where an illuminated glass sculpture of the diva stands on a stage and the baron sits listening to a jewel-encrusted box containing a cylinder of her last performance.[53] A stray bullet pierces the box as the baron holds it in his arms to flee. "Her voice—her voice!" he cries, "They have destroyed her voice!" Before the baron can escape and trap Franz in the dynamited room according to his plan, a prearranged electric charge detonates the dynamite that in turn demolishes the castle. Franz somehow survives the blast, only to discover that the baron, crushed under the rubble, secretly had made the recording at the final concert and ever since had been listening to it each night while staring at La Stilla's statue. The villain of *Le Château des Carpathes* thus literally transforms the woman singer into a machine, her voice a mechanical ruse that ensnares men, and the phonograph becomes implicated in an uncanny, ultimately manipulative sensual fantasy.[54]

While the Verne novel offers—to say the least—a tale of odd Freudian entanglements with communications technology, its use of the phonograph suggests it had a profound impact both on Conan Doyle, who reworked it in one of his own stories several years later, and also, one suspects, on Stoker, whose *Dracula* echoes and inverts it in curious ways. Conan Doyle's "The Story of the Japanned Box," published in the *Strand* in 1899, derives its major elements from the Verne novel but implies that the manipulative power of the phonograph can be used beneficially as a form of self-restraint. "The Japanned Box" is, like Verne's work, a gothic send-up but takes place in a dilapidated English, not Transylvanian, castle; the threat has moved back closer to home. "It sent a chill to my heart when first I came there," the narrator, a private tutor named Colmore, recounts, "those enormously thick grey walls, the rude crumbling stones, the smell as from a sick animal which exhaled from the rotting plaster of the aged building."[55] The theme of decay dominates this tale: the rotting castle reflects the moral and emotional state of its owner, the widower John Bollamore, an aristocrat with an air of evil about him, from his "brindled hair, shaggy eyebrows, . . . small, pointed Mephistophelian beard, and lines upon his brow and round his eyes as deep as if they had been carved with a pen-knife" to his "weary, hopeless looking eyes" (3–4).

Bollamore, like Verne's Baron de Gortz, is an older, enigmatic recluse "with the snarl of a furious wild beast," spending all his time in his tower study with a photo of his dead wife and the mysterious black box of the story's title (8). Soon Colmore hears "tales of mysterious visitors there, and of voices over-heard by the servants," and discovers from a steward that Bollamore hides a secret past: decades ago he had been known as "'Devil' Bollamore . . . the leader of the fastest set, bruiser, driver, gambler, drunkard. . . . The greatest rip and debauchee in England!" (5). One night, while walking outside, Colmore hears a sound from the study window: "It was a voice—the voice undoubtedly of a woman. It was low—so low that it was only in that still night air that we could hear it, but, hushed as it was, there was no mistaking its feminine tim-bre. It spoke hurriedly, gaspingly for a few sentences, and then was silent—a piteous, breathless, imploring sort of voice" (6). Open to gothic suggestion, Colmore concludes the worst, that Bollamore must be leading "a double and dubious life" by keeping a woman prisoner in "some medieval passage" in the castle: "I conceived a horror of the man," Colmore remarks (7).

As in Verne's novel, such gothic fears are revealed to derive from perfectly "scientific" grounds and nearly identical ones at that. Colmore, under the ef-fects of chlorodyne for neuralgia, falls into a "semi-conscious state" on a se-cluded settee in the library and overhears Bollamore enter and take some-thing—readers familiar with Verne's novel already know this will be a phonograph—out of the japanned box he carries: "I heard a strange, crisp metallic clicking, and then the voice. . . . Yes, it was a woman's voice" (10). Like the cylinder record of La Stilla's final aria, "every word was clear, though faint—very faint, for they were the last words of a dying woman" (10). That voice is a far cry from the gossipy chatter of the phonograph in "The Voice of Science": "'I am not really gone, John,' said the thin, gasping voice. 'I am here at your very elbow, and shall be until we meet once more. I die happy to think that morning and night you will hear my voice. Oh, John, be strong, be strong, until we meet again'" (10). Bollamore's dead wife, it turns out, had "brought him back to manhood and decency" from his alcoholism, and she had pro-cured a phonograph once she knew she was dying in order to record a final message urging his self-restraint (6). Bollamore, in turn, vowed to listen to it twice a day to resist the temptation to revert to his degenerate state. As in Verne's tale and "The Voice of Science," the phonograph in this story occupies a feminine space, but in an ironic twist, Conan Doyle has that site at first *ap-pear* sinful—as seemingly the space, once again, of the kept woman—only to ultimately reveal it as the last bastion of propriety for a guilty man. And in an autobiographical vein, Conan Doyle incorporates his own disturbing memo-ries of an alcoholic and abusive father in the portrayal of the man tempered by the ailing wife-turned-machine. What is reinforced in this tale is not only the classic Victorian conception of the woman/wife as the voice of domestic disci-pline capable of containing unchecked male sloth, but also the sense that in the dying light of the nineteenth century, such a voice of self-control had become mechanical, a vanishing remnant of the past, and also was dying or perhaps already was dead. At the end of the tale, upon learning that Bollamore had been killed in a carriage accident, Colmore soberly adds, "I do not fancy it was a very unwelcome event to him" (10). The technology that had at first suggested to the narrator a secret life of vice instead ends up facilitating a monotonous pattern of solitary sobriety. In an increasingly isolated, libertine, and faithless age, Conan Doyle shows how the phonograph could manufacture an artificial communion with the past, out of which nevertheless might come self-mastery, even a bleak salvation.

SOUND BITES

EDISON'S own interaction with his invention, however, was more earthy and visceral. A story from an 1879 account of the origin of the phonograph described one way Edison discovered the principle behind the machine. "In the course of some experiments Mr. Edison was making with the telephone, a stylus attached to the diaphragm pierced his finger at the moment when the diaphragm began to vibrate under the influence of the voice, and the prick was enough to draw blood. It then occurred to him that if the vibrations of the diaphragm enabled the stylus to pierce the skin, they might produce on a flexible surface such distinct outlines as to represent all the undulations produced by the voice."[56] More painful still is part of the phonograph story concerning the inventor's deafness: "Edison's hearing deficit forced him when testing different materials' acoustic properties to follow the same bizarre technique he would use decades later when auditioning pianists for his phonograph records: clenching his teeth around a metal plate attached to the sounding apparatus, so that vibrations were conveyed through his resonating jawbone—meaning, in effect, that *he virtually heard through his teeth*."[57] Edison's daughter Madeleine recalled a related experience from her childhood:

> During the winter of 1912, what seemed to Madeleine like every night, a pianist would "pound out" waltzes in the downstairs den. Sometimes her papa would put his teeth on the piano—literally bite it—so that the vibrations resonated through his skull bones. . . . One evening, Madame Montessori [the educator] was a dinner guest at Glenmont while the waltzes were being auditioned, and the great lady huddled in the corner of the den weeping because Edison could not hear, and was putting his teeth in the side of the grand piano. . . . Edison's personal Disc Phonograph, preserved at the Laboratory, also shows teeth marks on its soft wood framework. (321)

It is one of the famous ironies of invention that the man behind the phonograph suffered from severe deafness. Less known, perhaps with good reason, is Edison's animalistic manner of close listening. As if to express his hunger to hear, Edison gnawed the grooves of his own incisors into the wood of the groove-machine. From pricking to biting, from blood to bone, there is something primal, piercing, about the phonograph, the needle, and the biting inventor, something, one might even say . . . vampiric.

So it should come as no surprise that along with such technological innovations as typewriters and Kodak cameras, diary-keeping phonographs play an important part in the action of the classic vampire novel that is, in the words of one of the characters, "nineteenth century up-to-date with a vengeance."[58] With a narrative that is at once *about* and (supposedly) communicated *through* such gadgetry, *Dracula* may appear to be, as Jennifer Wicke has put it, a consumptive tale that is the "first great *modern* novel in British literature."[59] Yet at the heart of Stoker's text lurks a distinctly late-Victorian fascination with the primacy of the voices that pulse through it. For *Dracula* explores the occult dimension of "Primal Sound," the kind of sublime tones that Rilke imagined might be revealed if one were to play back with a phonograph needle the groove of the coronal suture of the skull.[60] In *Dracula*, Stoker, as had Edison and Rilke, associates blood and bones with tones. Not only the ancient powers of the count, but also the modern ones of the phonograph, ensure that speaking and hearing in the fin-de-siècle world of *Dracula* are draining and confusing. Yet it is the phonograph and other tools of modernity featured in the novel that allow the band of heroes to harness sound collectively and defeat the vampire with scientific and professional mastery.

Phonographic representations in *Dracula* go beyond merely the literal. The text of *Dracula* itself emerges from sound, that is, sound-*writing*. The first lines of the novel proper—"Jonathan Harker's Journal / (*kept in shorthand*)"— indicate the importance of sound-capture for this famous opening section of gothic imprisonment and for the chain of events it triggers. Jonathan may be a naive solicitor, but he is also revealed to be, as his surname suggests, an experienced listener, a "harker," who first hears and reports sounds of ominous foreboding: the incessant howling of Dracula's wolves and the "harsh, metallic whisper" of his hypnotic, otherworldly voice (64). Harker's method of recording these experiences, moreover, is phonography, the phonetic shorthand system devised by Isaac Pitman in 1837 and so coined by him in 1840 with the publication of his best-selling *Phonography, or Writing by Sound*, which became the standard Victorian shorthand manual, reaching over twelve editions by the time a new one appeared in 1897, the year *Dracula* was published (and the year Pitman died).[61] Harker, then, acts as a kind of human phonograph, a sound-recorder whose modern hieroglyphs keep his journal safe from the count's prying eyes. But Harker, trapped literally in the castle, is also *used* by Dracula as a language machine, much as Edison had envisioned phonographs would be used for language tutorials: "as yet I only know your tongue through books," the count tells him, "To you, my friend, I look that I know it to speak . . . by our talking I may learn the English intonation" (31–32). The distinctly alien sound of Dracula's arrival on English soil, however, betrays his outsider status: "A little after midnight came a strange sound from over the sea, and high overhead the air began to carry a strange, faint, hollow booming" (103). The count himself acquires a kind of phonographic presence in the disembodied voice that Mina Harker, once bitten and nursed by him, hears and must obey: "When my brain says 'Come!' to you, you shall cross land or sea to do my bidding" (371).[62]

The emphasis on sound and voice in the novel is encapsulated in the phonograph that Stoker indicates records Dr. Seward's medical and personal diary. Used as a medical tool within the text, then, the phonograph records a literal "Voice of Science." But in ways more provocative than Conan Doyle's phonograph stories, the machine in *Dracula* acts as a locus of sexual anxiety and symbolism among Seward, Lucy Westenra, and Mina. As he goes to become, as Van Helsing puts it, a "bigamist," to give blood to the drained and nearly vampiric Lucy whom he loves, Seward makes a point of noting that he "take[s his] cylinder with [him]" so as to "complete [his] entry on Lucy's phonograph" (227, 184–85). Following Lucy's graphic death scene in the graveyard, Mina desires access to the secrets of Seward's machine: "I had never seen one, and was much interested" (283). Listening to the "hollow cylinders of metal covered with dark wax" on which Seward confesses his unrequited love for Lucy, Mina senses and covets a new intimacy between the doctor and herself: as Mina says to him, "'That is a wonderful machine, but it is cruelly true. It told me, in its very tones, the anguish of your heart. It was like a soul crying out to almighty God. No one must hear them ever again! . . . none other need now hear your heart beat, as I did'" (284–86). Once Mina begins to transcribe Seward's cylinders, this new intimacy lends to their restrained professional interactions a sensual charge:

> After dinner I came with Dr Seward to his study. He brought back the phonograph from my room, and I took my typewriter. He placed me in a comfortable chair, and arranged the phonograph so I could touch it without getting up, and showed me how to stop it in case I should want to pause. Then he very thoughtfully took a chair, with his back to me, so that I might be as free as possible, and began to read. I put the forked metal to my ears and listened.
>
> When . . . done, I lay back in my chair powerless. (287)

In a work with so many scenes of sublimated sexuality, it is tempting to read this act of private listening as a moment with autoerotic implications for the character who satisfies standard Victorian masculine *and* feminine gender expectations—as bold, resourceful, New Woman vampire-hunter, as well as dutiful secretary, wife, and mother to Jonathan and his band of ineffective men. But the scene more directly suggests the power of hearing and sound in this novel both to consummate and consume. So Mina can claim writing in her journal to be "like whispering to one's self and listening at the same time" (96–97). At the end of the novel, when Van Helsing hypnotizes the bitten and suckled Mina to, in his words, "tell what the Count see and hear" in order to lead the men to Dracula's hiding place, she repeats the same sounds with "un-

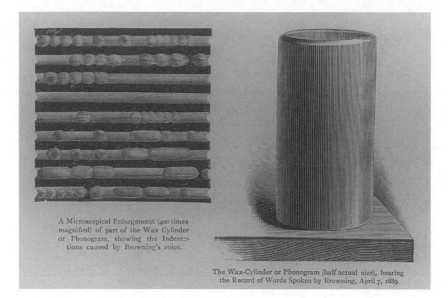

A Microscopical Enlargement (400 times magnified) of part of the Wax Cylinder or Phonogram, showing the Indentations caused by Browning's voice.

The Wax-Cylinder or Phonogram (half actual size), bearing the Record of Words Spoken by Browning, April 7, 1889.

FIGURE 4.6. THE BROWNING CYLINDER, WITH AN ENLARGEMENT OF THE GROOVES "SHOWING THE INDENTATIONS CAUSED BY BROWNING'S VOICE." FROM THE SECOND VOLUME OF *Black and White* (12 DECEMBER 1891): 780. ARMSTRONG BROWNING LIBRARY, BAYLOR UNIVERSITY, WACO, TEXAS.

varied" words, over and over, like a broken record: "lapping waves, rushing water, and creaking masts" (415, 430). It is entirely in keeping with her established intimate connection with sound-writing and sound-writers (both human and mechanical) that Mina Harker is herself an expert recorder, transmitter, and replayer.[63]

Stoker may indeed have been influenced by his knowledge of Irving's recordings at Little Menlo, his listening experience at Tennyson's house, and by Verne's *Le Château des Carpathes* to bring a phonograph into *Dracula*, but the workings of the machine take on their own symbolic significance within his story. In terms that became the source of years of legal wrangling over patent infringement, Edison's 1878 phonograph patent stated that the device worked by "indenting" marks on a yielding surface.[64] Thus, an illustrated enlargement of the grooves of the Browning cylinder could call attention to "the Indentations caused by Browning's voice" (figure 4.6). *Dracula* is in a way a novel of *indentations*, most concretely, perhaps, in Stoker's use of the phonograph but also in the inescapable bites of vampire teeth and the impress of typewriter hammers by which Mina has "made manifest" the entire manuscript (6). It is, of course, this indentation, this typing and hiding of manifest copies, that Stoker would have us believe allows the "evidence" to survive, despite Dracula's attempt to destroy it by setting fire to the "original" manuscript and cylinders (367). The ancient count can only be defeated by the heroes' altogether more cold-blooded professional labor, in Kittler's words, their "mechanical discourse processing": "Stoker's *Dracula* is no vampire novel but rather the written account of our bureaucratization. Anyone is free to call this a horror novel as well."[65]

Put another way, the means to combat the "reverse colonization" that Stephen Arata has identified underlying Dracula's mission to England is through a technological imperialism whose mechanisms ultimately consume its warriors.[66] "How many of us begin a new record with each day of our lives?" Seward naively asks into his phonograph, unaware that his daily ritual of recording enacts precisely this (96). Harker the phonographer longs to escape from "the groove of [his] life" on the careerist track; yet his wife Mina finally must become a phonographic medium to track Dracula down (243). The vampire whom Renfield calls "Master" and who longs endlessly to reproduce his race burns the master cylinders of Seward and the others; yet the original recordings have already been transcribed, and by the end of the novel, both Seward and Harker ironically have become masters themselves in hierarchies of professional reproduction: "You were only student then; now you are master," Van Helsing tells Seward, while upon the death of his overseer, Harker rises "from clerk to master" (157, 206). The novel that alleges to be a copy of a copy has many masters, but no master take. Instead, in their phonographic resourcefulness, the Western victors oddly seem to echo the toothy Transylvanian.[67] A lethal stake strikes the vampire heart, while a stylus on a cylinder summons the human past; for each, the path to the grave is through the groove:

> I seize the palpitating air. . . .
> All lips that breathe are mine

But whose mouth is it anyway that constructs this imperial archive of "metallic whispers"? The count's, with his piercing canines, or the doctor's, with his resonant needles? Dracula cries: "This man belongs to me!" (55). Seward sighs: "How I miss my phonograph!" (431). Stoker, through all their rush to bite and engrave, keeps tight-lipped.

If *Dracula* only nibbles at the possibilities for serious problems with the notion of a phonographic voice, Joseph Conrad's *Heart of Darkness*, first serialized in *Blackwood's* two years later, feasts on them. "Voice," that foundational yet slippery term of textual criticism—"that shibboleth of the humanist literary tradition," in Garrett Stewart's words—is on trial in Conrad's novella.[68] Through an exploration of the relations between sound and speech, *Heart of Darkness* conveys the inherent insufficiency of making a record of the voice. Addressing the question of what it "would mean to write a work of literature . . . within this new paradigm of sound and inscription," Conrad uses what has been called "phonographic logic" to show that in the wake of the phonograph, the concept of "voice" has become "a part-object standing for nothing beyond itself."[69] Edward Said has claimed that with Conrad "we are in a world being made and unmade more or less all the time," yet it might be more helpful to consider the world of *Heart of Darkness* as one perpetually sounded and re-sounded.[70] For this is not only an "Edison-haunted, electrical text,"[71] but also one deeply invested in attempting to record an aural landscape of fierce mutterings and menacing silences. References to the phonograph in Conrad's letters from this period have shown that the author was familiar with the machine. The phonograph is everywhere and nowhere in *Heart of Darkness*, literally absent though always present in metaphorical associations and residual effects.

In January 1885, the *New York Times* published "The Phonograph in Africa," a remarkable op-ed piece that shed light on the mingled dynamics of technology and imperialism Conrad later examined in his novella. The author of the column contended that "two travelers who are about to try to cross the African continent" planned to put the phonograph to its first practical use to "obtain specimens of Central African languages" and bring these back West for further study. But the author went on to raise suspicions of these seemingly innocuous motives:

> It is possible that the two travelers are wicked and ambitious men, who . . . have conceived the idea of introducing a new religion into Central Africa and of ruling the entire country in the character of high priests. Nothing could be easier than to carry such a scheme into effect. The travelers could describe the phonograph as a new and improved portable god, and call upon the native Kings to obey it. A god capable of speaking, and even of carrying on a conversation, in the presence of swarms of hearers would be something entirely new in Central Africa, where the local gods are constructed out of solid billets of wood, and are hopelessly dumb. There is not a Central African living who would dare to refuse to obey the phonograph god, and the two travelers, as its only authorized priests, could bring the greater part of the continent into subjection for as long a time as they could keep their portable god in good repair and working order.[72]

In this disturbing "techno-colonial dream," the travelers use the peculiar linguistic features of the new technology to conquer central Africa effortlessly. The phonograph becomes all-powerful not only in physical presence but also because it captures "the social power of the ruler's voice."[73] In other words, it is the ability of the machine to command speech that compels African subjugation. It is unclear from the historical record whether these explorers ever set out, or for that matter even existed, for phonographs had their first official use in ethnographic fieldwork five years later, when the anthropologist Jesse Walter Fewkes recorded Passamaquoddy and Zuni Pueblo in the Americas.[74] But it is striking that even as early as 1885, the notion of a "wicked and ambitious" ideology of recorded language was imagined as lurking in the mechanisms of one of the marvels of the age.

In *Le Château des Carpathes*, Verne had begun to suggest how the phonograph might invite such devious manipulations of speech, but it was for Conrad to confront the ways in which "phonographic logic" could corrupt the integrity of the individual voice within the context of diabolical imperialist practices.[75] As described by Marlow, Kurtz is indeed a kind of phonographic god, one ultimately revealed to be nothing more nor less than a "wicked and ambitious" voice of manipulation and conquest. "I had never imagined him as doing, you know, but as discoursing," Marlow says, "The man presented himself as a voice."[76] The devoted Russian states the case simply: "You don't talk with that man—you listen to him" (88). Kurtz's voice mesmerizes natives and colonists alike. When the armed tribesmen approach his hut, it is only his voice that pacifies them (97). Kurtz's "weirdly voracious" mouth, open wide "as though he had wanted to swallow all the air, all the earth, all the men before him," echoes both Dracula's all-consuming mouth and the gaping horned mouth of the fin-de-siècle phonograph that seizes the "palpitating air" (97). Hearing Kurtz utter "I am glad," Marlow rhapsodizes about the disjunction between Kurtz's wasted body and majestic voice: "The volume of tone he emitted without effort, almost without the effort of moving his lips, amazed me. A voice! A voice! It was grave, profound, vibrating, while the man did not seem capable of a whisper" (98). "A voice! A voice!" Marlow later repeats over Kurtz's deathbed, "It rang deep to the very last. It survived his strength to hide in the magnificent folds of eloquence the barren darkness of his heart. . . . The shade of the original Kurtz frequented the bedside of the hollow sham, whose fate it was to be buried presently in the mould of primeval earth" (110). Kurtz's greed for ivory has reduced him to a speaking shell of the "original," a corrupted copy degenerated into darkness. Merely that remnant of identity, his voice, remains. Like Browning on record, Kurtz becomes a hollow replica on an ivory-shaded cylinder of totemic power.

Marlow is on the one hand Kurtz's auditor, his phonographer, the only one who can play him back, so to speak, to the Intended and the unnamed narrator. But on the other, Marlow is Conrad's Harker, actively listening to his surroundings, struggling to make sense of the "violent babble of uncouth sounds" of natives, the "tremor of far-off drums . . . weird, appealing, suggestive, and wild," and the "high stillness" and impenetrable hush of the thick growth of forest around him as he journeys to Kurtz (38, 39, 58). In *Heart of Darkness*, the "ringing grooves of change" of "Locksley Hall" sound not progressive but doomed. The colonial railway building Marlow encounters is "a rapacious and pitiless folly," marked by "a heavy and dull detonation" of mindless blasting, set off against the ominous noise of violated nature: "The rapids were near, and an uninterrupted, uniform, head-long, rushing noise filled the mournful silence of the grove, where not a breath stirred, not a leaf moved, with a mysterious sound—as though the tearing pace of the launched earth had suddenly become audible" (32, 34). On his trek to the Inner Station, Marlow travels like a needle in grooves around the hollow core of an engraved continent, tracing and relaying "paths, paths, everywhere; a stamped-in network of paths spreading over the empty land" (39). He sounds the landscape like a stylus, using a "sounding-pole" to guide his steamer along the narrow groove of the Congo on the "track" of Kurtz (74, 105). The doubling effect that critics often have observed between Marlow and Kurtz unites them too in their appropriated voicings. That their dialogue is subsumed in dual layers of narrative calls into question the reliability and clarity of it: "I found myself lumped along with Kurtz . . . ," Marlow says after an uncomfortable talk with the manager, "I was unsound!" (101). Sounding and unsound, voicing and voiced, Marlow becomes at once listener, archive, and nested narrator; or needle, record, and harnessed talking machine.

Heart of Darkness manages to crystallize into moments of remarkable dialogical precision, what in the wake of mass media we now would call "sound bites." Perhaps no shorter work of modern fiction has contributed so many quotable lines to the pop culture lexicon. People who have not even read the work (and perhaps not even seen *Apocalypse Now*, let alone *Apocalypse Now Redux*) still are familiar with some of its famous tags: "Exterminate all the brutes!" "Mistah Kurtz—he dead," and, of course, "The horror! The horror!" (84, 112).[77] Sound bites are themselves phonographic phenomena—snippets of endlessly recycled recorded speech, catchphrases standing in for the whole of a particular event or experience. But Kurtz's final words do more: they point to the risks the phonograph would bring to the world in the century ahead. In its self-contained echo, "The horror! The horror!" is perhaps the greatest needle-skip (or more precisely, needle-stick) in modern literature, the summative judgment that insists on voicing not a unified, coherent singularity but a divided, paralyzed vision of self that persists throughout modernist writing. The needle-skip (or stick), with its connotations of immobility and hollow repetition, recurs in the work of those who were themselves discomforted by the successor to the cylinder phonograph, the more insidious gramophone: in Eliot's "Love Song" (1917), with Prufrock's faint "Do I dare? Do I dare?"; in Faulkner's *Absalom, Absalom!* (1936), with Quentin Compson's tortured "*I dont hate it! I dont hate it!*"; and most explicitly in Woolf's *Between the Acts*, with the chuffing machine's monotonous "*Dispersed are we. . . . Dispersed are we.*"[78] Kurtz's last confession lies in a scratched groove on which moderns reinscribed their own voices.

What is more, *Heart of Darkness* explores the untranslatability of sound as it bears on the limits of vision. "Of course, in this you fellows see more than I could then. You see me, whom you know . . . ," Marlow comments midway through his tale (50). But the narrator of the novella immediately undermines this assertion:

> It had become so pitch dark that we listeners could hardly see one another. For a long time already he, sitting apart, had been no more to us than a voice. . . . The others might have been asleep, but I was awake. I listened, I listened on the watch for the sentence, for the word, that

would give me the clue to the faint uneasiness inspired by this narrative that seemed to shape itself without human lips in the heavy night-
air of the river. (50)

The blindness of this scene calls to mind lines from Eliot's 1925 "The Hollow
Men," the epigraph of which is one of those infamous sound bites lifted from
Heart of Darkness ("Mistah Kurtz—he dead"): "The eyes are not here / There
are no eyes here."[79] Ironically, Marlow, who "did not see the man in the name
[Kurtz] any more than you do," also cannot be seen, but only heard, like Kurtz,
as a disembodied voice (50). Through Marlow, Conrad suggests, finally, that
the phonographic dynamic of the severed voice—the act of listening to an invisible source—even the act of oral narrative itself—fails to capture the
essence of lived experience: "I've been telling you what we said—repeating
the phrases we pronounced,—but what's the good? They were common
everyday words—the familiar, vague sounds exchanged on every waking day
of life. But what of that? They had behind them, to my mind, the terrific sug-
gestiveness of words heard in dreams, of phrases spoken in nightmares" (107).
The disembodied voices of Kurtz and Marlow, the acts of retelling and replaying by Marlow and the unnamed narrator, are not enough to clarify or resus-
citate the past, the silent, or the dead, but only conjure them in mysterious,
incomplete, and distant ways. Marlow recognizes that his reproduction of
Kurtz is itself inadequate, even as it emerges from the amorphous, corrupt
babble of his narrative:

> He was very little more than a voice. And I heard him—it—this voice—
> other voices—all of them were so little more than voices—and the
> memory of that time itself lingers around me, impalpable, like a dying
> vibration of one immense jabber, silly, atrocious, sordid, savage, or
> simply mean, without any kind of sense. Voices, voices—even the girl
> herself—now— (80)

"His last word—to live with," the Intended begs Marlow (123). But in the
phonograph-text of *Heart of Darkness*, words, and voices, no longer possess the
kind of authenticity, masterful finality, and authority the grieving woman
wants. First-time readers of the tale (and even some experienced ones) fall into
the trap Conrad lays when they claim that "it is not Kurtz's voice but Marlow's
that we hear as readers."[80] Is it? The initial vocal conflation of the text, Marlow
as replayer of Kurtz's oratorical fragments, is amplified by the fact that there is
a second level of listening and replaying, the anonymous harker who sits in silence on the Thames, waiting for the word he thinks will resolve Marlow's "in-
conclusive experience," the clue that, when (and if) it arrives, surely opens
more doors than it closes. In their earlier fictions, Conan Doyle and Stoker had
stopped short of deep investigation of the effect of voice recording technology
on the craft of fiction making itself. But Conrad is less cautionary than he is
wise to the ambiguous fissures that modern repetition opens up. His *Heart of
Darkness* enacts the narrative cost—or is it gain?—of technological progress.

CODA: THE VICTOR DOG

IN DECEMBER 1898 and January 1899, as Conrad was in Kent writing the story that would work to undermine Victorian faith in the recorded voice, Francis Barraud was in London painting the canvas that would become one of the most recognizable representations of voice in the twentieth and twenty-first centuries. Barraud, whose father and uncle were well-known Victorian animal painters, and who himself had made a respectable if undistinguished career as an artist exhibiting work at the Royal Academy from 1881 on, found his life forever changed in 1887, when his brother Mark died, leaving to Francis his fox terrier Nipper, so named for his tendency to bite the backs of people's legs. The rest is commercial art history: "We had a phonograph," Barraud later wrote, "and I often noticed how puzzled he was to make out where the voice came from. It was certainly the happiest thought I ever had."[81] In February 1899, Barraud filed an application for copyright of his painting, listed as "Dog Looking at and Listening to a Phonograph" (figure 4.7). But the Royal Academy refused to exhibit the painting, and the Edison Bell Company, the phonograph marketers of London, refused to buy it: "One well-known man objected on the score that no one would know what the dog was doing."[82] Finally, in September 1899, the London Gramophone Company agreed to purchase the painting on the condition that Barraud paint over his original phonograph with a disk gramophone, which he did soon afterward. The alteration in the painting foreshadowed the impending shift in technology during the ensuing decade, when the device that had inspired active, personal engagement with recording became eclipsed by the commercially dominant playback-only gramophone, which reproduced mass-marketed disks but could not make records. With the beginning of the new century, Barraud's famous image of a voice being mechanically reproduced itself underwent mass reproduction. In January 1900, the painting first appeared in advertising on that month's British Record Supplement, and by the end of 1901 it had received trademarks on behalf of the Gramophone Company in England and the Victor Talking Machine Company in the United States. On this arc from the individually crafted to the corporate-branded, Barraud's Nipper eventually became better-known as "The Victor Dog," which was also the title James Merrill much later chose for his often-reprinted poem honoring, among other things, the mass-marketed classical LP record.

In its juxtaposition of a quintessential Victorian dog portrait with that of a speech machine, "His Master's Voice" heralds the uneasy divide between Victorian aura and modern echo, between the initial allure of recording voices that Tennyson felt and the ultimate hollowness of mechanical repetition that Conrad foresaw. But perhaps the painting also hints at what was reduced and demeaned as the experience of reality yielded to the simulacrum of replication in a phonographic, or rather, gramophonic, world.[83] For in the painting, it is the master who barks, not the dog. The title too has a buried meaning, one implicit in the power relations of capturing speech: In the

FIGURE 4.7. PHOTOGRAPH TAKEN C. 1899 BY FRANCIS BARRAUD OF HIS "DOG
LOOKING AT AND LISTENING TO A PHONOGRAPH" BEFORE HE PAINTED OVER THE
PHONOGRAPH WITH A GRAMOPHONE. PUBLIC RECORD OFFICE: COPY 1/147 F.1.

wake of the phonograph, can it be that the dog's—and, by extension,
our—Master has become Voice?[84] For Barraud portrays the machine with an
audience of a loyal canine, not devoted humans. And as the centerpiece of
the parlor or den, the gramophone indeed became the great domesticator.[85]
In retrospect, might the illustration (figure 4.4) of Browning's followers huddled around the phonograph just possibly appear in a different light? . . .
those poor dogs. The small linguistic shift from "The Master's Voice" as represented in the Browning illustration to "His Master's Voice" as heard by Nipper eight years later marked a larger cultural one. In the cases of Browning,
Tennyson, Conan Doyle, and even Stoker, the phonograph served to attract
and unite curious Victorians in an intimate, uncanny community, but by the
turn of the century, for skeptics like Conrad, the principles of the machine
only appeared to subdue, diminish, and isolate speakers and listeners alike.
So too the inherent *activity* of Victorian phonography, the attempt to create
idiosyncratic Libraries of Voices, with all the marvels and risks that involved,
yielded to the passivity of modern listening to disks, when gramophone companies took the prospect of home recording away from the masses and more

FIGURE 4.8. FRANCIS BARRAUD WITH COPIES OF "HIS MASTER'S VOICE,"
1922. EMI RECORDS (U.K.) LTD.

thoroughly commercialized the production of records. It is a heavy irony that Barraud, elderly and broke, became a slave to his own creation, grinding out two dozen commissioned reproductions of "His Master's Voice" canvases, all identical to the first, down to the phonograph painted over with a gramophone. A photo of the artist from 1922 shows him in his studio surrounded by his "His Master's Voice" copies, hunched over another on his easel and gazing out with a despairing look (figure 4.8). By the time of his death two years later, Barraud had become a mechanical artist trapped by his own trademark, a late Victorian whom modernity, in more ways than one, had contracted to Victor. Like that of a powerful god or a good dog, the call of the recorded voice proved impossible to resist.

⍋ APPENDIX ⍋

Dickens's Prospectus
for the Cheap Edition (1847)

[What follows is the text of Dickens's prospectus for the Cheap Edition (see the discussion in chapter 1). The prospectus was inserted in part 6 of *Dombey and Son* (March 1847). A slightly revised version was inserted in part 7 of *Dombey* (April 1847), and the address was reprinted separately inside the front cover of the first monthly part of the 1847 Cheap Edition of *Pickwick Papers*. The manuscript of the prospectus, in Dickens's hand and including his unused dedication, is in the Berg Collection at the New York Public Library. Revisions to the later version and a significant variation from the manuscript are indicated in the notes.]

Cheap Edition of the Works of

Mr. Charles Dickens.

On SATURDAY, the 27th of MARCH, will commence,[1]

In Weekly Numbers,

Containing Sixteen clear and handsomely printed pages, small 8vo,

double columns,

PRICE THREE HALFPENCE EACH,

And in Monthly Parts, sewed in a Wrapper;

A New Edition of

THE WORKS OF

MR. CHARLES DICKENS.

The Works to be comprised in this Cheap Edition will be:—

	s.	d.
THE PICKWICK PAPERS,[2] which, completed in about Thirty-two Numbers, will cost	4	0
NICHOLAS NICKLEBY, 32 Numbers	4	0
SKETCHES BY "BOZ," 20 Numbers	2	6
OLD CURIOSITY SHOP, 24 Numbers	3	0
BARNABY RUDGE, 24 Numbers	3	0
AMERICAN NOTES, 12 Numbers	1	6
OLIVER TWIST, 20 Numbers	2	6
MARTIN CHUZZLEWIT, 32 Numbers	4	0

ADDRESS.

ON the 31st March, 1836, the Publication of "THE POSTHUMOUS PAPERS OF THE PICKWICK CLUB" was begun, in what was then a very unusual form, at less than one-third of the price in the whole of an ordinary novel, and in Shilling Monthly Parts. On Saturday, the 27th of March, 1847, the proposed Re-issue, unprecedented, it is believed, in the history of Cheap Literature, will be[3] commenced.

It is not for an author to describe his own books. If they cannot speak for themselves, he is likely to do little service by speaking for them. It is enough to observe of these, that eleven years have strengthened in their writer's mind every purpose and sympathy he has endeavoured to express in them; and that their re-production in a shape which shall render them easily accessible as a possession by all classes of society, is at least consistent with the spirit in which they have been written, and is the fulfilment of a desire long entertained.

It had been intended that this CHEAP EDITION, now announced,[4] should not be undertaken until the books were much older, or the Author was dead. But the favour with which they have been received, and the extent to which they have circulated, and continue to circulate, at five times the proposed price, justify the belief that the living Author may enjoy the pride and honour of their widest diffusion, and may couple it with increased personal emolument.

This belief is supported by the conviction, that the CHEAP EDITION will in no way clash or interfere[5] with that already existing. The existing edition will always contain the original illustrations, which, it is hardly necessary to add, will constitute[6] no part of the CHEAP EDITION; and its form is perfectly distinct and different. Neither will any of the more recent writings of the Author; those now in progress of publication, or yet to come; appear in the CHEAP EDITION, until after the lapse of A VERY CONSIDERABLE PERIOD, and when their circulation in the original form shall, by degrees, and in the course of years, have placed them on a level with their predecessors.

To become, in his new guise, a permanent inmate of many English homes, where, in his old shape, he was only known as a guest, or hardly known at all: to be well thumbed and soiled in a plain suit that will bear a great deal, by children and grown people, at the fireside and on the journey: to be hoarded on the humble shelf where there are few books, and to lie about in libraries like any familiar piece of household stuff that is easy of replacement: and to see and feel this—not to die first, or grow old and passionless: must obviously be among the hopes of a living author, venturing on such an enterprise. Without such hopes it never could be set on foot. I have no fear of being mistaken in acknowledging that they are mine; that they are built, in simple earnestness and grateful faith, on my experience, past and present, of the cheering-on of very many thousands of my countrymen and countrywomen, never more numerous or true to me than now;—and that hence this CHEAP EDITION is[7] projected.

CHARLES DICKENS.

A new Preface to each Tale will be published on its conclusion in Weekly Parts. A Frontispiece to each Tale, engraved on Wood from a Design by some eminent Artist, will also be given at the same time. The whole Text will be carefully revised and corrected throughout, by the Author.

For a Specimen of the page of THE CHEAP EDITION, the reader is referred to the other side.

LONDON: CHAPMAN & HALL, 186, STRAND:

JOHN MENZIES, EDINBURGH; CUMMING & FERGUSON, DUBLIN;[8]

AND SOLD BY ALL BOOKSELLERS IN TOWN AND COUNTRY.

[This is followed by a sample page from the Cheap Edition text of *Pickwick Papers*, chapter 13, beginning "The noise and bustle which ushered in the morning . . ."][9]

≈ NOTES ≈

INTRODUCTION

1. Charles Wheatstone, "Experiments on Audition" (1827), *The Scientific Papers of Sir Charles Wheatstone* (London: Taylor and Francis, 1879), 30–35.

2. W. H. Preece, "The Microphone," *Nature* 18 (20 June 1878): 209; Preece, "The Phonograph," *Journal of the Society of Arts* 26 (1878): 534.

3. George Eliot, "Shadows of the Coming Race," in *Impressions of Theophrastus Such*, ed. Nancy Henry (London: Pickering, 1994), 138. Similarly, Latimer, the protagonist of Eliot's gothic short story "The Lifted Veil" (serialized in 1859 and published for the first time in book form in 1878), is a clairvoyant driven out of his mind by the thoughts of those around him, which become amplified and reverberate inside his head; he develops what might be called, in the terms of the day, a microphonic psychosis.

4. "The Microphone," *The Spectator* 51 (23 May 1878): 662–63. Most spectacularly, the writer concluded, "the new instrument may enable us not merely to see, but to *hear* light. . . . May it not be possible, with the help of the microphone to give us a true rainbow music, — a music really caused by the sound of the same waves which, in their effect on the optic nerve, produce the vision of the rainbow?" (663). The late Victorian desire for underlying natural order and analogous design lay behind a recurring subject in the pages of *Nature* in the 1870s for the possibility of so-called colour-music, as contributors offered ingenious theories for correspondence models of the color spectrum with the musical octave.

5. George Eliot, *Middlemarch*, ed. David Carroll (Oxford: Clarendon, 1986), 189; hereafter cited in text. Preece, "The Microphone," 209.

6. G. J. Symons, ed., *The Eruption of Krakatoa and Subsequent Phenomena: Report of the Krakatoa Committee of the Royal Society* (London: Trübner, 1888), 87.

7. Quoted in Tom Simkin and Richard S. Fiske, *Krakatau 1883: The Volcanic Eruption and Its Effects* (Washington, D.C.: Smithsonian Institution Press, 1983), 367.

8. R. M. Ballantyne, *Blown to Bits; or, The Lonely Man of Rakata* (London: Nisbet, 1889), 374. See also Richard D. Altick, "Four Victorian Poets and an Exploding Island," *Victorian Studies* 3 (1960): 249–60.

9. A representative sampling of important recent work on Victorian sight-related subjects would include: Jonathan Crary, *Techniques of the Observer: On Vision and Modernity in the Nineteenth Century* (Cambridge, Mass.: MIT Press, 1990); James Krasner, *The Entangled Eye: Visual Perception and the Representation of Nature in Post-Darwinian Narrative* (New York: Oxford University Press, 1992); *Victorian Literature and the Victorian Vi-*

sual Imagination, ed. Carol T. Christ and John O. Jordan (Berkeley: University of California Press, 1995); Jennifer Green-Lewis, *Framing the Victorians: Photography and the Culture of Realism* (Ithaca, N.Y.: Cornell University Press, 1996); *Vision in Context: Historical and Contemporary Perspectives on Sight*, ed. Martin Jay (London: Routledge, 1996); Nancy Armstrong, *Fiction in the Age of Photography: The Legacy of British Realism* (Cambridge, Mass.: Harvard University Press, 1999); Kate Flint, *The Victorians and the Visual Imagination* (Cambridge: Cambridge University Press, 2000); Lynda Nead, *Victorian Babylon: People, Streets and Images in Nineteenth-Century London* (New Haven, Conn.: Yale University Press, 2000); and Gerard Curtis, *Visual Words: Art and the Material Book in Victorian England* (Aldershot, U.K.: Ashgate, 2002).

10. Nearly a century after *Middlemarch*, John Cage entered an anechoic chamber, where he heard his heart beat and blood flow, prompting his remark that "there is no such thing as silence" and his notorious "silent piece," *4'33"*, in which a pianist sits onstage without playing. See John Cage, *Silence* (Middletown, Conn.: Wesleyan University Press, 1961), 51. On *4'33"*, see Douglas Kahn, "John Cage: Silence and Silencing," in his *Noise Water Meat: A History of Sound in the Arts* (Cambridge, Mass.: MIT Press, 1999), 161–99.

11. Both Jonathan Rée and Melba Cuddy-Keane have used the term "auscultation" to formulate a more precise means to discuss and analyze sound in the context of cultural studies, the former in a "philosophical history" that centers on the phenomenon of deafness, the latter in a study of sound in Virginia Woolf's life and novels, yet the term and the verb form of it have principally Victorian origins (the *Oxford English Dictionary* lists one seventeenth-century appearance of "auscultation" before 1833, and the first appearance of "auscultate" is given as in Thackeray, *Philip*, 1862). See Rée, *I See a Voice: Deafness, Language and the Senses—A Philosophical History* (New York: Metropolitan, 1999), 53, and Cuddy-Keane, "Virginia Woolf, Sound Technologies, and the New Aurality," *Virginia Woolf in the Age of Mechanical Reproduction*, ed. Pamela L. Caughie (New York: Garland, 2000), 71.

12. Jonathan Sterne, "Mediate Auscultation, the Stethoscope, and the 'Autopsy of the Living': Medicine's Acoustic Culture," *Journal of Medical Humanities* 22 (2001): 135, 123. In an approach that dovetails with my own about literary culture and is one of the most thorough discussions of the significance of the stethoscope, Sterne argues for the central place of auscultation in nineteenth-century medicine, and that Laennec's real innovation was in "*listening* to the body": "at the level of clinical practice, it was the technique of listening that did more than any other single technique to render the medical body as a dynamic field of action" (117, 129).

13. Eliot acknowledges the novelty of Lydgate's possession of the stethoscope, noting that use of the instrument "had not become a matter of course in practice at that time" (*Middlemarch*, 279). Stethoscopes were advertised for sale in London in 1820, but it was not until the mid-1830s that they were in regular use in examinations by English doctors. In an anonymous poem titled "Auscultation Extraordinary" in an 1829 issue of the *Lancet*, the author satirically speculated the stethoscope might be used to "take 'reports'" of "private meetings" (*Lancet*, 1829: 1.96), while nearly twenty years later, the American doctor and man of letters Oliver Wendell Holmes, who had received his medical education in Paris, published "The Stethoscope Song," a comic poem warning of relying too exclusively on one's ears (*The Complete Poetical Works of Oliver Wendell Holmes*, ed. Horace E. Scudder [Boston: Houghton Mifflin, 1908], 60–61). Charles Newman dates the scientific revolution in medicine from Laennec and the introduction of auscultation and discusses the incremental English adoption of the stethoscope in his

The Evolution of Medical Education in the Nineteenth Century (London: Oxford University Press, 1957), 83–96. See also W. F. Bynum, *Science and the Practice of Medicine in the Nineteenth Century* (Cambridge: Cambridge University Press, 1994), 40–41, 47, for more on the adoption of the stethoscope in England and Eliot's use of it in *Middlemarch*.

14. Charles Dickens, *The Mystery of Edwin Drood*, ed. Margaret Cardwell (Oxford: Clarendon, 1972), 35–36.

15. Samuel Taylor Coleridge, *The Friend*, ed. Barbara E. Rooke, vol. 4 in *The Collected Works of Samuel Taylor Coleridge* (London: Routledge and Kegan Paul, 1969), 1:367; William Wordsworth, "On the Power of Sound," *Wordsworth: Poetical Works*, ed. Thomas Hutchinson and Ernest de Selincourt (Oxford: Oxford University Press, 1936), 185–87. See also "Wordsworth's Mighty World of Eye and Ear" and "Coleridge's Blessed Interval" in Kerry McSweeney's *The Language of the Senses: Sensory Perceptual Dynamics in Wordsworth, Coleridge, Thoreau, Whitman, and Dickinson* (Montreal: McGill-Queen's University Press, 1998), 41–97. A classic treatment of the Romantics' conception of hearing as manifested in their poetry is to be found in the work of John Hollander, whose studies on music, voice, and the lyric range from his *Images of Voice: Music and Sound in Romantic Poetry* (Cambridge: Heffer, 1970), to "Wordsworth and the Music of Sound," *New Perspectives on Coleridge and Wordsworth*, ed. Geoffrey H. Hartman (New York: Columbia University Press, 1972), 41–84, and *Vision and Resonance: Two Senses of Poetic Form* (New York: Oxford University Press, 1975). Pairing musical compositions with poetry in revealing ways, Lawrence Kramer considers Beethoven's works alongside Wordsworth's lyrics in analyses that offer a kind of counterpoint to Hollander's, in *Music and Poetry: The Nineteenth Century and After* (Berkeley: University of California Press, 1984), 25–90. Scott Brewster takes a more techno-theoretical approach, by way of Derrida and Barthes, in his consideration of Romantic poetry "as a strange and uncertain type of telephony," in "*Tintern*abulation: Poetry Ringing in the Ears," in *Sensual Reading: New Approaches to Reading and Its Relation to the Senses*, ed. Michael Syrotinski and Ian Maclachlin (Lewisburg, Pa.: Bucknell University Press, 2001), 69–82.

16. Charles Lamb, "A Chapter on Ears," *The Essays of Elia* (London: Dent, 1923), 46.

17. By 1838, Dickens's copies of Lamb's works were "both cut and both soiled." See his letter to Dr. Henry Belcombe, 8 February 1838, in *The Letters of Charles Dickens*, Pilgrim edition, ed. Madeline House, Graham Storey, Kathleen Tillotson, et al., 12 vols. (Oxford: Clarendon, 1965–2002), 7:789.

18. These are included in his *Scientific Papers*. Wheatstone came from a family of music publishers and instrument-makers, a background that influenced his work in the science of sound. For more on the popularity of one of the many bona fide musical instruments he invented, see Allan W. Atlas, *The Wheatstone Concertina in Victorian England* (Oxford: Clarendon, 1996).

19. William Hyde Wollaston, "On Sounds Inaudible by Certain Ears," *Philosophical Transactions of the Royal Society* 110 (1820): 306–14; D. C. Goodman, "Wollaston, William Hyde," *Dictionary of Scientific Biography*, ed. Charles Coulston Gillispie (New York: Scribner's, 1976), 14:492.

20. For more on this transformation, see James Loudon's 1901 presidential address to the American Association for the Advancement of Science, "A Century of Progress in Acoustics," *Science*, n.s., 14 (27 December 1901), 987–95; see also the extended discussion of the development of the architectural division of the science of sound, the "New Acoustics" that originated at the turn of the century, in Emily Thompson's *The Soundscape of Modernity: Architectural Acoustics and the Culture of Listening in America, 1900–1933* (Cambridge, Mass.: MIT Press, 2002), 59–113.

21. William Wright, *Practical Observations on Deafness, and Noises in the Head, and Their Treatment on Physiological Principles, Shewing the Injurious and Often Irremediable Consequences of Violent Applications, as Exemplified in the Case of Field Marshall His Grace the Duke of Wellington* (London: Wesley, 1853), 1, 3. Wright made the dedication to Wellington in *On the Varieties of Deafness, and Diseases of the Ear, with Proposed Methods of Relieving Them* (London: Hurst, Chance, 1829).

22. Alfred Tennyson, "Ode on the Death of the Duke of Wellington" (1852), *The Poems of Tennyson*, 2d ed., ed. Christopher Ricks (Berkeley: University of California Press, 1987), 2:482, ll. 8–12.

23. Thomas Hood, "A Tale of a Trumpet," *The Complete Poetical Works of Thomas Hood*, ed. Walter Jerrold (London: Frowde, 1906), 605, ll. 268–69.

24. William Wright, *Fishes and Fishing: Artificial Breeding of Fish, Anatomy of Their Senses, Their Loves, Passions, and Intellects* (London: Thomas Cautley Newby, 1858), 86–87.

25. As Steven Connor puts it, the nineteenth century "saw an energetic revival of schemes for the systematic representation of sound, encouraged by German historical and comparative phonology," and the phonograph "came as the culmination of a range of different attempts through the nineteenth century to formalize and control sound" (*Dumbstruck: A Cultural History of Ventriloquism* [Oxford: Oxford University Press, 2000], 347; "The Modern Auditory I," in *Rewriting the Self: Histories from the Renaissance to the Present*, ed. Roy Porter [London: Routledge, 1997], 215–16). Similarly, James Lastra analyzes the function of inscription as it bears on the phonograph in *Sound Technology and the American Cinema: Perception, Representation, Modernity* (New York: Columbia University Press, 2000) to argue that "the conceptual pair inscription/ simulation worked above all to normalize a new series of conditions that had come to define the technologically mediated relationships between perception, representation, and meaning" (22).

26. James Clerk-Maxwell, "The Rede Lecture," *Nature* 18 (6 June 1878): 163.

27. "The Sun-Voice," *All The Year Round*, n.s., 46 (19 February 1881): 418.

28. Geoffrey Winthrop-Young and Michael Wutz, "Translators' Introduction," Friedrich A. Kittler, *Gramophone Film Typewriter*, trans. Winthrop-Young and Wutz (Stanford, Calif.: Stanford University Press, 1999), xxviii.

29. "The Phonograph and Its Future," *Nature* 18 (30 May 1878): 116.

30. Joseph Conrad, "Author's Note" (1917), *Heart of Darkness*, ed. Robert Hampson (New York: Penguin, 1995), 11.

31. Henry Thompson, "Telephone London," *Living London*, ed. George R. Sims (London: Cassell, 1901), 115.

32. See particularly Ong's classic defenses of sound, or, at least, a kind of romanticized preliterate sound, in *The Presence of the Word* (Minneapolis: University of Minnesota Press, 1967) and *Orality and Literacy: The Technologizing of the Word* (London: Methuen, 1982).

33. For Derrida's positioning of *l'ecriture* over *lecture*, see *Of Grammatology*, trans. Gayatri Chakravorty Spivak (Baltimore, Md.: Johns Hopkins University Press, 1976).

34. Rée, *I See a Voice*, 6.

35. T. V. F. Brogan, "Sound," *New Princeton Encyclopedia of Poetry and Poetics*, ed. Brogan and Alex Preminger (Princeton, N.J.: Princeton University Press, 1993), 1172.

36. R. Murray Schafer, *The Tuning of the World* (New York: Knopf, 1977), repr. as *The Soundscape: Our Sonic Environment and the Tuning of the World* (Rochester, Vt.: Destiny, 1994); hereafter cited in text.

37. The problem of noise pollution has become more alarming since the 1970s, even as Schafer's terminology has entered the mainstream press. An article in a popular nature magazine focuses on the attempts by Gordon Hempton to "save the soundscape of our national parks" by founding the politically active organization One Square Inch of Silence and, "with 'Fritz,' a binaural microphone the size and shape of a human head," producing high-fidelity recordings of "sound-rich" natural spaces to be sold on CDs and other digital formats to "zoos, museums, filmmakers, and businesses developing advertisements" (Jane Braxton Little, "Desperately Seeking Silence," *Audubon* 102 [January–February 2000]: 70–73).

38. Three anthologies have taken sound as their explicit focus, typically in conjunction with a consideration of technology and modern poetics: *Wireless Imagination: Sound, Radio, and the Avant-Garde*, ed. Douglas Kahn and Gregory Whitehead (Cambridge, Mass.: MIT Press, 1992); *Sound States: Innovative Poetics and Acoustical Technologies*, ed. Adalaide Morris (Chapel Hill: University of North Carolina Press, 1997); *Close Listening: Poetry and the Performed Word*, ed. Charles Bernstein (New York: Oxford University Press, 1998). Kahn gives particular attention to John Cage and avant-garde music in his *Noise Water Meat: A History of Sound in the Arts* (Cambridge, Mass.: MIT Press, 1999).

39. Peter Gay provides an extended consideration of the way European concert audiences over the nineteenth century gradually adopted a "worshipful silence," prompting introspection and perfecting "the art of silent listening," while James Johnson examines Parisian audience behavior practices across a wider timespan; see Peter Gay, *The Naked Heart*, vol. 4 of *The Bourgeois Experience, Victoria to Freud* (New York: Norton, 1995), 11–35; and James H. Johnson, *Listening in Paris: A Cultural History* (Berkeley: University of California Press, 1995). Studies on the politics of music and noise in French history, on the cultural, psychological, and political significance of the sounds of church bells in French village life, and on the value of sound, speech, and noise in early modern English drama and culture, include: Jacque Attali, *Noise: A Political Economy of Music*, trans. Brian Massumi (Minneapolis: University of Minnesota Press, 1985); Alain Corbin, *Village Bells: Sound and Meaning in the 19th-Century French Countryside*, trans. Martin Thom (New York: Columbia University Press, 1998); and Bruce R. Smith, *The Acoustic World of Early Modern England: Attending to the O-Factor* (Chicago: University of Chicago Press, 1999). James Lastra's genealogy of the film soundtrack, which has implications for considerations of the phonograph as well, is found in his *Sound Technology and the American Cinema*, and new interest in early film sound also has produced the collection *The Sounds of Early Cinema*, ed. Richard Abel and Rick Altman (Bloomington: Indiana University Press, 2001). Also relevant here is Jonathan Sterne's *The Audible Past: Cultural Origins of Sound Reproduction* (Durham, N.C.: Duke University Press, 2003), which appeared as this book went to press. In a tongue-twist on the Derrida-Ong debate, Garrett Stewart has developed an intricate and influential analysis of literary puns, echoes, and graphemes, while arguing for reading as a distinctly interior-voiced practice, in his *Reading Voices: Literature and the Phonotext* (Berkeley: University of California Press, 1990).

40. Leigh Eric Schmidt, *Hearing Things: Religion, Illusion, and the American Enlightenment* (Cambridge, Mass.: Harvard University Press, 2000); Mark M. Smith, *Listening to Nineteenth-Century America* (Chapel Hill: University of North Carolina Press, 2001). I adapt the term "acoustic archaeology" from the use of it to refer either (a) to attempts to replay buried "signals" on grooves in various plastic media from antiquity, such as pots or paintings; or, more commonly, (b) to audio restoration, such as the kind that theoret-

ically might be done on the famous 18-and-a-half minute gap on one of Nixon's Watergate reel-to-reel tapes. See Richard G. Woodbridge, "Acoustic Recordings from Antiquity," *Proceedings of the IEEE* 57 (1969): 1465–66; M. Kleiner and P. Astrom, "The Brittle Sound of Ceramics — Can Vases Speak?" *Archaeology and Natural Science* 1 (1993): 66–72; and Jack Hitt, "Eavesdropping on History," *New York Times Magazine*, 3 December 2000, 132–36.

41. Peter Bailey, "Breaking the Sound Barrier," *Popular Culture and Performance in the Victorian City* (Cambridge: Cambridge University Press, 1998), 194–211. As if to echo Bailey, Smith sets out the beginnings of a methodological framework in his "Sound Matters: An Essay on Method" (the closing chapter of his book *Listening*), which reviews historians' traditional discomfort with sound and suggests it is time to move away from "ocularcentrism" and toward "acoustemology" (262).

42. Steven Connor, "The Modern Auditory I," 219. Connor crafts such a narrative in his ambitious and essential *Dumbstruck*, which does not identify itself as a soundscape study per se but as a history of what he calls "vocalic space" (12).

43. George Henry Lewes, "Dickens in Relation to Criticism," *Fortnightly Review* 17 (1872): 149.

CHAPTER 1

1. The draft of Babbage's letter to Princess Victoria is in the British Library, Add. 37190, f. 147. Babbage received an official reply from John Conroy two days later stating that the Duchess of Kent was "much gratified" and "deeply sensible of the importance of the work you have sent the Royal Highness the Princess Victoria." Conroy sent another reply on 12 June to say that Babbage's "high attainments render your attention particularly acceptable to the Princess, who has been trained to regard with the highest feelings of consideration, all those, who so labour, for the benefit of the country." Babbage also sent a copy of the book to King William IV, who, according to Mary Fox, received it "*most* graciously" about three weeks before his death (Add. 37190, ff. 150, 218, 162).

2. Babbage had interests in cryptography, optics, economics, and geology, among other fields. Over a period of a decade beginning in the 1820s, he spent more than £20,000 of his own and government money on futile attempts to build his Difference Engine and gained notoriety as an outspoken critic of, on the one hand, the Royal Society and, on the other, street musicians (see chapter 2). Babbage claimed that "a list of his writings" was his best biography and to look at one is to realize what a polymath he was. See Alfred W. Van Sinderen, "The Printed Papers of Charles Babbage" (*Annals of the History of Computing* 2 [1980]: 169–85), for an accurate list of his publications and a biographical overview. For more on his life, and whether or not to consider Babbage a "pioneer" of modern computing, see Jay Clayton, "Hacking the Nineteenth Century," in *Victorian Afterlife: Postmodern Culture Rewrites the Nineteenth Century*, ed. John Kucich and Dianne F. Sadoff (Minneapolis: University of Minnesota Press, 2000), 191–92, 200.

3. Babbage's unofficial contribution was written as an extension of and reply to (but not, as is sometimes claimed, a parody of) the eight treatises that had preceded it in the series, which had been subsidized by the Earl of Bridgewater to demonstrate "the Power, Wisdom, and Goodness of God, as manifested in the Creation," and authored for a commission of £1000 each by eminent clerics and doctors. Babbage was neither, of course, and he resented that the authors had received payment for their work, believing it compromised their integrity. He revised and expanded his book for a

new edition the following year (1838). For a detailed account of the earlier treatises, see W. H. Brock, "The Selection of the Authors of the Bridgewater Treatises," *Notes and Records* 21 (1966): 162–79, and John M. Robson, "The Fiat and Finger of God: The Bridgewater Treatises," in *Victorian Faith in Crisis: Essays on Continuity and Change in Nineteenth-Century Religious Belief*, ed. Richard J. Helmstadter and Bernard Lightman (Stanford, Calif.: Stanford University Press, 1990), 71–125. Brock notes that Babbage's "extraordinary" contribution is a "Tristram Shandy of a book" and "was written in opposition to [William] Whewell's denial in his Bridgewater Treatise that pure and applied mathematicians could marshal natural theological arguments from mathematics" (173).

4. Charles Babbage, *The Ninth Bridgewater Treatise: A Fragment*, vol. 9 of *The Works of Charles Babbage*, ed. Martin Campbell-Kelly (New York: New York University Press, 1989), 29. All references to Babbage's work will be to this, the second, edition unless otherwise stated; significant revisions to the first edition will be noted. In studies of Babbage, consideration of the *Treatise* typically is dwarfed by that of his work on the Difference and, later, Analytical Engines, but two of the more recent discussions of the book that have useful summaries of the main argument of the *Treatise* are Anthony Hyman, *Charles Babbage: Pioneer of the Computer* (Oxford: Oxford University Press, 1982), 136–38, and Doron Swade, *The Cogwheel Brain: Charles Babbage and the Quest to Build the First Computer* (London: Little, Brown, 2000), 79–80. Swade points out that the Difference Engine provided a physical model of causation that "was compelling in ways that philosophical speculation was not" (80). Yet the physical and philosophical in this case are closely intertwined: like the machines that Babbage never completed, the *Treatise* was provocative rather than prescriptive, a belated Romantic formulation that ushered in the Victorian age alongside which it had originated as if by (as Babbage coyly claimed) "accidental circumstances" (British Library, Add. 37190, f. 147). An older but invaluable reading of the *Treatise* in the context of debates over the status of miracles in pre-Darwinian natural theology can be found in Walter Cannon's "The Problem of Miracles in the 1830's," *Victorian Studies* 4 (1960): 23–26, 31, which addresses the influence of Babbage's book on Robert Chambers's *Vestiges of the Natural History of Creation* (London: John Churchill, 1844).

5. Babbage here cites as his source a sentence from Laplace's *Théorie analytique des probabilités* on the path taken by "une simple molécule d'air ou de vapeurs" (*Ninth Bridgewater Treatise*, 35), but the influence of Wollaston, whose work on the subjective reception of sounds Babbage refers to in chapter 14 ("Thoughts on the Nature of Future Punishments," 57), is also apparent (see William Wollaston, "On Sounds Inaudible by Certain Ears," *Philosophical Transactions of the Royal Society* 110 [1820]: 306–14). Before Laplace and Wollaston, Lamarck had proposed as the conductor of sound not air but an omnipresent "invisible fluid": "un fluide invisible, très-subtil, singuliérement, élastique, d'un rarité extrême, pénétrant facilement tous les corps, répandu dans toutes les parties de notre globe, et conséquement dans son atmosphère" (Jean Baptiste Lamarck, "Mémoire sur la matière du son" [*An* 8 (1800)], repr. in *Hydrogéologie* [Paris, *An* X (1802)], 255). There may be other influences at work on Babbage as well: H. W. Buxton suggests that the theory has much in common with a dogma of the Mimansa, that "sound was eternal and uncreated" and that "it was equally indestructible and continued to vibrate through Time," although he adds that when asked, Babbage "stated that the existence of such a doctrine was entirely unknown to him, either as a dogma of religion, or doctrine of Indian philosophy" (*Memoir of the Life and Labours of the Late Charles Babbage Esq. F.R.S.*, ed. Anthony Hyman [Cambridge, Mass.: MIT Press; Los

Angeles: Tomash, 1988], 343). In his biography of Babbage, Hyman, meanwhile, identifies a theological anticipation in Chaucer's *House of Fame*, "though naturally without so
clear a physical basis" (*Charles Babbage*, 141).

6. For "woman," the first edition reads "even."

7. Lyell, who critiqued the *Treatise* in proof and sent some of it on to Adam Sedgwick at Cambridge for further criticism when Babbage refused to delete what Lyell
considered offensive passages, wrote to Babbage that the ninth chapter was "not equal
to the rest . . . the whole too as it stands is too much like the arrow shot into the air in
Virgil and when there is no mark aimed at it ought at least[,] as in the poetry[,] hands to
turn into a bright, clear and beautiful burning meteor," adding that he found the end of
the chapter "not [in] good taste" (Letter to Babbage, May 1837, British Library Add.
37190, f. 185; see also Leonard G. Wilson, *Charles Lyell: The Years to 1841: The Revolution in
Geology* [New Haven, Conn.: Yale University Press, 1972], 461–62). Hill's comment is
taken from his *Geometry and Faith: A Fragmentary Supplement to the Ninth Bridgewater
Treatise* (New York: Francis, 1849), 39. Buxton's appraisal that Babbage's chapter was
"too remarkable not to attract special notice" is in his *Memoir*, 342. Henry P. Babbage's
comments, dated "Nov 1887," are written inside the front cover of the copy of the first
edition of the *Treatise* in Harvard's Houghton Library, shelf mark *74–434.

8. A copy of the first (1837) edition is listed in the catalog made after Dickens's
death of his library at Gad's Hill. See the *Catalogue of the Library of Charles Dickens from
Gadshill Reprinted from Sotheran's "Price Current of Literature" Nos. CLXXIV and CLXXV*,
ed. J. H. Stonehouse (London: Piccadilly Fountain Press, 1935), 9. Dickens's citation of
Babbage's *Treatise* is from his 27 September 1869 speech at the Birmingham and Mid-
lan Institute, in Charles Dickens, *The Speeches of Charles Dickens*, ed. K. J. Fielding (Oxford: Clarendon, 1960), 399. Douglas Kahn discusses the reference in his *Noise Water
Meat: A History of Sound in the Arts* (Cambridge, Mass.: MIT Press, 1999), 210–12. Nearly
ten years earlier, however, in "Night Walks," first published in the 21 July 1860 issue of
All the Year Round and collected in the first series of *The Uncommercial Traveller* (1861),
Dickens had cited Babbage in similar terms ("for ever and ever," "eternal space") to describe the sound of church clock chimes as they echo through the nighttime streets of
London: "When a church clock strikes, on houseless ears in the dead of the night, it
may be at first mistaken for company, and hailed as such. But, as the spreading circles
of vibration, which you may perceive at such a time with great clearness, go opening
out, for ever and ever afterwards widening perhaps (as the philosopher has suggested)
in eternal space, the mistake is rectified, and the sense of loneliness is profounder"
("The Uncommercial Traveller: Night Walks," *The Uncommercial Traveller and Other Papers 1859–70*, ed. Michael Slater and John Drew [London: Dent, 2000], 154). Dickens's
friendship with Babbage dates at least from 1840, which is the year he is listed by
William Macready as attending one of Babbage's renowned soirées (*Diaries of William
Charles Macready, 1833–1851*, ed. William Toynbee [New York: Putnam's, 1912], 2:59), at
which Babbage sometimes showed off his automaton, the "Silver Lady," and where
there typically were, in the words of occasional guest Charles Darwin, "a good mixture
of pretty women" and opportunities to "see the *World*" (*The Correspondence of Charles
Darwin*, ed. Frederick Burkhardt and Sydney Smith [Cambridge: Cambridge University Press, 1985–], 2:8, 175). For more on the erotic undercurrents of these gatherings,
see Clayton, "Hacking," 187–88. The earliest correspondence from Dickens to Babbage
that has been published dates from the following year. See his letter to Babbage,
17 June 1841, in *The Letters of Charles Dickens*, Pilgrim edition, ed. Madeline House, Graham Storey, Kathleen Tillotson, et al., 12 vols. (Oxford: Clarendon, 1965–2002), 2:307.

Unless otherwise noted, all references to Dickens's letters will be to this edition and cited by volume and page number.

9. Charles Dickens, *Dombey and Son*, ed. Alan Horsman (Oxford: Clarendon, 1974), 333. All references to the novel will be to this edition and will be cited parenthetically in text.

10. The revised Oxford World's Classics edition of *Dombey*, the most extensively annotated version available, glosses this figure as "unidentified" (Charles Dickens, *Dombey and Son*, ed. Alan Horsman, intro. and notes by Dennis Walder [Oxford: Oxford University Press, 2001], 957). It should not be a surprise that it is Babbage, however, for Dickens makes direct and indirect reference to him throughout his writings: for example, in his characterizations of Mr. Slug the mathematician and Mr. Crinkles the inventor of a pickpocketing machine in *The Mudfog Papers* (1837–1838), Dickens satirized aspects of Babbage's public persona; moreover, shortly after beginning *Dombey*, Dickens wrote in a letter to his close friend and biographer John Forster in reference to the lack of political support for financial assistance in emigration schemes that "not all the figures that Babbage's calculating machine could turn up in twenty generations, would stand in the long run against the general heart"; Babbage's frustration in attempting to obtain governmental support for his Difference Engine influenced Dickens's portrayal of the inventor Daniel Doyce and the conception of the Circumlocution Office in *Little Dorrit* (1855–1857); and finally, Dickens quoted the *Treatise* in "Night Walks" and his 1869 speech (see Clayton, "Hacking," 188–92, for more on the examples from the two pieces of fiction mentioned; for Dickens's letter, see the one to Forster, [24 and 25 August 1846], 4:609). What distinguishes the citation in *Dombey* is that it appears to be the only instance in the fiction where Dickens directly recapitulates Babbage's philosophy (as opposed to his personality or the notoriety of his troubles with his invention): a critical moment in a critical novel, for this philosophy had an implicit influence on Dickens's career as novelist and public figure.

11. Kathleen Tillotson, *Novels of the Eighteen-Forties* (London: Oxford University Press, 1954), 157. See also Edgar Johnson, who writes that "with a creative vitality hardly surpassed by any of the books between it and *Pickwick*, [*Dombey*] leaves all its predecessors far behind in structural logic, intellectual power, and social insight" (*Charles Dickens: His Tragedy and Triumph*, 2 vols. [New York: Simon and Schuster, 1952], 2:643).

12. In writing *Dombey*, Dickens "also created himself as Dombey, the linear, purposive, selfish architect of a unique destiny" (Gabriel Pearson, "Towards a Reading of *Dombey and Son*," in *The Modern English Novel: The Reader, the Writer and the Work*, ed. Gabriel Josipovici [New York: Barnes and Noble, 1976], 57). In *Partings Welded Together: Politics and Desire in the Nineteenth-Century English Novel* (London: Methuen, 1987), David Musselwhite agrees in principle with Pearson but views the authorial shift in negative terms: "The nomadic 'Boz' has given way to the despotic Dickens" (208). As Richard Altick notes, Forster himself labeled *Dombey* "the turning point of [Dickens's] career," and Altick describes it as "the first novel he meticulously planned from beginning to end" ("Varieties of Readers' Response: The Case of *Dombey and Son*," *Yearbook of English Studies* 10 [1980]: 70). Roger B. Henkle reiterates Forster's point (and Johnson's and Tillotson's) when he refers to *Dombey* as "the pivotal novel in Dickens's career" ("The Crisis of Representation in *Dombey and Son*," in *Critical Reconstructions: The Relationship of Fiction and Life*, ed. Robert Polhemus and Roger B. Henkle [Stanford, Calif.: Stanford University Press, 1994], 90).

13. Letter to Forster, [25–26 July 1846], 4:590.
14. Letter to Forster, [25–26 July 1846], 4:593.

15. Letter to Forster, [21 December 1847], 5:211.

16. Letter to the Countess of Blessington, 2 March 1846, 4:510.

17. Letters to Forster, [13 and 14 August 1846], 4:602; [30 August 1846], 4:612; [?4 January 1847], 5:2; [7 February 1847], 5:23; [26 September 1846], 4:625–26; to Georgina Hogarth, [9 March 1847], 5:33; to Frances Burnett, 31 March 1848, 7:885. One of the classic treatments of this turbulent period is Steven Marcus's chapter "Dickens from *Martin Chuzzlewit* to *Dombey and Son* 1844–1848," in his *Dickens from Pickwick to Dombey* (New York: Basic, 1965), 269–92. Also useful is Robert Patten's discussion of the anxious questions surrounding the writing and publishing of *Dombey*: "would it sell, sell widely, sell enough to repay his debts and reconfirm his popularity?" (*Charles Dickens and His Publishers* [Oxford: Clarendon, 1978], 182–97; 184).

18. See David Trotter, *Circulation: Defoe, Dickens, and the Economies of the Novel* (New York: St. Martin's, 1988), esp. 104ff. See also Laura C. Berry, "In the Bosom of the Family: The Wet-Nurse, the Railroad, and *Dombey and Son*," *Dickens Studies Annual* 25 (1996): 8, 14.

19. John Butt and Kathleen Tillotson, *Dickens at Work* (London: Methuen, 1957), 92.

20. Letter to Forster, [18 July 1846], 4:586. Speculation on the origins of the name "Dombey" range from initials ("D" for Dickens [Marcus, *Dickens from Pickwick to Dombey*]) to anagrams ("Embody" [Robert Newsom, "Embodying *Dombey*: Whole and In Part," *Dickens Studies Annual* 18 (1989): 197–219]) to religion ("Paul Dombey" and the dome of St. Paul's Cathedral). All of these suggestions have their merits; another possibility is that "Dombey" is a combination of "Dom" and "Bey," a Western prefix and a common nineteenth-century Eastern suffix, both roughly translating as titles of respect akin to "master." A stretch, perhaps, but this makes some sense, as Dombey ("Master-master") is portrayed as Domination personified. In the process, he remains hollow, lacking a heart, or in grammatical terms, a base. The combination of the two titles also suggests the international reach of Dombey's mercantile business, indicating his mastery, one would assume from his success, of both Eastern and Western markets.

21. See Gerhard Joseph, "Change and the Changeling in *Dombey and Son*," *Dickens Studies Annual* 18 (1989): 187; for more on Little Paul as a victim of middle-class culture, see Marcus, *Dickens from Pickwick to Dombey*, 329.

22. Aural obstacles not only play a prominent role in the novel, but they also occupied Dickens as he composed it: "This question of the boy [Walter Gay] is very important. . . . Let me hear all you think about it. Hear! I wish I could," he wrote Forster from Lausanne as he began *Dombey*, and he commented from Kent as he approached the end of the writing, "Vagrant music is getting to that height here, and is so impossible to be escaped from, that I fear Broadstairs and I must part company in time to come. Unless it pours of rain, I cannot write half-an-hour without the most excruciating organs, fiddles, bells, or glee-singers" (Letters to Forster, [25–26 July 1846], 4:593; [?8–9 September 1847], 5:162–63). Equally unhappy composing *Dombey* amidst the "quiet" in Switzerland and the "vagrant music" of Kent, Dickens seems to imply that what he most needs to write is not silence but the distinctive bustle and buzz of busy London.

23. See Tillotson, *Novels of the Eighteen-Forties*, 189–93; J. Hillis Miller, *Charles Dickens: The World of His Novels* (Cambridge, Mass.: Harvard University Press, 1958), 148–49; and Julian Moynahan, "Dealings with the Firm of Dombey and Son: Firmness *versus* Wetness," in *Dickens and the Twentieth Century*, ed. John Gross and Gabriel Pearson (Toronto: University of Toronto Press, 1962), 131. In "Dickens and Dombey: A Daughter after All," Nina Auerbach claims that the sea is Florence's realm because "its voice is quiet and its language is private," and that the waves contribute to the overall "polar-

ized vision" in *Dombey* between male and female spheres (*Romantic Imprisonment: Women and Other Glorified Outcasts* [New York: Columbia University Press, 1986], 117, 128). This argument has been rebutted by Newsom in "Embodying *Dombey*" (199) and by Jeremy Tambling, who writes that Auerbach "simply wishes a set of concepts onto the railway" when she construes it as a masculine force to offset the feminized sea ("Death and Modernity in *Dombey and Son*," *Essays in Criticism* 43 [1993]: 310). To this one could add that it is the son, Paul, and not Florence, who initially hears the waves and whom the waves ultimately take, and that the novel instead offers a critique of the problematic and confining nature of gender roles and expectations that, for example, doom the frail son to death for not being able to withstand the social priming that succeeding his father in business necessitates.

24. "What Are the Wild Waves Saying?" with music by Stephen Glover, lyrics by J. E. Carpenter (1849), sold sufficiently well to be followed by Glover's "A Voice from the Waves," with lyrics by Richard Ryan (1851).

25. The slippery question of meaning in and of the novel is taken up at length by Susan Horton, in *Interpreting Interpreting: Interpreting Dickens's Dombey* (Baltimore, Md.: Johns Hopkins University Press, 1979). While Horton offers a critique of all manners of reading *Dombey*, she really is out to make clear the sheer impossibility of creating a "perfect" or totalizing criticism of Dickens's works. Garrett Stewart makes the point that within the novel the waves offer a "lulling signifier without a signified," in *Death Sentences: Styles of Dying in British Fiction* (Cambridge, Mass.: Harvard University Press, 1984), 65. This is good as far as it goes but, as I suggest below, the waves also may be speaking in more significant and fantastic ways to, and especially for, Dickens the aspiring professional author.

26. In the second edition of the *Treatise*, Babbage further delineated the voice of the waves by claiming that they uttered an abolitionist message. He added a coda to the ninth chapter that included extracts from 1835 and 1837 articles, citing incidents of mass drownings of human "cargo" off of slave ships at sea. As he put it: "Interrogate every wave which breaks unimpeded on ten thousand desolate shores, and it will give evidence of the last gurgle of the waters which closed over the head of [the] dying victim: confront the murderer with every corporeal atom of his immolated slave, and in its still quivering movements he will read the prophet's denunciation of the prophet king" (39).

27. Patricia Ingham, in "Speech and Non-Communication in *Dombey and Son*" (*Review of English Studies* 30 [1979]: 144–53), demonstrates how "speech and its failure to communicate become central to two of the main concerns of the novel," Little Paul's short life and readers' impressions of Dombey, and that "the rest of the novel is a suitable backcloth in this" (144). Ingham is strong on the ways in which Paul seeks, but does not find, meaning in his world, arguing that "Paul is anything but knowing" (146–47).

28. For more on these developments, see especially Gillian Beer, "'Authentic Tidings of Invisible Things': Vision and the Invisible in the Later Nineteenth Century," *Vision in Context: Historical and Contemporary Perspectives on Sight*, ed. Teresa Brennan and Martin Jay (New York: Routledge, 1996), 85–98, and her "Helmholtz, Tyndall, Gerard Manley Hopkins: Leaps of the Prepared Imagination" and "Wave Theory and the Rise of Literary Modernism," both in *Open Fields: Science in Cultural Encounter* (Oxford: Clarendon, 1996), 242–72, 295–318.

29. Moynahan, "Dealings," 128.

30. There is something of a critical tradition of reading Shakespearean echoes in *Dombey*, but especially of reading Dombey as a kind of Lear. For a thorough treatment

of the influence of *Lear* on *Dombey*, see Alexander Welsh's chapters "Dickens as Dombey" and "Dombey as King Lear," in *From Copyright to Copperfield: The Identity of Dickens* (Cambridge, Mass.: Harvard University Press, 1987). But also see Valerie Gager's effective rebuttal of Welsh's and others' claims about the influence of *Lear* on the novel, in her *Shakespeare and Dickens: The Dynamics of Influence* (Cambridge: Cambridge University Press: 1996), 11–15. I am reluctant to agree that Dombey "*must* be granted the status of tragic hero" (Welsh, *From Copyright to Copperfield*, 83, emphasis added). This largely depends on the extent to which one feels sympathy for him, since the novel does, after all, adhere to the formal conventions of comedy; but then Dombey is hardly a comic hero either. A more appropriate Shakespearean influence for the construction of Dombey's character is a tragicomic romance like *The Winter's Tale* or *Cymbeline*, as Gager and Anny Sadrin discuss (Gager, *Shakespeare and Dickens*, 13; Sadrin, *Parentage and Inheritance in the Works of Charles Dickens* [Cambridge: Cambridge University Press: 1994], 49–51).

31. Gager mentions parallels between the Dombey-Carker and Othello-Iago relationships, although she argues most thoroughly, if not (for this reader) convincingly, that the underlying Shakespearean echoes in *Dombey* are those of *Macbeth* (*Shakespeare and Dickens*, 184–85, 212–22).

32. For more on Carker as a "deployment of sexuality" and an alternative to Dombey's sexual repression, see Robert Clark's "Riddling the Family Firm: The Sexual Economy in *Dombey and Son*," *ELH* 51 (1984): 79.

33. See Gillian Gane, "The Hat, the Hook, the Eyes, the Teeth: Captain Cuttle, Mr. Carker, and Literacy," *Dickens Studies Annual* 25 (1996): 120. Gane makes some excellent points about the power Carker derives from the various ways he reads in the novel, but I think she overstates her case when she concludes both that "Mr. Carker is of course Dickens," a by-now-familiar, yet still simplistic conclusion which originated with Marcus (*Dickens from Pickwick to Dombey*, 346), and, even more problematically, that "we too are Carkers," which while it cleverly elides readers' own "hyperliteracy" with the villain's, ignores the fact that most of us are not lust-driven Machiavels with dark sexual secrets and a deadly attraction to high-speed trains.

34. Edmund Wilson, "Dickens: The Two Scrooges," in *The Wound and the Bow: Seven Studies in Literature* (1941; Athens: Ohio University Press, 1997), 55–56.

35. Letters to Forster, [?4 January 1847], 5:2; [10 February 1847], 5:24; to James K. Shuttleworth, 21 June 1847, 5:96; to Lord Albert Conyngham, 10 February 1847, 5:25; to Forster, 17 February 1847, 5:30; to W. Harrison Ainsworth, 18 March 1847, 5:37; to Henry Austin, 26 April 1847, 5:60; to Lewes, 15 June 1847, 5:91; to Forster, [18 October 1846], 4:637; 9 April 1847, 5:55.

36. On the irony of this development, see Gane, "The Hat, the Hook," 115.

37. See, for instance, Tillotson, *Novels of the Eighteen-Forties*, 200; Marcus, *Dickens from Pickwick to Dombey*, 311; Herbert Sussman, *Victorians and the Machine* (Cambridge, Mass.: Harvard University Press, 1968), 51–58; Harlan S. Nelson, "Staggs's Gardens: The Railway through Dickens' World," *Dickens Studies Annual* 3 (1974): 43–52; F. S. Schwarzbach, *Dickens and the City* (London: Athlone, 1979), 110. For a consideration of the impact of the railway on the spatial representation of London, with reference to *Dombey*, see Lynda Nead, *Victorian Babylon: People, Streets and Images in Nineteenth-Century London* (New Haven, Conn.: Yale University Press, 2000), 34–36.

38. Dickens, "A Flight" (1851), *"Gone Astray" and Other Papers from Household Words*, ed. Michael Slater (London: Dent, 1998), 29.

39. Humphry House, *The Dickens World* (London: Oxford University Press, 1941), 145.

40. Murray Baumgarten, "Railway/Reading/Time: *Dombey & Son* and the Industrial World," *Dickens Studies Annual* 19 (1990): 69. This is one the most suggestive essays on the role of the railway in the novel, and it has substantially influenced my thinking about the growth of railway culture as it relates to the work.

41. Nelson, "Staggs's Gardens," 50.

42. Dickens's ambiguous response to the roar of the railway can be usefully juxtaposed with that of Henry David Thoreau, whose time at Walden overlapped by a year with the serialization of *Dombey*. Thoreau's famous chapter on "Sounds" in *Walden* begins with descriptions of the sounds of trees and birds but soon becomes dominated by the sound of the train, which he transforms into bird sound by way of analogy: "the rattle of railroad cars, now dying away and then reviving like the beat of a partridge"; "The whistle of the locomotive penetrates my woods summer and winter, sounding like the scream of a hawk sailing over some farmer's yard." The celebration of the sublimity of natural sound had been present early on in his work: in 1841, he wrote in his journal, "I drink in a wonderful health—a cordial—in sound. The effect of the slightest tinkling in the horizon measures my own soundness. I thank God for sound it always mounts, and makes me mount." Yet despite this love for natural sound, or perhaps because of it, the train, and the telegraph (which he called "the poetry of the R[ail]R[oad]"), come to fascinate him; he hears in them a confirmation of man's worthiness and progress, and a prophesy of "a golden age": "when I hear the iron horse make the hills echo with his snort like thunder, shaking the earth with his feet, and breathing fire and smoke from his nostrils, . . . it seems as if the earth had got a race now worthy to inhabit it" (see Thoreau, *Walden and Resistance to Civil Government*, ed. William Rossi [1854; New York: Norton, 1992], 77, 78; Thoreau, entry for 9 March 1852, *Journal 4: 1851–1852*, ed. Leonard N. Neufeldt and Nancy Craig Simmons [Princeton, N.J.: Princeton University Press, 1992], 383; Thoreau, entry for 3 March 1841, *Journal 1: 1837–1844*, ed. Elizabeth Hall Witherall, William L. Howarth, Robert Sattelmeyer, and Thomas Blandny [Princeton, N.J.: Princeton University Press, 1981], 277; and *Walden*, 78).

43. Wolfgang Schivelbusch, *The Railway Journey*, trans. Anselm Hollo (New York: Urizen, 1979), 66.

44. Jack Simmons, *The Victorian Railway* (London: Thames and Hudson, 1991), 245ff.; Charles Wilson, *First with the News: The History of W. H. Smith 1792–1972* (London: Cape, 1985), 99ff.; Michael Freeman, *Railways and the Victorian Imagination* (New Haven, Conn.: Yale University Press, 1999), 86–89. See also G. R. Pocklington, *The Story of W. H. Smith & Son*, 4th ed., rev. Gwen Clear (London: privately printed, 1949), 11, for more on the first W. H. Smith railway bookstall, opened at Euston station on 1 November 1848.

45. Altick, "Varieties of Readers' Response," 74–75.

46. Altick, *The English Common Reader* (Chicago: University of Chicago Press, 1957), 299; Margaret Dalziel, *Popular Fiction 100 Years Ago* (London: Cohen and West, 1957), 79–81; Robert A. Colby, "That He Who Rides May Read: W. H. Smith & Son's Railway Library," *Wilson Library Bulletin* 27 (1952), 302–3. Pocklington writes that Elizabeth Gaskell's *Cranford* was Smith's first yellowback, issued in 1857 (209). Among the best overviews of these developments is Raymond Williams's "The Growth of the Reading Public," in his classic *The Long Revolution* (London: Chatto and Windus, 1961), 156–72.

47. Patten, *Dickens and His Publishers*, 161 n. 3.

48. "Cheap Literature," *British Quarterly Review* 29 (1 April 1859): 326.

49. "Railway Circulating Libraries," *Punch* 16 (1849): 61.

50. "Railway Literature," *Dublin University Magazine* 34 (1849): 280.

51. In other words, the train here is not simply Dickens's image of "an engine of death," as Auerbach has it, but Dickens's image of *Dombey's* image of an engine of death, which is to say that the scene is meant to tell readers more about Dombey's mindset than Dickens's attitude toward the railway. See Auerbach, "Dickens and Dombey," 117, as well as Sussman, who claims that the train is an "objective correlative for the emotional blight of Dombey's mind" (*Victorians and the Machine*, 55–56). In his consideration of *Dombey* as a "revolutionary narrative," Ian Duncan concurs, writing that the narrator's description is filtered through "Dombey's own morbid fascination" (*Modern Romance and Transformations of the Novel: The Gothic, Scott, Dickens* [Cambridge: Cambridge University Press, 1992], 252, 245).

52. Charles Dickens and Wilkie Collins, "The Lazy Tour of Two Idle Apprentices," in *Christmas Stories* (Oxford: Oxford University Press, 1956), 665–66.

53. Of the numerous critical treatments of this passage, two deserve mention for different reasons: Garrett Stewart's, which is one of the most convincing in its claim that Carker's death is an act of "displacement" for Dombey the onlooker, and that it symbolizes Dombey's "death undergone by proxy" (*Death Sentences*, 17); and Nina Auerbach's, which is right to see Carker's trip as a recapitulation of Dombey's railway ride, but reads Carker's demise as "the final explosion of death, a giant eruption of the maleness he had tried to soften with his wiles" ("Dickens and Dombey," 123). Carker is torn apart as if in a "jagged mill"; he does not explode or erupt.

54. Dickens's revision of this passage for the 1867 edition made the reference to the express more explicit: "It don't stop."

55. Marcus, *Dickens from Pickwick to Dombey*, 311.

56. References to Dickens's address in the prospectus are to the version included in part 6 of *Dombey* in March 1847. The address (but not the rest of the prospectus) was reprinted in volume 1 of Dickens's *Collected Papers*, ed. Arthur Waugh, Hugh Walpole, Walter Dexter, and Thomas Hatton (Bloomsbury: Nonesuch, 1937), under the heading "Address in the Cheap Edition of *Pickwick Papers*. 1847" (64–66), and in Simon Nowell-Smith, "The 'Cheap Edition' of Dickens's Works [First Series] 1847–1852," *The Library*, 5th ser., 22 (1967), 246. The prospectus was written by Dickens and inserted by Chapman and Hall in parts 6 and 7 of *Dombey* (March and April 1847), and the address was reprinted on the inside front cover of the first monthly part of the 1847 *Pickwick*. As far as I can ascertain, neither the prospectus nor the address has been included in editions of either novel since (although excerpts can be found in Patten, *Charles Dickens and His Publishers*, 190–92). For the entire text of the prospectus, see the appendix.

57. Letter to Emile De La Rue, 24 March 1847, 5:42.

58. The distinction made in note 53 (above) about Carker's method of dying is significant if one reads his death metafictionally, as a pulping analogous to the operation of a paper mill on old rags or paper. In this sense, the death scene confirms Carker's status as villain in a particular kind of "pulp fiction"—one whose author, while writing, had determined to republish his earlier output on cheap paper made from those mills. Carker's death thus not only shows him becoming pulp for the mill that is Dickens the novelist and expressive dynamo, but also is emblematic of the central activity that will drive the republishing and recycling of Dickens's canon. This process is one Dickens will describe in explicit terms two years later, in "A Paper-Mill," a first-person account of the process of manufacturing cheap paper set against the soundscape of the noise of a steam engine ("the murmuring and throbbing of a mighty giant, labouring hard"). The narrator momentarily becomes "a bale of rags," moves through the mill, and, Carker-like, is "worried into smaller shreds—torn cross-wise at

the knives," then boiled and cut again, to emerge, finally, as "fawn-coloured pulp" (Dickens and Mark Lemon, "A Paper-Mill" [1850], in *Charles Dickens' Uncollected Writings from Household Words 1850–1859*, ed. Harry Stone [Bloomington: Indiana University Press, 1968], 1:138–40). Compare Thoreau's explicit connection between the train, the cargo, and print production in *Walden*: "This car-load of torn sails [to be pulped for paper] is more legible and interesting now than if they should be wrought into paper and printed books. Who can write so graphically the history of the storms they have weathered as these rents have done? They are proof-sheets which need no correction" (81).

59. That Dickens claimed for himself the position of "conductor" of his new publication should come as no surprise, given his identification as professional writer with the express train. The term was common enough for editors of periodicals, but for him it held special resonance. As he saw it, *Household Words* would be his vehicle for journalistic expression, the literary train he would both conduct and fuel. Alison Winter indicates the influence of mesmerism and musical contexts on Dickens's choice of word here, as well as the mesmeric aspects of his public readings, for which, conductor-like, he often held a baton, in her excellent *Mesmerized: Powers of Mind in Victorian Britain* (Chicago: University of Chicago Press, 1998), 321–22.

60. Letter to Forster, [?1 February 1850], 6:26: "But I rather think the VOICE is it." The vestiges of this title are evident in the closing paragraph of Dickens's "A Preliminary Word" (1850), which introduced the first issue of *Household Words* and, as what Michael Slater calls an "editorial manifesto," had an indirect antecedent in the address to the Cheap Edition: "All the voices *we* hear cry Go on! The stones that call to us have sermons in them, as the trees have tongues, as there are books in the running brooks, as there is good in everything! They, and the Time, cry out to us Go on! . . . Go on, is all we hear, Go on! In a glow already, with the air from yonder height upon us, and the inspiriting voices joining in this acclamation, we echo back the cry, and go on cheerily!" (*The Amusements of the People and Other Papers: Reports, Essays and Reviews 1834–51*, ed. Michael Slater [London: Dent, 1996], 175, 178–79). Slater cites Shakespeare's *As You Like It* 2.1 as the source for "The stones that call to us" (177). But note the echoes of Babbage's chapter in the idea of the air as filled with voices; the implicit analogy between Dickens's swift steps onward and upward and this pivotal moment in his "career"; and the Dickensian "hallucination" (to borrow Lewes's term) of a chorus of natural voices that commands him and his readers, "Go on!" This command might well be, for the professional author, "what the waves are always saying." The unused dedication is housed with the manuscript of the prospectus to the Cheap Edition in the Berg Collection, was reprinted in John Forster's *The Life of Charles Dickens*, ed. J. W. T. Ley (London: Palmer, 1928), 448–49, and is included in a note to the appendix.

61. Consider Babbage's observation earlier in the *Treatise* in a discussion of the history of printing: "Until printing was very generally spread, civilization scarcely advanced by slow and languid steps; since this art has become cheap, its advances have been unparalleled, and its rate of progress vastly accelerated. . . . It is to the easy and cheap methods of communicating thought from man to man, which enable a country to sift, as it were, its whole people, and to produce, in its science, its literature, and its arts, not the brightest efforts of a limited class, but the highest exertions of the most powerful minds amongst a whole community" (13 14). This is another version of the paradox Dickens confronts in the Cheap Edition: for "the highest exertions" of the "most powerful" thinkers to be able to influence civilization, what is required is "easy and cheap" printing.

62. Goldie Morgentaler, *Dickens and Heredity: When Like Begets Like* (Basingstoke, U.K.: Macmillan, 2000), 57: "In a mercantile world where everything is a matter of trade . . . women represent the most obvious example of human beings as commodities."

63. See also Ingham on Edith's speech and ability to use silence as a communicative weapon ("Speech and Non-Communication," 150–51), and her later discussion of Edith in *Dickens, Women, and Language* (Toronto: University of Toronto Press, 1992), 87–110.

64. In a different approach, Morgentaler sees naming in *Dombey* as "linked to the corrupting influence of capitalism" and aligns the "repetitive naming" at the end to the seventeenth- and eighteenth-century concept of preformation: "The repetitive naming allows Dickens to work his happy ending by suggesting that each new generation affords the one before it an opportunity for expiation and exculpation" (*Dickens and Heredity*, 61–62).

65. Marcus, *Dickens from Pickwick to Dombey*, 283.

66. Letter to Forster, [11 October 1846], 4:631. The touring, of course, went on to take an immense profit, and, some argue, the ultimate price—his life.

67. Stephen Connor, *Dumbstruck: A Cultural History of Ventriloquism* (Oxford: Oxford University Press, 2000), 315; Altick, "Varieties of Readers' Response," 81. Given Dickens's concern with hearing and being heard in *Dombey*, it is uncannily apt that Connor claims the best representation of ventriloquism in Dickens is Captain Cuttle's friend Jack Bunsby; he considers this fitting for a novel in which "the governing principle seems to be that of 'unutterable intelligence'" (315–16).

68. For another view, and a very provocative political interpretation of Dickens's readings, see Helen Small, "A Pulse of 124: Charles Dickens and a Pathology of the Mid-Victorian Reading Public," *The Practice and Representation of Reading in England*, ed. James Raven, Helen Small, and Naomi Tadmor (Cambridge: Cambridge University Press, 1996), 263–90.

69. Charles Dickens, *Our Mutual Friend*, ed. Michael Cotsell (Oxford: Oxford University Press, 1989), 198. The chapter from the *Treatise* that had so affected Dickens plays a central role in "The Automaton-Ear," a fascinating but long out-of-print short story by Florence McLandburgh published three years after the Inimitable's death. In the tale, a college professor reads a paraphrase of Babbage's passage on the permanence of sound and becomes obsessed with creating "an instrument which could catch these faint tones vibrating in the air and render them audible"—and this was four years before Edison invented the phonograph. He succeeds and determines to test the device on the ears of a deaf-mute domestic, but once she has miraculously heard through the machine, she attempts to steal it. In the ensuing struggle the professor murders her, only to find that he continues to hear her "strange grating noise" through the machine. At the end, he discovers that she is actually alive and well, and that his whole experience was a bout of "monomania," including the building of the machine ("The Automaton-Ear," *Scribner's Monthly* 5 [1872–1873]: 711–20). Kahn and Connor discuss the tale in *Noise Water Meat*, 212–14, and *Dumbstruck*, 359–61, respectively.

70. The events are recounted in detail in T. W. Hill, "The Staplehurst Railway Accident," *Dickensian* 38 (1942): 147–52; Johnson, *Charles Dickens*, 2:1018–20; and Peter Ackroyd, *Dickens* (London: Sinclair-Stevenson, 1990), 959–61. Hill notes that the Tidal Express was "so called because it ran at a different time, altered every few days, depending on the state of the tide in the harbours concerned" (148). As the name for a train, "Tidal Express" is a railway version of "What the Waves Were Always Saying," a phrase that merges the waves and rails that dominate *Dombey*. What is more, it is a particularly apt

train for close association with Dickens, who was his own kind of "title express": a driven novelist who constantly produced, and who approached the titling of his books with new seriousness (and who, it should be said, was not at a loss for titles from which to choose).

71. Letter to Thomas Mitton, 13 June 1865, 11:56.

72. Letter to Forster, [?13 June 1865], 11:55. Jill L. Matus's "Trauma, Memory, and Railway Disaster: The Dickensian Connection" (*Victorian Studies* 43 [2000/2001]: 413–36) is an excellent consideration of Dickens's knowledge of trauma in the wake of the accident and the manifestations of this in his late ghost story "The Signalman." This story was part of "Mugby Junction" (1866), the Christmas collaboration inspired by the accident, which contains Dickens's final conjunction of the noisy train with his career. This time he displaces it onto the central character Jackson, who imagines that in "a shadowy train," he sees "no other than the train of a life," his own, attendant with which, "with many a clank and wrench, were lumbering cares, dark meditations, huge dim disappointments, monotonous years, a long jarring line of the discords of a solitary and unhappy existence." After realizing that "there were so many Lines. . . . And then so many of the Lines went such wonderful ways, so crossing and curving among one another, that the eye lost them," Jackson chooses to live at the railway junction, a setting suggestive of Dickens's self-consciousness about taking a turn in his career away from print and toward performance. As the lines of track are "lost" by the eye, so Dickens's lines in his public readings are "lost" by the eyes of readers—but "found" by the ears of listeners. As if to echo this connection, Jackson later describes himself as "an unintelligible book with the earlier chapters all torn out, and thrown away" (Dickens, "Mugby Junction," in *Christmas Stories*, ed. Ruth Glancy [London: Dent, 1996], 608–9, 615, 627). The shift to public reading was borne out by the fact that Dickens turned the four chapters he contributed to "Mugby Junction" into three different reading scripts (one of which, "The Signalman," was never performed).

73. Comment to Charles Collins, quoted in Ackroyd, *Dickens*, 961.

74. Letter to Charles Fechter, 17 June 1865, 11:59–60.

75. Letter to Augustus Tracey, 15 June 1865, 11:59.

CHAPTER 2

1. From a manuscript in the Dickens House Museum, quoted in Fred Kaplan, *Dickens: A Biography* (New York: William Morrow, 1988), 450.

2. Letter to Forster, [?1 November 1864], *The Letters of Charles Dickens*, Pilgrim edition, ed. Madeline House, Graham Storey, Kathleen Tillotson, et al., 12 vols. (Oxford: Clarendon, 1965–2002), 10:447. Unless otherwise noted, all references to Dickens's letters will be to this edition and cited by volume and page number.

3. Edgar Johnson, *Charles Dickens: His Tragedy and Triumph*, 2 vols. (New York: Simon and Schuster, 1952) 2:1017; Kaplan, *Dickens*, 451. A good discussion of Leech's professional relationship with Dickens on the Christmas books can be found in Jane R. Cohen, *Charles Dickens and His Original Illustrators* (Columbus: Ohio State University Press, 1980), 142–49.

4. Letter to M. T. Bass, [May 1864], in Michael T. Bass, *Street Music in the Metropolis: Correspondence and Observations on the Existing Law, and Proposed Amendments* (London: Murray, 1864), 41.

5. Quoted in W. P. Frith, *John Leech: His Life and Work*, 2 vols. (London: Bentley, 1891), 2:297.

6. *Times* (London), 2 May 1856, 9.

7. *Times*, 2 July 1860, 8–9.

8. Peter Bailey, "Breaking the Sound Barrier," in his *Popular Culture and Performance in the Victorian City* (Cambridge: Cambridge University Press, 1998), 206.

9. H. J. Dyos, "Some Historical Reflections on the Quality of Urban Life," in *Exploring the Urban Past: Essays in Urban History*, ed. David Cannadine and David Reeder (Cambridge: Cambridge University Press, 1982), 69.

10. These can be found in the chapter "Neighbours and Nuisances" in Thea Holme, *The Carlyles at Home* (London: Oxford University Press, 1965), 58–76. Holbrook Jackson claims that Carlyle "was probably pathological" in his attitude toward noise, but then there were many other urban workers echoing the same pathology ("Listening to Reading," *The Reading of Books* [London: Faber and Faber, 1946], 118).

11. From Thomas Carlyle's letter to Jane Welsh Carlyle, 28 July 1853, in *The Collected Letters of Thomas and Jane Welsh Carlyle*, ed. C. R. Sanders, K. J. Fielding, et al., 29 vols. to date (Durham, N.C.: Duke University Press, 1970–), 28:231; his note to a letter from Jane Welsh Carlyle, 19 December 1853, 28:342; and his letter to Jane Welsh Carlyle, 29 July 1853, 28:233. All references to Thomas and Jane Welsh Carlyle's letters will be to this edition and cited by volume and page number.

12. Letter to Jane Welsh Carlyle, 8 July 1853, 28:185; to Jean Carlyle Aitken, 8 February 1853, 28:38.

13. Letter to Jean Carlyle Aitken, 11 August 1853, 28:245.

14. From Carlyle's journal, c. 17 August 1853, quoted in *Froude's Life of Carlyle*, ed. and abr. John Clubbe (Columbus: Ohio State University Press, 1979), 521.

15. Letter to Charles Redwood, 5 August 1853, 28:240.

16. Jenni Calder, *The Victorian Home* (London: Batsford, 1977), 15.

17. Alain Corbin, *Village Bells: Sound and Meaning in the 19th-Century French Countryside*, trans. Martin Thom (New York: Columbia University Press, 1998), x, xii; see also Bruce R. Smith, *The Acoustic World of Early Modern England: Attending to the O-Factor* (Chicago: University of Chicago Press, 1999); Mark M. Smith, *Listening to Nineteenth-Century America* (Chapel Hill: University of North Carolina Press, 2001); and Emily Thompson, *The Soundscape of Modernity: Architectural Acoustics and the Culture of Listening in America, 1900–1933* (Cambridge, Mass.: MIT Press, 2002).

18. Jacques Attali, *Noise: The Political Economy of Music*, trans. Brian Massumi (Minneapolis: University of Minnesota Press, 1985), 6; hereafter cited in text.

19. For approaches that are complementary to Corbin's and Attali's claims, see Eric Wilson ("Plagues, Fairs, and Street Cries: Sounding Out Society and Space in Early Modern London," *Modern Language Studies* 25.3 [1995]: 1–42), who studies "chapbooks, plague pamphlets, street cries, and ballads" as well as "the economic rhythms of voice and sound" in the soundscapes of Tudor and Stuart London (8–9). See also Bruce Smith, *The Acoustic World*, which offers "an ecology of voice, media, and community" for the primarily oral culture of early modern England (29). Mark M. Smith shows in *Listening to Nineteenth-Century America* "how important aurality, listening, and hearing were to the process of creating real and abiding notions of slavery and freedom, North and South, especially during the last three decades prior to the Civil War" (6–7). In *The Soundscape of Modernity* Thompson studies the ways, in tandem with urban industrialization, "new kinds of noises began to offend" in the early decades of the twentieth century (116–17).

20. James Winter, *London's Teeming Streets, 1830–1914* (London: Routledge, 1993), 71; Lucio Sponza, *Italian Immigrants in Nineteenth-Century Britain: Realities and Images*

(Leicester: Leicester University Press, 1988), 163–65; David R. Green, "Street Trading in London: A Case Study of Casual Labour, 1830–60," in *The Structure of Nineteenth-Century Cities*, ed. James H. Johnson and Colin G. Pooley (London: Croom Helm, 1982), 138. For an early account of street trader cries and music, see Charles Knight, "Street Noises," in *London*, ed. Charles Knight (London: Knight, 1841), 129–44. Knight's predictions are optimistic but fail to account for rising immigration and decreasing middle-class patience: "we are still advancing; and in a few years the [1839] Act which protects housekeepers from the nuisance of street musicians will be a dead letter" (142, 144).

21. Henry Mayhew, *London Labour and the London Poor* (1861; reprint New York: Dover, 1968), 3:158–204.

22. Medicus, "The Organ Nuisance," *Times*, 20 March 1851, 6.

23. The most detailed study of Italian immigration in Victorian London is Sponza, *Italian Immigrants*. For a survey that primarily focuses on the twentieth century, see Terri Colpi, *The Italian Factor: The Italian Community in Great Britain* (Edinburgh: Mainstream, 1991). The literature on English views toward foreigners and immigrants during the period is, of course, vast; a very selective list of studies includes Robin Cohen, *Frontiers of Identity: The British and the Others* (London: Longman, 1994), especially chapter 1, "Six Frontiers of a British Identity," 5–36; Panikos Panayi, *Immigration, Ethnicity, and Racism in Britain, 1815–1945* (Manchester: Manchester University Press, 1994); and Colin Holmes, *John Bull's Island: Immigration and British Society, 1871–1971* (London: Macmillan Education, 1988).

24. Knight, *London*, 142; "A Paterfamilias," "An Unneighbourly Act," *Good Words* (1864): 698. This is indeed one of the only published defenses of the musicians in this period of which I am aware.

25. [Charles Manby Smith], "Music-Grinders of the Metropolis," *Chambers's Edinburgh Journal*, n.s., 17 (27 March 1852): 197; hereafter cited in text.

26. Ronald Pearsall, *Victorian Popular Music* (Newton Abbot, U.K.: David and Charles, 1973), 192. For those who want to gauge the accuracy of the responses for themselves, performances of restored barrel organs, organettes, and a barrel piano are included on the recording *Music of the Streets*, Saydisc CSDL 340 (1983).

27. Mayhew, *London Labour*, 3:180.

28. In fact, as John Zucchi explains, the first Savoyards of note in England were children who arrived in the sixteenth century as chimney-sweeps and also played hurdy-gurdies, exhibited animals native to Savoy such as groundhogs, and put on magic lantern shows. However, unlike their predecessors, "the new Savoyards [those arriving in the later nineteenth century] were not from the Duchy of Savoy but from the Duchy of Parma." See John Zucchi, *The Little Slaves of the Harp: Italian Child Street Musicians in Nineteenth-Century Paris, London, and New York* (Montreal: McGill-Queen's University Press, 1992), 18.

29. For more on the confusion over "Savoyard" origins, see Sponza, *Italian Immigrants*, 40–41. Savoy's and Nice's surrender was the result of a series of secret treaties in 1859–1860 between Napoleon III and Cavour, who all the while publicly vowed not to give up the regions. An enthusiastic supporter of Italian unity, England responded to the decision with shock: Lord Palmerston began to regard Cavour "as a puppet of imperial France and thoroughly untrustworthy" (*The Making of Italy, 1796–1870*, ed. Denis Mack Smith [New York: Walker and Company, 1968], 304).

30. David Thomson provides a summary of the events leading up to the unification of Italy in 1871, with details about the role of Cavour in Savoy, in *Europe since Napoleon*, 2nd ed. (New York: Knopf, 1962), 263–71. Details can be found in Arthur James Whyte,

The Evolution of Modern Italy (New York: Norton, 1959), 129–30; Denis Mack Smith, *Italy: A Modern History*, 2nd ed. (Ann Arbor: University of Michigan Press, 1969), 24–25; and Harry Hearder, *Cavour* (London: Longman, 1994), 155–59. Still not surpassed for its focus is Derek Beales's *England and Italy 1859–60* (London: Nelson, 1961), which devotes an entire chapter to the Savoy controversy (131–62).

31. Cavour's epithet is taken from Denis Mack Smith, *Cavour* (New York: Knopf, 1985), 200.

32. Letter from "Chelone," reprinted in Bass, *Street Music*, 76; *Examiner* articles quoted in Bass, 70, 92, 96.

33. Quoted in Bass, *Street Music*, 109–10.

34. [Charles Collins], "An Unreported Speech," *All The Year Round* 6 (16 November 1861): 180.

35. Quoted in Bass, *Street Music*, 8–9.

36. Leonore Davidoff, *The Best Circles: Society, Etiquette and the Season* (London: Cresset, 1986), 92.

37. John Tosh, *A Man's Place: Masculinity and the Middle-Class Home in Victorian England* (New Haven, Conn.: Yale University Press, 1999), 17.

38. While Victorian leisure is conventionally considered a public phenomenon, it had its more intimate manifestations inside homes, as Bailey and others have argued. The artistic and intellectual classes who played and worked at home further complicate an understanding of the spatial situation of leisure. Indeed, it is partly this group's lack of such separation that led them to suffer increasing anxiety about urban disturbances. For they considered street music an insult to their status as both homeowners and at-home workers, or more concisely, as individuals with overlapping "occupations."

39. T. R. Gourvish, "The Rise of the Professions," in *Later Victorian Britain, 1867–1900*, ed. T. R. Gourvish and Alan O'Day (New York: St. Martin's, 1988), 14, 20.

40. W. J. Reader, *Professional Men: The Rise of the Professional Classes in Nineteenth-Century England* (London: Weidenfeld and Nicolson, 1966), 66.

41. Gourvish, "The Rise of the Professions," 32.

42. Reader, *Professional Men*, 148.

43. For more on the effects of street music on "the thickening but still soft skin of the middle class," see Sponza, *Italian Immigrants*, 171–72.

44. John Burnett, *A Social History of Housing 1815–1985*, 2nd ed. (London: Methuen, 1986), 113; see also Leonore Davidoff and Catherine Hall, *Family Fortunes: Men and Women of the English Middle Class, 1780–1850* (Chicago: University of Chicago Press, 1987), 364–69.

45. Bailey, "Breaking the Sound Barrier," 209.

46. Norma Clarke, "Strenuous Idleness: Thomas Carlyle and the Man of Letters as Hero," in *Manful Assertions: Masculinities in Britain since 1800*, ed. Michael Roper and John Tosh (London: Routledge, 1991), 26, 41. As Carlyle tellingly put it, his intent was to have the study "be made nearly *cock*-proof" (letter to Jane Welsh Carlyle, 27 July 1853, 28:226; emphasis in original). Similar anxieties over masculinity manifest in Thomas's concern with the protection the soundproof room ostensibly would afford him, as the exposed and vulnerable man of letters: "I feel as if the mercy [of the soundless room] were already *wrought* for me; as if my dextrous dauntless little lie[u]tenant [the builder] had already (in some way) *delivered* the unprotected man, and covered him safe again" (letter to Jane Welsh Carlyle, 29 July 1853, 28:233).

47. Thomas Carlyle's commentary, in Jane Welsh Carlyle, *Letters and Memorials of Jane Welsh Carlyle*, ed. James Anthony Froude (London: Longmans, Green, 1883), 2:230.

48. Letter to John A. Carlyle, [27 June 1852], 27:189.

49. Letter to Thomas Carlyle, [10 August 1852], 27:216.

50. Letter to Alexander Carlyle, 8 April 1853, 28:100.

51. *Times*, 2 July 1860, 9.

52. Winter, *London's Teeming Streets*, 72; a fuller discussion of the Babbage case can be found on 71–79. Mary Lloyd's reminiscence is representative: "I remember one day Mr. Babbage came down to Richmond quite in low spirits at the persecution he had received regarding the organs, etc., and I was much shocked to find when I called on some friends in Manchester Square, that there was a subscription started to encourage the organs to worry him! He told me with a dismal face that one day when he was walking in the city and just going to cross a street, a pretty little girl cried out 'There goes old Babbage!' He was then engaged in five actions about the brass bands, and organs, and he was in correspondence with Sir Richard Mayne, and the Home Office, for power to suppress them" (*"Sunny Memories," Containing Personal Recollections of Some Celebrated Characters* [London: Women's Printing Society, 1880], 65).

53. Charles Babbage, "A Chapter on Street Nuisances" (1864), reprinted in *Passages in the Life of a Philosopher*, vol. 11 of *The Works of Charles Babbage*, ed. Martin Campbell-Kelly (New York: New York University Press, 1989), 253; hereafter cited in text.

54. Babbage's list of interruptions is reproduced in a letter to M. T. Bass, in Bass, *Street Music*, 20–22. In the draft of a 12 July 1860 letter to Sir Richard Mayne, Babbage provided an equally colorful list: "Amongst some thousand nuisances comprising: Organs; Brass-bands; Fiddlers; Harps; Punch; Pantomime, Monkeys, Military; Dancing and Musical; Athletes; Ladies and Gentlemen walking on stilts and looking inquiringly in at the Drawing Room windows; Hindu or Mohammedan imposters beating monotonous drums, or showing insanity; troups of Scotch imposters dancing with bagpipes, even more inharmonious than the genuine instrument; it is obviously impossible for the householder to enjoy any quiet" (quoted in Anthony Hyman, *Charles Babbage: Pioneer of the Computer* [Oxford: Oxford University Press, 1982], 247). Note the way the anxious homeowner includes along with all the other noisemakers "Pantomime" and those outside who might peer "inquiringly in at the Drawing Room windows," from which one can infer that his quest for "quiet" is really a desire for territorial defense and distance.

55. Connections between the value of the scholars' time and that of their quiet space deserve further exploration; I can only touch on some here. Andrew Halliday commented tongue-in-cheek in an article written from the perspective of a wearied aristocratic street-music admirer: "Labour has its duties no doubt; but property has its rights. What is Mr. Babbage's calculation machine to me? . . . The machine I require is an organ to play to me when I am dull, and want to kill time" ("The Battle of the Barrels," *All The Year Round* 11 [11 June 1864], 423). As Halliday suggests here, to "kill time" is to be "dull" and shun intellectual pursuits. The implication is that to protect time, as Babbage attempts to do, is to preserve them. The quotation from Halliday ironically demonstrates how claims about space ("property has its rights") could be used by the wealthy to defend street musicians even as the claiming of space, such as Carlyle's of his study, was used to deflect them. For more on eighteenth- and nineteenth-century attitudes toward time as a condition of work, see E. P. Thompson, "Time, Work-Discipline and Industrial Capitalism," in *Customs in Common* (New York: New Press, 1991), 352–403.

56. F. M. L. Thompson, *The Rise of Respectable Society: A Social History of Victorian Britain, 1830–1900* (Cambridge, Mass.: Harvard University Press, 1988), 257.

57. A detailed summary of the events is given in Sponza, *Italian Immigrants*, 176–81; the full text of Bass's proposed bill is printed in Bass, *Street Music*, 120, hereafter cited in text, and the emended bill as passed appears in Sponza, *Italian Immigrants*, 341.

58. The letter also appears, but without the signers' names other than Dickens's, in the Nonesuch Dickens (*The Letters of Charles Dickens*, ed. Walter Dexter [Bloomsbury: Nonesuch, 1938], 3:389–90) and is reprinted (again without signers' names) with a brief commentary in Lillian Ruff, "How Musical Was Charles Dickens?" (*Dickensian* 68 [1972]: 36), and the Pilgrim edition of the letters (10:388–89).

59. What *is* certain is that Leech was most anxious to sign the letter. On 16 May 1864, Dickens wrote to Leech, who appears to have been impatient for official action on the part of the author, "I cannot send you the letter to P. A. [*sic*] Bass tonight, because I find I have no letter paper here without my engraved address. But it shall follow speedily" (10:396). Leech, already in failing health, had at this point five months to live.

60. Kaplan, *Dickens*, 478. The letter also is mentioned in another biography: Norman Mackenzie and Jeanne Mackenzie, *Dickens: A Life* (Oxford: Oxford University Press, 1979), 339.

61. Karen Chase and Michael Levenson, *The Spectacle of Intimacy: A Public Life for the Victorian Family* (Princeton: Princeton University Press, 2000), 143, 151.

62. On this subject, see Joseph F. Lamb, "Symbols of Success in Suburbia: The Establishment of Artists' Communities in Late Victorian London," in *Victorian Urban Settings: Essays on the Nineteenth-Century City and Its Contexts*, ed. Debra N. Mancoff and D. J. Trela (New York: Garland, 1996), 57–73.

63. Dickens to W. C. Macready, 22 April 1865, 11:33.

64. Dickens's attitude toward organ grinders worked its timely way into his contribution to the 1863 Christmas number of *All The Year Round*, "Mrs Lirriper's Lodgings." In terms that evoke the explosive behavior of Babbage and Leech, the landlady Lirriper recounts the defensive tactics used by her boarder Major Jemmy Jackson "when it got about among the organ-men that quiet was our object": "he made lion and tiger war upon them to that degree without seeing it I could not have believed it was in any gentleman to have such a power of bursting out with fire-irons walking-sticks water-jugs coals potatoes off his table the very hat off his head, and at the same time so furious in foreign languages that they would stand with their handles half turned fixed like the Sleeping Ugly—for I cannot say Beauty" (*Christmas Stories*, ed. Ruth Glancy [London: Dent, 1996], 515–16).

65. Peter Bailey, *Leisure and Class in Victorian England* (London: Routledge and Kegan Paul, 1978), 173. My chapter is indebted to many of the claims put forth in this study. Bailey discusses leisure as a "play discipline to complement the work discipline that was the principal means of social control in an industrial capitalist society" (5). Clearly, the Bass act was a form of "play discipline" and "social control," though not one enacted with the intention of morally uplifting the working classes. Bailey emphasizes urban leisure as distinct from work in time and place of practice, and the subject of this part of my argument is the anxiety that results when the two intermingle—when London street organs grind into the workplace that itself overlaps with the home.

66. In Bass, *Street Music*, 46–47, 53, 52, 15, 73–75.

67. *Observations on the Abuse of Toleration Permitted to the Itinerants Who Prowl About the Streets of London with Machines Assuming to be Music Played Mechanically by the Hand* (London: Doughty and Wilkins, 1863), 3.

68. The aesthetic attitude expressed in George Dodd's "Music in Poor Neighborhoods," which appeared in Dickens's *Household Words*, typified the condescension of the

middle classes: "while the German bands and the monster organs, albeit somewhat rough and noisy, do certainly familiarise the ear with much German and Italian music of a superior kind, it is the evening music, however, the music listened to within a building when the labours of the day are over, that somewhat embarrasses our licensing magistrates and our Lord Chamberlains." Dodd granted that the poor have "a want, a tendency, a natural yearning" for music, and hazarded that it "may lead to good, if properly managed," that is, performed according to acceptable middle-class standards and in appropriate venues ([George Dodd], "Music in Poor Neighborhoods," *Household Words* 12 [8 September 1858]: 138, 141). Yet the categories Dodd employed—between "daytime" and "evening," and "indoor" and "outdoor," music—while convenient tags for expressing and managing class distinction, as Bass's act would go on to do, were also as subjective and unstable as any of the other attempts to define what constituted "music" in these debates. What the concepts of "indoors" and "evening" might actually *mean* to "the horn-handed artisan" or "the tile workman, and his wife and children," who did not necessarily lay claims to either home ownership or leisurely evenings, was never considered (137, 140–41).

69. Richard Middleton, "Popular Music of the Lower Classes," in *The Romantic Age, 1800–1914*, ed. Nicholas Temperley (London: Athlone, 1981), 70.

70. Dave Russell, *Popular Music in England, 1840–1914: A Social History* (Montreal: McGill-Queen's University Press, 1987), 65; Mayhew, *London Labour*, 3:175.

71. [Charles Mackay], "Music and Misery," *All The Year Round* 20 (15 August 1868): 230–33; Pearsall, *Victorian Popular Music*, 194.

72. Edward Jacobs, "Disvaluing the Popular: London Street Culture, 'Industrial Literacy,' and the Emergence of Mass Culture in Victorian England," in *Victorian Urban Settings*, 94; hereafter cited in text.

73. Bailey, "Breaking the Sound Barrier," 207; Robert D. Storch, "The Policeman as Domestic Missionary: Urban Discipline and Popular Culture in Northern England, 1850–1880," *Journal of Social History* 9 (1976): 483, 496.

74. Sponza, *Italian Immigrants*, 178–79. The amendments attempted to clarify what constituted a "reasonable Cause" for asking musicians to depart. The original provision (1839) had specified illness or other "reasonable Cause"; Bass's proposal did not require any reason at all; and the amended act struck a balance, specifying illness "or on account of the Interruption of the ordinary Occupations or Pursuits of any Inmate of such House, or for other reasonable or sufficient Cause." As to the effectiveness of this new wording, see my conclusion to this chapter.

75. Letter of 18 August 1864, in Sophia Elizabeth De Morgan, *Memoir of Augustus De Morgan* (London: Longman, Green, 1882), 324.

76. Bruce Haley, *The Healthy Body and Victorian Culture* (Cambridge, Mass.: Harvard University Press, 1978), 5–6. Following Haley's study, there has of course appeared much work on the subject, especially feminist approaches that help to compensate for his focus on the Victorian male. Others have dealt with neurosis in the culture and in cultural productions. See, for instance, George Frederick Drinka, *The Birth of Neurosis: Myth, Malady, and the Victorians* (New York: Simon and Schuster, 1984), and Janet Oppenheim's excellent *"Shattered Nerves": Doctors, Patients, and Depression in Victorian England* (Oxford: Oxford University Press, 1991).

77. Athena Vrettos, *Somatic Fictions: Imagining Illness in Victorian Culture* (Stanford, Calif.: Stanford University Press, 1995), 3. See also Miriam Bailin, *The Sickroom in Victorian Fiction: The Art of Being Ill* (Cambridge: Cambridge University Press, 1994).

78. Florence Nightingale, *Notes on Nursing: What It Is, and What It Is Not* (New York: Appleton, 1860), 44–58; hereafter cited in text.

79. In the brief note on music Nightingale included at the end of the section, she wrote, without a trace of irony: "The finest piano-forte playing will damage the sick, while an air, like 'Home, sweet home,' or 'Assisa a piè d'un salice,' on the most ordinary grinding organ, will sensibly soothe them—" (*Notes on Nursing*, 57–58). Her judgment here did not quite hit the mark; the ensuing street music battles proved her conclusion about the organs wrong indeed.

80. *Times*, 10 November 1857, 6.

81. While many scholars have noted the sensory elements of social reformers' growing fascination with urban others, few have discussed the particularly complex problem of hearing. In *The Politics and Poetics of Transgression* (Ithaca, N.Y.: Cornell University Press, 1986), for example, Peter Stallybrass and Allon White write of the "transformation of the senses" that Victorian policing enacted, arguing that an "increased regulation of touch" arose between lower and middle classes during the period, as well as a new emphasis on visual and olfactory senses (as in "The Great Stink" of 1858). See their chapter, "The City: The Sewer, the Gaze, and the Contaminating Touch," 125–48.

82. Babbage, "Chapter," 264, 255; Bass, *Street Music*, 109.

83. Frith, *John Leech*, 2:260.

84. Frith, *John Leech*, 2:267; Simon Houfe, *John Leech and the Victorian Scene* (Suffolk: Antique Collectors' Club, 1984), 196.

85. An apocryphal incident that has acquired some of the same notoriety as Leech's confrontations is Anthony Trollope's November 1882 apparent altercation with an organ grinder or German bandsman playing outside his window, which supposedly agitated the author so much that it led to his fatal stroke several hours later (N. John Hall, *Trollope: A Biography* [Oxford: Oxford University Press, 1991], 513–14).

86. J. W. T. Ley, "John Leech: Dickens's Friendship with the Great 'Punch' Artist," *Dickensian* 13 (1917): 202; Kaplan, *Dickens*, 452; John Ruskin, "Lecture V — The Fireside: John Leech and John Tenniel," in *The Art of England: Lectures Given in Oxford* (Orpington: Allen, 1884), 178–79; Charles Dickens, "Review: *The Rising Generation*," *The Amusements of the People and Other Papers: Reports, Essays and Reviews 1834–51*, ed. Michael Slater (London: Dent, 1996), 144, 147. Omitting any reference to the organ grinder works, Ley goes on to call Leech's art "graceful and kindly, yet thoroughly masculine" ("John Leech," 202). See also Cohen, who writes that "Dickens ranked Leech, along with Cruikshank, among the best caricaturists of all time," while Thackeray is quoted as saying, "'Leech is the sort of man who appears once in a century'" (*Dickens and His Original Illustrators*, 149, 151).

87. Frith, *John Leech*, 2:297.

88. Silver, from an account dated January 1864, quoted in Houfe, *John Leech*, 199.

89. In a letter to the *Times* published 20 May 1864, Leech called for "some more summary mode . . . of indicting" musical "foul-mouthed foreigners" (6).

90. Quoted in M. H. Spielmann, *The History of "Punch"* (London: Cassell, 1895), 440.

91. James Greenwood, "The Private Life of a Public Nuisance," *London Society* 11 (1867): 226.

92. H. R. Haweis, *Music and Morals* (New York: Harper, 1872), 458; hereafter cited in text.

93. Adolphe Smith, *Street Life in London* (1877; reprint, New York: Blom, 1969), 121, 125.

94. Richard Rowe, *Life in the London Streets, or, Struggles for Daily Bread* (London: Nimmo, 1881), 274.

95. See Sponza, *Italian Immigrants*, 181. An author who identified himself only as "A London Physician" offered an attack on the ineffectiveness of the act and a familiar de-

fense of the ill in *The Nuisance of Street Music; or, a Plea for the Sick, the Sensitive, and the Studious* (London: Renshaw, 1869).

96. James Sully, "Civilization and Noise," *Fortnightly Review* 24 (1878): 711; hereafter cited in text.

97. For the rise of the science of acoustical engineering and the realities of the problems Sully anticipates, see Thompson, "The New Acoustics, 1900–1933" and "Noise and Modern Culture, 1900–1933," in *The Soundscape of Modernity*, 59–168. The claims of the 1860s about the *bestiality* of street music resonated in the terms of "Animal Music," one of Sully's later articles, in which he elaborated on arguments first set out by Charles Darwin and Herbert Spencer over the relationship between the "sub-human music" of animal noises and "our own highly developed art of tone": "How terrible, how lacerating to the ear of a musical man are the cries which occasionally issue from our Zoological Gardens!" (*Cornhill Magazine* 40 [1879]: 606).

98. G. B. Shaw, "The Barrel-Organ Question," *Morning Leader* (27 November 1893), reprinted in *Shaw's Music: The Complete Musical Criticism in Three Volumes*, ed. Dan H. Laurence (London: Max Reinhardt, The Bodley Head, 1981), 3:43; hereafter cited in text.

99. Lawrence Baron, "Noise and Degeneration: Theodor Lessing's Crusade for Quiet," *Journal of Contemporary History* 17 (1982): 165, 173.

100. Arthur Symons, "The Barrel-Organ," *Amoris Victima (1897); Amoris Victimia (1940)* (New York: Garland, 1984), 44.

101. Letter to Henry Eliot, 8 September 1914, in *The Letters of T. S. Eliot*, ed. Valerie Eliot (San Diego: Harcourt, 1988), 55.

102. T. S. Eliot, "Portrait of a Lady," *Collected Poems 1909–1962* (San Diego: Harcourt, 1970), 10–11.

103. Calder, *The Victorian Home*, 31.

104. Thompson, *The Rise of Respectable Society*, 332.

CHAPTER 3

1. George Eliot, *Daniel Deronda*, ed. Graham Handley (Oxford: Clarendon, 1984), 3; hereafter cited in text.

2. Sally Shuttleworth, *George Eliot and Nineteenth-Century Science: The Make-Believe of a Beginning* (Cambridge: Cambridge University Press, 1984), 201. See also Gillian Beer, who claims that answering the opening question of the novel "will take up much of the book" (*Darwin's Plots: Evolutionary Narrative in Darwin, George Eliot and Nineteenth-Century Fiction* [London: Routledge and Kegan Paul, 1983], 207).

3. George Eliot, *Middlemarch*, ed. David Carroll (Oxford: Clarendon, 1986), 189; hereafter cited in text.

4. The tag of "post-realist" is taken from Bryan Cheyette's discussion of the novel, although it echoes the general sentiment that *Deronda* moves, formally and thematically, beyond anything else Eliot and most other Victorian novelists wrote (*Constructions of "The Jew" in English Literature and Society: Racial Representations, 1875–1945* [Cambridge: Cambridge University Press, 1993], 53–54).

5. George Henry Lewes to John Blackwood, [22 November 1875], in *The George Eliot Letters*, ed. Gordon S. Haight, 9 vols. (New Haven, Conn.: Yale University Press, 1954–1978), 6:193.

6. The pioneering work here is, of course, Beer's *Darwin's Plots*, which, it does not seem too much to say, has had on Eliot criticism nearly the extent of impact that Darwin did on Eliot.

7. Albert Einstein to Mileva Marić, early August 1899, quoted in David Cahan, "Introduction: Helmholtz at the Borders of Science," *Hermann von Helmholtz and the Foundations of Nineteenth-Century Science*, ed. David Cahan (Berkeley: University of California Press, 1993), 2.

8. Hermann von Helmholtz, "The Physiological Causes of Harmony in Music" (1857), in *Selected Writings of Hermann von Helmholtz*, ed. Russell Kahl (Middletown, Conn.: Wesleyan University Press, 1971), 75–108. Beer discusses Helmholtz's use of wave theory, as well as the indirect influence, on Eliot, Hardy, and Whitman, of his use of the wave metaphor in his work on acoustics: see her "Helmholtz, Tyndall, Gerard Manley Hopkins: Leaps of the Prepared Imagination," in *Open Fields: Science in Cultural Encounter* (Oxford: Clarendon, 1996), 245–48; and "'Authentic Tidings of Invisible Things': Vision and the Invisible in the Later Nineteenth Century," in *Vision in Context: Historical and Contemporary Perspectives on Sight*, ed. Teresa Brennan and Martin Jay (New York: Routledge, 1996), 85–98, especially 88ff.

9. Russell Kahl, "Introduction," *Selected Writings of Hermann von Helmholtz*, xxix.

10. Beer, "'Authentic Tidings of Invisible Things,'" 91. Beer analyzes Helmholtz's influence on the meter and sound of Hopkins's poetry, as well as provides details on Ellis and his contribution to the disagreement over the proper English terminology for Helmholtz's *klangfarbe* (which Tyndall, instead of "timbre," translated as "clangtint," a word Hopkins called "the very worst compound I ever heard in English"), in "Helmholtz, Tyndall, Gerard Manley Hopkins," 267–72.

11. Ernest Glen Wever explains that Helmholtz was not the first to postulate a resonance theory of hearing. That distinction belongs to the seventeenth-century anatomy professors Caspar Bauhin and Joseph DuVerney, whose resonator theory prominently figured in the unpublished work of Joseph Sauveur, the sound theorist who coined the term "acoustics" in 1701. But, as Wever goes on to show, because Helmholtz was able to incorporate the contemporaneous principles and observations of Georg Ohm, Max Müller, and Alfonso Corti, he was able to make a much more detailed and elegant, and hence convincing, case for his own resonance theory, which I discuss below (see Wever, *Theory of Hearing* [New York: Dover, 1970], 10–33; Richard Semmens, *Joseph Sauveur's 'Treatise on the Theory of Music': A Study, Diplomatic Transcription and Annotated Translation*, Studies in Music 11 [London, Ontario: University of Western Ontario Press, 1986], 14–19).

12. Hermann von Helmholtz, *On the Sensations of Tone as a Physiological Basis for the Theory of Music*, trans. from 3rd ed. (1870) by Alexander J. Ellis (London: Longmans, Green, 1875), 33; hereafter cited in text.

13. Helmholtz, *Sensations of Tone*, 221; Gary Hatfield, "Helmholtz and Classicism: The Science of Aesthetics and the Aesthetics of Science," in *Helmholtz and the Foundations of Nineteenth-Century Science*, 526.

14. For more on the discoveries by others that contributed to Helmholtz's theory, see Wever, *Theory of Hearing*, 25–33, and the concluding chapter "Helmholtz' Synthesis" in V. Carlton Maley, Jr., *The Theory of Beats and Combination Tones, 1700–1863* (New York: Garland, 1990), 120–36.

15. William Baker, *The George Eliot–George Henry Lewes Library: An Annotated Catalogue of Their Books at Dr. Williams's Library, London* (New York: Garland, 1977), 91–92.

16. Peter Allan Dale, *In Pursuit of a Scientific Culture: Science, Art, and Society in the Victorian Age* (Madison: University of Wisconsin Press, 1989), 105. Dale notes that Lewes's first published reference to Helmholtz was in his *Life and Works of Goethe*, that he made "a special effort to visit" Helmholtz in Heidelberg in 1868, and that he was

reading him regularly in 1869 (104, 302 n. 8); Lewes notes in his journal that he and Eliot were shown "Helmholtz's Sirene and Vocal tuning forks" in Freiburg in July 1868 (*George Eliot Letters*, 4:458–59). Kate Flint discusses Helmholtz's influence on Lewes's *Problems of Life and Mind* in *The Victorians and the Visual Imagination* (Cambridge: Cambridge University Press, 2000), 256. Laura Otis provides an overview of Helmholtz's and Lewes's uses of metaphor, and analyzes the webs of telegraphy, railways, and language in *Middlemarch*, in her *Networking: Communicating with Bodies and Machines in the Nineteenth Century* (Ann Arbor: University of Michigan Press, 2001), 69–78, 81–119.

17. George Eliot, *The Journals of George Eliot*, ed. Margaret Harris and Judith Johnston (Cambridge: Cambridge University Press, 1998), 135. Alison Byerly also refers to this entry, but her lone comment on Helmholtz, that his *Sensations of Tone* "suggested that music produces, not specific emotions, but rather a sympathetic mood or frame of mind," while adequate as far as it goes, does not convey the precision and depth of his work, which likely appealed to Eliot and which I consequently have tried to touch on here (*Realism, Representation, and the Arts in Nineteenth-Century Literature* [Cambridge: Cambridge University Press, 1997], 138). After my work on this chapter was completed, I took part in a panel, "Acoustic Victorians," in which Kay Young discussed the influence of Helmholtz's theories about hearing on *Middlemarch* in her paper "*Middlemarch* and the Problem of Other Minds Heard," presented at the Society for the Study of Narrative Literature conference, Houston, Texas, March 2001.

18. William Baker, *Some George Eliot Notebooks: An Edition of the Carl H. Pforzheimer Library's George Eliot Holograph Notebooks, MSS 707, 708, 709, 710, 711* (Salzburg: Institut für Anglistik und Amerikanstik, Universität Salzburg, 1984), 2:48 (Folio 48, Notebook 708, undated). Baker neither identifies the source of the quotation nor notes the reference to sympathetic vibration. It is possible that Eliot may have arrived at this particular example of the phenomenon from reading another account of it besides Helmholtz: for instance, the earliest published one by Galileo in his *Dialogues Concerning Two New Sciences* (1638; available in the complete works that Eliot and Lewes owned), or the widely circulated discussion of "sympathetic communication of vibration" by John Herschel in his article on sound (dated 3 February 1830) in the *Encyclopaedia Metropolitana*, or David Brewster's description of "sympathetic communication" in his recapitulation of Herschel's article from his published letters to Walter Scott (dated 24 April 1832), or Max Müller's description (derived from Helmholtz) of the sympathetic vibration of piano strings in "The Physiological Alphabet," the third of his *Lectures on the Science of Language*, second series, which Eliot read in 1864, or, as a final example (after 1871), one of James Sully's descriptions of the resonance theory in his articles in the *Fortnightly Review* and *Westminster Review*. None of these sources, however, mentions the specific example that Eliot invokes, and the approximate dating of the entry suggests that a likely inspiration was indeed Helmholtz, whom she had just been reading. See Galileo Galilei, *Dialogues Concerning Two New Sciences*, trans. Henry Crew and Alfonso de Salvio (New York: McGraw-Hill, 1963), 91, 94–95; J. F. W. Herschel, "Sound," *Encyclopaedia Metropolitana*, 2d division, ed. Edward Smedley, Hugh James Rose, and Henry John Rose (London: Fellowes, 1845), 2:783; David Brewster, *Letters on Natural Magic Addressed to Sir Walter Scott, Bart.* (New York: Harper and Brothers, 1843), 169–70; Max Müller, *Lectures on the Science of Language Delivered at the Royal Institution of Great Britain in February, March, April, and May, 1863* (London: Longman, Green, Longman, Roberts, and Green, 1864), 106–7; and James Sully, "The Basis of Musical Sensation," *Fortnightly Review* 17 (1872): 434, and "Recent Experiments with the Senses," *Westminster Review*, n.s., 42 (1872): 185. Eliot also might have read Bacon's musings on the possibility

of "sympathy" between strings on a viol, bells, and pipes in his *Sylva Sylvarum: or, a Natural History* (1627; vol. 4 of *The Work of Francis Bacon, Lord Chancellor of England*, ed. Basil Montagu [London: William Pickering, 1826], 137–38; see also Penelope Gouk, "Some English Theories of Hearing in the Seventeenth Century: Before and After Descartes," in *The Second Sense: Studies in Hearing and Musical Judgment from Antiquity to the Seventeenth Century*, ed. Charles Burnett, Michael Fend, and Penelope Gouk [London: The Warburg Institute, 1991], 98–99). Eliot would have known that Jean-Phillipe Rameau theorized the sympathetic vibration of strings in his *Traité de l'harmonie* (1722) to explain the concept of harmony; Eliot also may have been aware that this metaphor was appropriated by mesmerists to describe the magnetizer-subject relationship (see Phyllis Weliver, *Women Musicians in Victorian Fiction, 1860–1900: Representations of Music, Science and Gender in the Leisured Home* [Aldershot, U.K.: Ashgate, 2000], 66–71).

19. George Eliot, *Scenes of Clerical Life*, ed. Thomas A. Noble (Oxford: Clarendon, 1985), 56, 42; hereafter cited in text. The three stories that comprise *Scenes* were begun in September 1856, published in *Blackwood's* in 1857, and in volume form in 1858.

20. Byerly writes that "from the Romantics, [Eliot] borrows the idea of music as a supremely authentic mode of representation" (*Realism, Representation, and the Arts*, 106), while Karen B. Mann discusses Eliot's fondness for Wordsworth's poem in *The Language That Makes George Eliot's Fiction* (Baltimore, Md.: Johns Hopkins University Press, 1983), 60.

21. George Eliot, *The Mill on the Floss*, ed. Gordon Haight (Oxford: Clarendon, 1980), 193–94; hereafter cited in text.

22. Weliver makes a similar point about this passage in her discussion of women and music in *The Mill, Middlemarch*, and *Deronda*, in *Women Musicians in Victorian Fiction*, 194.

23. Mann, *The Language That Makes George Eliot's Fiction*, 63.

24. George Eliot, *Romola*, ed. Andrew Brown (Oxford: Clarendon, 1993), 320–21.

25. John Tyndall, *Sound* (London: Longmans, Green, 1867), 220, 241. Tyndall's singing flames are the subject of "Lecture VI," 217–54. For more on Tyndall's operation of the flames, see Charles A. Taylor, "Tyndall as Lecture Demonstrator," *John Tyndall: Essays on a Natural Philosopher*, ed. W. H. Brock, N. D. McMillan, and R. C. Mollan (Dublin: Royal Dublin Society, 1981), 207–9. *Sound* is deeply indebted to Helmholtz, as Tyndall indicates in his preface; the final lecture closes with a recapitulation of "synchronism" (sympathetic vibration) and an admiring summary of the resonance theory of hearing (320–25). As Beer points out, Müller had preceded Tyndall in popularizing Helmholtz in England: in a series of lectures delivered at the Royal Institution in 1863 and published the following year, Müller had publicized Helmholtz's theory of combination tones ("Helmholtz, Tyndall, Gerard Manley Hopkins," 247; see also my n. 8. Beer discusses Tyndall's role in disseminating Helmholtz's work on 246 and 248–50).

26. Flint, *The Victorians and the Visual Imagination*, 244–45.

27. Weliver, *Women Musicians in Victorian Fiction*, 172. See also Weliver's very useful discussion of Sully's treatment of harmony (172–79).

28. James Sully, "Recent Experiments with the Senses," 185. A revised version was included as "Recent German Experiments with Sensation" in Sully's *Sensation and Intuition: Studies in Psychology and Aesthetics* (London: King, 1874), 37–72.

29. James Sully, "George Eliot's Art," *Mind* 6 (1881): 388; hereafter cited in text. For a discussion of Sully's comments on the "visible" and "invisible" as they relate to *Deronda*, see Flint, *The Victorians and the Visual Imagination*, 251–55.

30. Beer, "'Authentic Tidings of Invisible Things,'" 91.

31. See, for example, Beryl Gray, *George Eliot and Music* (New York: St. Martin's, 1989), 100–19.

32. Peter Brooks, *Body Work: Objects of Desire in Modern Narrative* (Cambridge, Mass.: Harvard University Press, 1993), 254.

33. Emily Auerbach, *Maestros, Dilettantes, and Philistines: The Musician in the Victorian Novel* (New York: Lang, 1989), 166. See also William Baker, *George Eliot and Judaism* (Salzburg: Institut für Englische Sprache und Literatur, Universität Salzburg, 1975), 231.

34. See Gordon Haight, "George Eliot's Klesmer," in *Imagined Worlds: Essays on Some English Novels and Novelists in Honour of John Butt*, ed. Maynard Mack and Ian Gregor (London: Methuen, 1968), 210–12; Gray, *George Eliot and Music*, 103; Baker, *George Eliot and Judaism*, 234.

35. Nicholas Royle makes a similar connection between the names in his *Telepathy and Literature: Essays on the Reading Mind* (Oxford: Blackwell, 1991), 96. For the parallels between the role of the (foreign) orchestral conductor and that of the mesmerist, with particular attention to the cases of Berlioz and Wagner, see Alison Winter, *Mesmerized: Powers of Mind in Victorian Britain* (Chicago: University of Chicago Press, 1998), 309–20.

36. Mary Burgan, "Heroines at the Piano: Women and Music in Nineteenth-Century Fiction," in *The Lost Chord: Essays on Victorian Music*, ed. Nicholas Temperley (Bloomington: Indiana University Press, 1989), 57–66. See also Auerbach, who claims foreign musicians were perceived as "demonic Don Juans, men who led lives of scandal and intrigue," in *Maestros*, 32.

37. Although Byerly writes that music and mesmerism often were associated in the Victorian period, and that "Mr. Arrowpoint's refusal to countenance Klesmer's engagement to [Catherine Arrowpoint] is part of a larger social attitude in which music masters had come to represent a variety of seductive foreign influences," she discusses Klesmer in the familiar terms of foreigner and Jew, not mesmerist (*Realism, Representation, and the Arts*, 139–41).

38. Ruth Solie's "'Tadpole Pleasures': *Daniel Deronda* as Music Historiography" (*Yearbook of Comparative and General Literature* 45/46 [1997/1998]: 87–104) is enlightening on the ways the novel stages the contemporary debate "between Wagnerian progressivism and the gradual formation of a musical canon" (87).

39. George Eliot, *Felix Holt, The Radical*, ed. Fred C. Thomson (Oxford: Clarendon, 1980), 11.

40. Alexander Welsh, *George Eliot and Blackmail* (Cambridge, Mass.: Harvard University Press, 1985), 264–65.

41. Graham Handley, "Introduction," *Daniel Deronda*, ed. Graham Handley (Oxford: Oxford University Press, 1998), xxi.

42. Garrett Stewart, *Reading Voices: Literature and the Phonotext* (Berkeley: University of California Press, 1990), 214. Stewart discusses Grandcourt's interactions as "an effete depreciation of all converse" and also considers the "phonotextual" aspects of the language of *Deronda* (214–16).

43. George Eliot, *Armgart*, in *Collected Poems*, ed. Lucien Jenkins (London: Skoob, 1989), 144. Rosemarie Bodenheimer reads Armgart's loss of voice as reflecting Eliot's anxiety that she would not be able to write as well as she had (anxiety Eliot conquered with nothing less than *Middlemarch*), in *The Real Life of Mary Ann Evans: George Eliot, Her Letters and Fiction* (Ithaca, N.Y.: Cornell University Press, 1994), 178–79.

44. Gillian Beer, *George Eliot* (Bloomington: Indiana University Press, 1986), 10. Beer characterizes the silences of *Deronda* as "a terrifying seal over the crowded and various

discourses of the text," a view elaborated by other commentators (214). See, for example, Ellen B. Rosenman, who claims that *Deronda* stages "the silencing of the woman" and that Gwendolen's "silence is its own sort of language, signifying an inner self that remains inaccessible," in "Women's Speech and the Role of the Sexes in *Daniel Deronda*," *Texas Studies in Language and Literature* 31 (1989): 237, 241. Royle claims that Eliot's "texts repeatedly evoke and question the perception of silence, and of something other, within or beyond it," that *Deronda* "works in silence," that such workings are "more complex and more strange" in this final novel, and that for these and other reasons, "it is no longer possible to think of this text as a 'novel,'" since the text "scarcely understands what it is doing"; it is rather "a hypnopoetics, a foresight-sympathy-saga-machine of a passionate vision of possibilities" (*Telepathy and Literature*, 91, 109). Finally, for a legal studies approach that reads Eliot's silences in the context of Victorian Divorce Court proceedings and the wake of the 1857 Divorce Act, with particular attention to Gwendolen's silence in *Deronda*, see Andrew Dowling, "'The Other Side of Silence': Matrimonial Conflict and the Divorce Court in George Eliot's Fiction," *Nineteenth-Century Literature* 50 (1995): 322–36.

45. John Cage, *Silence* (Middletown, Conn.: Wesleyan University Press, 1961), 51. A good discussion of *4'33"* is in Douglas Kahn's "John Cage: Silence and Silencing," in his *Noise Water Meat: A History of Sound in the Arts* (Cambridge, Mass.: MIT Press, 1999), 161–99.

46. Leavis's classic treatment of *Deronda* is in *The Great Tradition* (London: Chatto and Windus, 1948), 79–125, in which he desires to discard the "bad Jewish half" and rechristen (in both senses) the remainder *Gwendolen Harleth*. He belatedly recanted in a 1960 *Commentary* article, "George Eliot's Zionist Novel," reprinted as the introduction to the 1961 Harper edition of *Deronda*. James's "*Daniel Deronda*: A Conversation" has been reprinted as an appendix to *The Great Tradition* (249–66) and first appeared in *Atlantic Monthly* 38 (December 1876): 684–94.

47. Michael Ragussis argues for the importance of ideas of conversion in the novel, claiming that Daniel, in fact, "converts" Gwendolen over the course of their conversations: "we must read Deronda's story as a conversion story" (*Figures of Conversion: The Jewish Question & English National Identity* [Durham, N.C.: Duke University Press, 1995], 269, 286).

48. In an argument that centers on Mordecai as a telepathic medium in the novel, Royle discusses "the Daniel-Mirah-Mordecai triad" and Mordecai's Wordsworthian echoes (*Telepathy and Literature*, 98–102). I prefer to focus on a different triad, however, that, with Daniel at its center, creates for the novel a kind of cohesion that in the Leavisite critical tradition has been denied it.

49. Not, as some scholars have suggested, from "Vocalism," which was a later version of "Voices" that appeared after *Deronda* was published. In the first appearance of the poem in the 1860 *Leaves of Grass*, "Voices" was simply titled "No. 21" in a "Leaves of Grass" cluster, and did not become "Voices" until the 1872 edition. "Vocalism" was a fusion of two poems, "To Oratists" and "Voices," that first appeared in the edition of *Leaves of Grass* published the year after Eliot died. "To Oratists" and "Voices" had been included separately in the 1872 and 1876 editions, and "Voices" was in the 1868 London edition of Whitman's poems edited by W. M. Rossetti that Eliot likely owned. Eliot had quoted from *Leaves of Grass* in a review in an 1856 *Westminster Review* and apparently read (or reread) the volume in 1871. See the commentary on "Vocalism" in Walt Whitman, *Leaves of Grass: Comprehensive Reader's Edition*, ed. Harold W. Blodgett and Sculley Bradley (New York: New York University Press, 1965), 383 n, and the text of the poem

on 383–84, as well as in Walt Whitman, *Leaves of Grass: A Textual Variorum of the Printed Poems, Volume II: Poems, 1860–1867*, ed. Sculley Bradley, Harold W. Blodgett, Arthur Golden, and William White (New York: New York University Press, 1980), 308–10.

50. George Eliot to John Blackwood, 18 April 1876, *George Eliot Letters* 6:241 and n. 5.

51. Whitman, "Vocalism" (from the section formerly titled "Voices"), *Leaves of Grass: Comprehensive Reader's Edition*, 384, ll. 16–17.

52. Welsh, *George Eliot and Blackmail*, 264; Brooks, *Body Work*, 226.

53. Bodenheimer, *The Real Life of Mary Ann Evans*, 183. Alison Booth claims that *Deronda* combines religious and cultural history with the theatricals of the novel of manners, in *Greatness Engendered: George Eliot and Virginia Woolf* (Ithaca, N.Y.: Cornell University Press, 1992), 236.

54. James Mackay, *Alexander Graham Bell: A Life* (New York: Wiley, 1997), 75; Bell, quoted in Edwin S. Grosvenor and Morgan Wesson, *Alexander Graham Bell: The Life and Times of the Man Who Invented the Telephone* (New York: Abrams, 1997), 44.

55. Quoted in Ellen Stern and Emily Gwathmey, *Once Upon a Telephone: An Illustrated Social History* (New York: Harcourt Brace, 1994), 3. Avital Ronell claims that in his erroneous translation, Bell "had given Helmholtz a *hysterical* reading," in *The Telephone Book: Technology—Schizophrenia—Electric Speech* (Lincoln: University of Nebraska Press, 1989), 287.

56. This substantially abridged summary is taken from narratives of the famous story in Mackay, *Bell*, 92–129; Robert V. Bruce, *Bell: Alexander Graham Bell and the Conquest of Solitude* (Boston: Little, Brown, 1973), 122–45; and Rosario Joseph Tosiello, *The Birth and Early Years of the Bell Telephone System, 1876–1880* (New York: Arno, 1979), 4–11. James Lastra notes that Bell derived his telephone experiments from the "die-hard physiologist" Helmholtz's resonance theory of hearing, in *Sound Technology and the American Cinema: Perception, Representation, Modernity* (New York: Columbia University Press, 2000), 22, 40. Bell's interest in Helmholtz is also mentioned by Jonathan Sterne, amid a detailed consideration of later nineteenth-century sound reproduction technologies as "tympanic," with particular reference to Bell's work on the ear phonautograph, an ancestor of the telephone that required a real human ear in its mechanism, and in doing so treated the ear "*as a* mechanism," as "the source and object of sound reproduction"; according to Sterne, "Not only were the modern sound media *for* the ear, they were *of* the ear" ("A Machine to Hear for Them: On the Very Possibility of Sound's Reproduction," *Cultural Studies* 15 [2001]: 266, 260, 264).

57. William Thomson, "The British Association: Opening Address by Prof. Sir William Thomson," *Nature* 14 (14 September 1876): 427.

58. A. Graham Bell, "The Telephone," *Journal of the Society of Arts* 26 (1877–1878): 19.

59. Mackay, *Bell*, 169–73; "The Telephone at Windsor," *Times*, 16 February 1878, 5; William Tegg, *Posts & Telegraphs, Past and Present* (London: Tegg, 1878), 308–10; *The History of Bell's Telephone*, ed. Kate Field (London: Bradbury, Agnew, 1878), 64–65.

60. Peter Young, *Person to Person: The International Impact of the Telephone* (Cambridge: Granta, 1991), 11–13, 16; "Edison's Loud-Speaking Telephone," *Illustrated London News* 75 (15 November 1879): 462, 465; George Henry Lewes Diary, London, 20–21 March 1878, *George Eliot Letters* 7:16.

61. Kate Field, "Recollections by Kate Field," *New York Daily Tribune*, 24 December 1880, 5.

62. Baker's commentary, in George Henry Lewes, *The Letters of George Henry Lewes*, ed. William Baker (Victoria: ELS Monograph Series 65, 1995), 2:210.

63. George Eliot to Charles Ritter, 22 May 1878, *George Eliot Letters* 7:28. Eliot already had expressed wry curiosity about the other great acoustic invention of the period in a letter to Mme. Eugène Bodichon, 17 January 1878: "What do you say to the Phonograph, which can report gentlemen's bad speeches with all their stammering?" (7:7).

64. Bell in a letter to his father, 1 July 1875, quoted in Grosvenor and Wilson, *Alexander Graham Bell*, 62.

65. Henry James, unsigned notice in the *Nation* (24 February 1876), reprinted in *George Eliot: The Critical Heritage*, ed. David Carroll (London: Routledge, 1971), 363. James's use of the telegraph in his own work is discussed by John Carlos Rowe in "Spectral Mechanics: Gender, Sexuality, and Work in *In the Cage*," in Rowe's *The Other Henry James* (Durham, N.C.: Duke University Press, 1998), 155–80. For the ways in which James would come to assimilate the effects of telegraphy into his literary mode, see Richard Menke, "Telegraphic Realism: Henry James's *In the Cage*," *PMLA* 115 (2000): 975–90.

66. Interestingly, the first permanent transatlantic telegraph connection was established, after several expensive failures, in July 1866, during the period in which the novel is set, which speaks to the notable transatlanticism of *Deronda*, encompassed in the narrator's famous reference to the American Civil War as a means to situate Gwendolen's consciousness within an international context. Once more the narrator resorts to the language of aurality: this was "a time when the soul of man was waking to pulses which had for centuries been beating in him unheard" (*Deronda*, 109). In an argument that links the act of vivisection with the art of fiction and that concludes Gwendolen "conveys the impression of being animate, pre-existent, and available for vivisection," Richard Menke notes the restoration in the Clarendon edition of the novel of Eliot's earlier "unheard" for "unfelt," which he considers "an emendation confirmed by the connections Eliot and Lewes drew between the novelist and the listening physiologist" ("Fiction as Vivisection: G. H. Lewes and George Eliot," *ELH* 67 [2000]: 646, 641). I would add that the aural dimensions of technology as well as physiology are at play here: not only does the language hearken back to (at the same time that it broadens the implications of) the sympathetically resonant "heart-pulses that are beating under the mere clothes of circumstance and opinion" in "Janet's Repentance," but the temporal and geographic specificity of the passage also suggests a resonance with the "pulses" of the previously "unheard" transatlantic telegraph. The international reach of the telegraph in this period also relates, of course, to Britain's imperial concerns; on this topic, see Bruce J. Hunt, "Doing Science in a Global Empire," in *Victorian Science in Context*, ed. Bernard Lightman (Chicago: University of Chicago Press, 1997), 312–33.

67. Welsh, *George Eliot and Blackmail*, 53–58, 263.

68. The quoted phrases are Steven Connor's, from his discussion of the sexual and cultural significance of the telephone in *Dumbstruck: A Cultural History of Ventriloquism* (Oxford: Oxford University Press, 2000), 381, 382.

69. Ernest Jones, *The Life and Work of Sigmund Freud*, 3 vols. (New York: Basic, 1953–1957), 1:36.

70. Peter Gay, *Freud: A Life for Our Time* (New York: Norton, 1988), 34.

71. Sigmund Freud to Martha Bernays, 28 October 1883, quoted in Jones, *The Life and Work of Sigmund Freud*, 1:41.

72. Sigmund Freud to Martha Bernays, 26 August 1882, quoted in Jones, *The Life and Work of Sigmund Freud*, 1:174.

73. Marc Redfield, *Phantom Formations: Aesthetic Ideology and the Bildungsroman* (Ithaca, N.Y.: Cornell University Press, 1996), 135.

74. Sigmund Freud, "Recommendations to Physicians Practising Psycho-Analysis" (1912), in *The Standard Edition of the Complete Psychological Works of Sigmund Freud*, trans. James Strachey (London: Hogarth, 1953–1974), 12:115–16.

75. The lingering influence of mesmerism on psychoanalysis also lies behind Freud's analogy: the image of sympathetically vibrating strings and the "corps sonore" had been used to characterize the magnetizer-subject relationship (see n. 18 and Weliver, *Women Musicians in Victorian Fiction*, 67–71).

76. Friedrich Kittler, *Discourse Networks 1800/1900*, trans. Michael Metteer, with Chris Cullens (Stanford, Calif.: Stanford University Press, 1990), 284. Freud had a telephone in his flat as early as 1895, according to Young, *Person to Person*, 52.

77. Bernhard Seigert, "Switchboards and Sex: The Nut(t) Case," in *Inscribing Science: Scientific Texts and the Materiality of Communication*, ed. Timothy Lenoir (Stanford, Calif.: Stanford University Press, 1998), 87.

78. Brooks, *Body Work*, 278. Considering this point from a wider perspective, Eliot's and Freud's attraction to telephonic converse and metaphors partly can be attributed to the greater appeal electric technologies have tended to have during what W. Bernard Carlson has called "cultural traumas." See his "Electrical Inventions and Cultural Traumas: The Telephone in Germany and America, 1860–1880," in *Elektrizität in der Geistesgeschichte*, ed. Klaus Plitzner (Bassum: Verlag für Geschichte der Naturwiss. und der Technik, 1998), 143–54.

79. The prominent placement of "Impressions" in the title suggests Eliot's ongoing preoccupation with the aesthetic challenge presented by physiological processes—with "discovering impressions heretofore obscure and unknown," to use Sully's phrase from his "Recent Experiments with the Senses."

80. He also was interested in having an income while accumulating rejection letters from publishers (Bernard Shaw, *The Irrational Knot* [New York: Brentano's, 1905], x–xi).

81. Michael Holroyd, *Bernard Shaw* (New York: Random House, 1988), 1:77–78. In the preface to *Pygmalion*, Shaw notes his growing interest in phonetics in the late 1870s, his knowledge of Alexander Melville Bell, Bell's father and inventor of Visible Speech, and his acquaintance with the "London patriarch" Alexander J. Ellis, who had suggested the younger Bell read Helmholtz in the first place ([New York: Penguin, 2000], 6).

82. William Baker, "A New George Eliot Manuscript," *George Eliot: Centenary Essays and an Unpublished Fragment*, ed. Anne Smith (Totowa, N.J.: Barnes and Noble, 1980), 10. Baker speculates that the fragment was written between either early 1877 and mid-1878 or mid-1879 and late 1880.

CHAPTER 4

1. Alfred Tennyson, *The Poems of Tennyson*, 2nd ed., ed. Christopher Ricks (Berkeley: University of California Press, 1987), 2:130; hereafter cited in text by volume, page numbers, and/or line.

2. One of the best studies of machines in modernist writing is Hugh Kenner's *The Mechanic Muse* (New York: Oxford University Press, 1987). Kenner does not discuss the phonograph; he does, however, discuss the disembodied voice in relation to the spread of the telephone, characterizing the heteroglossic *The Waste Land* as a "telephone poem" (36).

3. Virginia Woolf, *Between the Acts* (New York: Harcourt Brace, 1941), 97–98. Representations of the gramophone and of sound in Woolf's work are beginning to receive

fuller attention. See Michele Pridmore-Brown, "1939–40: Of Virginia Woolf, Gramophones, and Fascism," *PMLA* 113 (1998): 408–21, and Bonnie Kime Scott, "The Subversive Mechanics of Woolf's Gramophone in *Between the Acts*," in *Virginia Woolf in the Age
of Mechanical Reproduction*, ed. Pamela L. Caughie (New York: Garland, 2000), 97–113.
For a sustained study of the "menacing sounds" of the early novels and the "hollow
echoes and apocalyptic sounds" of the later work, see Marilyn Kurtz's two chapters on
these subjects in her *Virginia Woolf: Reflections and Reverberations* (New York: Lang,
1990), 53–114, and for a different perspective, see Melba Cuddy-Keane, "Virginia Woolf,
Sound Technologies, and the New Aurality," in *Virginia Woolf in the Age of Mechanical
Reproduction*, ed. Caughie, 69–96.

4. I do not mean to suggest that literary responses to the telegraph and telephone
were less profound, only different in nature. For an excellent overview of the cultural significance of the telegraph, see Jay Clayton's "The Voice in the Machine: Hazlett, Hardy,
James," in *Language Machines: Technologies of Literary and Cultural Production*, ed. Jeffrey
Masten, Peter Stallybrass, and Nancy Vickers (New York: Routledge, 1997), 209–32.

5. Arthur Symons, "The Decadent Movement in Literature," *Harper's New Monthly
Magazine* 87 (1893): 867.

6. Evan Eisenberg, *The Recording Angel: Explorations in Phonography* (New York:
McGraw-Hill, 1987), 54, 57. In *Recorded Music in American Life: The Phonograph and Popular Memory, 1890–1945* (New York: Oxford University Press, 1999), William Howland
Kennedy attempts to challenge Eisenberg's "isolationist" model of phonograph listening by looking at the ways solitary listeners were in fact playing the same commercially
recorded cylinders at the same time and by considering the ways the repetitive function of the phonograph enabled an "enhanced sense of mastery" (3–4). Yet, as I argue in
this chapter, the private listening rituals need to be considered alongside private
recording rituals that resulted in the loss of, or at least in challenges to, some of the
forms of "mastery" late Victorians sought.

7. Ivan Kreilkamp, "A Voice without a Body: The Phonographic Logic of *Heart of
Darkness*," *Victorian Studies* 40 (1997): 237. Kreilkamp's article appeared as I was re-
searching and writing this, and it will be evident that I am indebted to it toward the end
of the chapter, though our differences are marked. While Kreilkamp deals exclusively
with Conrad's novella, I attempt to consider it alongside a longer line of literary, visual,
and historical representations of the phonograph that helped shape it.

8. Frank Andrews, *The Edison Phonograph: The British Connection* (London: City of
London Phonograph and Gramophone Society, 1986), xi; *Times* (London), 17 January
1878, 4; George L. Frow, "The Cylinder Phonograph in Great Britain," *Phonographs and
Gramophones: A Symposium* (Edinburgh: Royal Scottish Museum, 1977), 49.

9. "The Phonograph at the Royal Institution," *Graphic* 17 (16 March 1878): 259,
262, 268.

10. Thomas A. Edison, "The Phonograph and Its Future," *North American Review*
126 (1878): 530. In a superb theoretical approach to sound technology and the origins of
film in this period, James Lastra traces the development of "writing and simulation,"
which he identifies as "the master tropes through which the nineteenth century sought
to come to grips with the newness of technologically mediated sensory experience"
(*Sound Technology and the American Cinema: Perception, Representation, Modernity* [New
York: Columbia University Press, 2000], 21). He discusses the long history of the use of
the term "fugitive" in scientific discourse and claims that there was a shift from hearing
noise to hearing sound over the course of the century, characterized as "a counter-intellectual, counter-hierarchical sensitivity to the fugitive, the ephemeral, 'the back-

ground'" (48). In English literature, something like this is apparent in George Eliot's fiction from *Scenes of Clerical Life* on, though in her case one would be reluctant to call it "counter-intellectual" (see chapter 3 of this book).

11. Edison, "The Phonograph and Its Future," 533–34. Edison's interest in preserving the last words of dying men meant that to be asked to record was, in a sense, to be given a death sentence—rather, to be asked to supply one for oneself.

12. Thomas A. Edison, "The Perfected Phonograph," *North American Review* 146 (1888): 646–47; 649–50. Did Edison have in mind an eight-minute version of *Nickleby?* To get a sense of how exaggerated his claim was, consider that an unabridged audiobook edition of the novel (read by Alex Jennings [Audio Partners, 1998]) fills twenty-four cassettes and lasts thirty-six hours.

13. Oliver Read and Walter L. Welch, *From Tin Foil to Stereo: Evolution of the Phonograph*, 2nd ed. (Indianapolis: Sams, 1976), 137.

14. Jehu Junior [pseud.], "Men of the Day—No. CCCCXXI: Colonel George E. Gouraud," *Vanity Fair* 41 (13 April 1889): 269. The profile ended by noting that Gouraud was "a handsome, genial, warm-hearted host. His wife is pretty, amiable, engaging, and musical. He has sons at Harrow and in the nursery. He drives a tandem, and has his boots cleaned by electricity."

15. Robert Conot, *A Streak of Luck* (New York: Seaview, 1979), 270; Walter L. Welch and Leah Brodbeck Stenzel Burt, *From Tinfoil to Stereo: The Acoustic Years of the Recording Industry, 1877–1929* (Gainesville: University Press of Florida, 1994), 185 n. 4. In 1893, Gouraud earned the Congressional Medal of Honor for his performance at Honey Hill, South Carolina, 30 November 1864; the citation read, "While under severe fire of the enemy, which drove back the command, rendered valuable assistance in rallying the men."

16. Colonel Gouraud, "The Phonograph," *Journal of the Society of Arts* 37 (30 November 1888): 33. The imperial powers of the phonograph perhaps even deluded the publicist himself. According to George Frow, after falling out of favor with Edison much later on, Gouraud reputedly claimed toward the end of his life to be "Governor General of a 'do-it-yourself' empire in the Sahara Desert" ("The Cylinder Phonograph," 50). One of the last appearances of Gouraud that I have been able to trace, however, is in an 1898 report in the *New York Times* that indicates he was embarrassing the American Society in London with his fervent fund-raising efforts on behalf of an "Edison Chair of Science" for the proposed "Gordon Memorial College" to be founded in honor of the governor-general who had been killed in the siege of Khartoum in 1885. Gouraud died on 20 February 1912 in Vevey, Switzerland, one week after his son Bayard, captain of the Seventeenth Lancers, died on his way back to England from India. The author of the *New York Times* obituary wrote that "it is believed that the news of his son's death was the cause of the Colonel's sudden end" ("Col. George Gouraud Dead," *New York Times*, 20 February 1912, 3).

17. Friedrich Kittler, *Discourse Networks 1800/1900*, trans. Michael Metteer, with Chris Cullens (Stanford, Calif.: Stanford University Press, 1990), 236–38.

18. Quoted in Andrews, *The Edison Phonograph*, xiv–xv.

19. "The Phonograph's Salutation" was published in a commemorative sheet now housed in the Thomas A. Edison Papers, which also holds a transcription published in the British Press. Both Powers's and Edison's verses are in Read and Welch, *From Tin Foil to Stereo*, 413. Powers's poem later was collected in his *Lyrics of the Hudson* (Boston: Lothrop, 1891), 69–70, at which point he or his editor excised Gouraud's name and replaced "New trophies, Gouraud, yet are to be won" with "Well were your trophies

through the ages won." Gouraud provided a transcript of Edison's first phonogram to England in the *Standard* on 3o June 1888, in which he quotes the inventor as saying "Send me some good music from England," without a mention of Gladstone or balance sheets; but then again, it is more than likely Gouraud would have chosen to omit Edison's triplet in the interests of public relations (Edison Papers, [SC88] Unbound Clipping Series: 1888).

20. Quoted in "No Phonograms from Europe Yet," *New York Morning Sun*, July 1888, Edison Papers, Unbound Clipping Series: 1888.

21. Some of these recordings have been digitally remastered and one is available for listening on the Edison National Historic Site (ENHS) *Experimental Recordings* Web page: <http://www.nps.gov/edis/experimentgenre.htm> (as of 1 December 2002).

22. See the headnote to *The Captive* in *Seven Gothic Dramas, 1789–1825*, ed. Jeffrey N. Cox (Athens: Ohio University Press, 1992), 225.

23. Joseph Hatton, "An Irving Reminiscence," *In Jest and Earnest: A Book of Gossip* (London: Leandenhall, 1893), 135–37. It is not clear whether Irving changed the feminine pronoun to a "He" in his reading; without wanting to make too much out of his choice of text, it nevertheless is curious that he appeared to associate the phonograph, as Edison and businessmen did, with the feminine. Irving went on to make several cylinder recordings for Gouraud and others, including readings from *Richard III*, *Henry VIII*, and Tennyson's *Becket*. The Shakespeare excerpts are included on *Great Historical Shakespeare Recordings* (Naxos CD NA 220012).

24. "The Possibilities of the Phonograph. — By an Imaginative Artist," *Pall Mall Budget* 36 (16 August 1888): 19; "The First Interview Recorded by the Phonograph," *Pall Mall Gazette* 48 (24 July 1888): 2.

25. Steven Connor discusses the concurrent "evolution of ghost phenomena and the developing logic of technological communications" in the context of nineteenth-century spiritualism in "A Gramophone in Every Grave," in his *Dumbstruck: A Cultural History of Ventriloquism* (Oxford: Oxford University Press, 2000), 362–93.

26. A transcription of Collins's letter, addressed from Wimpole Street where he had moved in February 1888, can be found in the Edison papers, [D885o] Document File Series — 1888: (D-88-5o). It was not included in the list of "Unpublished Letters," in *The Letters of Wilkie Collins*, ed. William Baker and William M. Clarke (Basingstoke, U.K.: Macmillan, 1999). Clarke discusses Collins's move and his ailing state in his *The Secret Life of Wilkie Collins* (London: Allison and Busby, 1988), 181–84.

27. Despite rumors to the contrary, two recordings of Gladstone were made (the first on 22 November and the second on 18 December 1888), and at least one copy of the second of Gladstone's messages is available at the ENHS; a transcript is in the Edison Papers and was published in "Mr. Gladstone and Mr. Edison," *Times*, 11 January 1889, 5. According to Francis Arthur James, Powers's "The Phonograph's Salutation" was "said to have received the commendations of Mr. Gladstone himself" (*Thomas Alva Edison: Sixty Years of an Inventor's Life* [New York: Crowell, 1908], 155). Rumors continue to fly about the authenticity of "lost" recordings of other eminent Englishmen and women made during the 1880s and 1890s. A record that had long been thought to be of Oscar Wilde has been shown to be a fake, but the jury is still out on an 1888 cylinder supposedly of Queen Victoria reciting, bizarrely, what may just be the word "tomatoes." See Paul Tritton, *The Lost Voice of Queen Victoria* (London: Academy, 1991). Readers also can judge for themselves: the "Wilde" and Victoria recordings are included on the CD accompanying *Aural History: Essays on Recorded Sound* (London: National Sound Archive, British Library, 2001).

28. Lowell's letter to Gouraud, dated 31 March 1890, is bound with the Gladstone Correspondence in the British Library, Add. 44509, f. 291. His letter to James is dated four days earlier and was published in *New Letters of James Russell Lowell*, ed. M. A. De-Wolfe Howe (New York: Harper and Brothers, 1932), 336.

29. The significance of the Browning cylinder, in part, was as an ethnographic index; that is, the use to which it was put reflected what Erika Brady describes as the late-nineteenth-century obsession "at both the intellectual and the popular level with the acquisition and display of *indexic* items — objects directly connected, literally pointing to, and derived from their referent" (*A Spiral Way: How the Phonograph Changed Ethnography* [Jackson: University Press of Mississippi, 1999], 14).

30. Rudolf Lehmann, quoted in Michael Hancher and Jerrold Moore, "'The Sound of a Voice That Is Still': Browning's Edison Cylinder," *Browning Newsletter* 4 (1970): 22. As early as 1878, Preece had applied the words from Tennyson's "'Break, break, break'" to the phonograph: the "sound of a voice that is still" now "may be realized," he wrote (*The Phonograph; or, Speaking and Singing Machine, Invented and Patented by Thomas Alva Edison, with Extracts from the Principal Journals in England and America* [London: London Stereoscopic, 1878], 52).

31. The transcript is given in Hancher and Moore, "'The Sound of a Voice That Is Still,'" 25–26. I have adapted their version for use here, making some clarifications and alterations based on my own listening to the copy of the BBC cylinder recording held at the Library of Congress, call no. LWO 8527, reel 87. This is one of only a few complete copies available in the United States. A version is available on Disc 1 included with the collection edited by Elise Paschen and Rebekah Presson Mosby, *Poetry Speaks: Hear Great Poets Read Their Work from Tennyson to Plath* (Naperville, Ill.: Sourcebooks Mediafusion, 2001), but this copy omits Gouraud's introduction (which, as it turns out, is the most intelligible part of the recording).

32. H. R. Haweis, "Robert Browning's Voice," *Times*, 13 December 1890, 10. A summary of various accounts of the event can be found in Hancher and Moore, "'The Sound of a Voice That Is Still,'" 28–30.

33. Letter to Katharine Bradley, [December?] 1890, quoted in William S. Peterson, *Interrogating the Oracle: A History of the London Browning Society* (Athens: Ohio University Press, 1969), 29–30.

34. Bennett Maxwell, "The Steytler Recordings of Alfred, Lord Tennyson: A History," *Tennyson Research Bulletin* 3 (1980): 153. For this event, Gouraud also obtained recordings of Florence Nightingale and Kenneth Landfrey, the bugler at the charge, both of which are available on the LP *The Wonder of the Age: Mister Edison's New Talking Phonograph*, comp. Kevin Daly, Argo ZPR 122–23, and online (as of 1 December 2002) at *MSU Vincent Voice Library Sound Samples* <http://www.lib.msu.edu/vincent/samples.html>. The two Tennyson recordings Steytler obtained (an abbreviated "Charge of the Light Brigade" and "The Bugle Song" from *The Princess*) are available in edited form on Disc 1 accompanying *Poetry Speaks*, ed. Paschen and Mosby.

35. A nearly complete listing of the Tennyson cylinders is given in Sir Charles Tennyson's "The Tennyson Phonograph Records," *British Institute of Recorded Sound Bulletin* 3 (1956): 2–8; hereafter cited in text.

36. *Alfred, Lord Tennyson Reads from His Own Poems*, introduced by Sir Charles Tennyson, Craighill LP, TC 1; CRS audiocassette, CR 9000.

37. Philip Collins, *Reading Aloud: A Victorian Métier* (Lincoln: Tennyson Society, 1972), 4; Eric Griffiths, *The Printed Voice of Victorian Poetry* (Oxford: Clarendon, 1989).

38. Jed Rasula, "Understanding the Sound of Not Understanding," in *Close Listen-*

ing: Poetry and the Performed Word, ed. Charles Bernstein (New York: Oxford University Press, 1998), 234–35.

39. Robert Bernard Martin, *Tennyson: The Unquiet Heart* (Oxford: Clarendon, 1980), 574; Rasula, "Understanding," 235.

40. Bram Stoker, *Personal Reminiscences of Henry Irving* (New York: Macmillan, 1906), 1:220; hereafter cited in text.

41. Collins, *Reading Aloud*, 26.

42. Friedrich Kittler, *Gramophone Film Typewriter*, trans. Geoffrey Winthrop-Young and Michael Wutz (Stanford, Calif.: Stanford University Press, 1999), 83.

43. Mark Twain to William D. Howells, 4 April 1891, in *Mark Twain–Howells Letters: The Correspondence of Samuel L. Clemens and William D. Howells, 1872–1910*, ed. Henry Nash Smith and William M. Gibson (Cambridge, Mass.: Harvard University Press, 1960), 2:641.

44. Andrew Chatto to Mark Twain, 27 July 1888, quoted in Mark Twain, *Mark Twain's Notebooks & Journals*, ed. Frederick Anderson et al., 3 vols. to date (Berkeley: University of California Press, 1975–), 3:386–87 n. 292. Twain had telegrammed Edison from New York in May 1888, requesting an hour to test the phonograph, and in a letter a few days later told the inventor his experience was one of "vast satisfaction," ending on a note of punning desperation: "My case is pretty urgent and if you can give it a puissant push I shall be *unspeakably* obliged to you" (letter to Edison, 25 May 1888, Edison Papers, [D8805] Document File Series—1888: [D-88-05]; emphasis added). Gouraud quoted Twain as saying that he "'had been carrying a book round inside of himself for more than a year, delaying deliverance only through sheer dread of the labour of writing'" ("First Interview," *Pall Mall Gazette*, 2).

45. Mark Twain, *The American Claimant* (New York: Webster, 1892), 176–77. Hatton, meanwhile, expressed similar exasperation in a column entitled "Where Is the Phonograph?" in which he griped that "it would take a Babbage to calculate the miles of paragraphs that have been written in praise of the phonograph as a machine to idealize and lighten the work of the author, the journalist, the clerk, and the polite letter-writer," but still complained that he didn't have one yet (*In Jest and Earnest*, 134).

46. Quoted in Conot, *A Streak of Luck*, 109.

47. The definitive study of ventriloquy is Connor's *Dumbstruck*, which recounts the history of throwing voices from the ancients to the present.

48. John Michael Gibson and Richard Lancelyn Green, "Introduction," in their edition of *The Unknown Conan Doyle: Uncollected Stories* (London: Secker and Warburg, 1982), xviii.

49. [Arthur Conan Doyle], "The Voice of Science," *Strand Magazine* 1 (1891): 312; hereafter cited in text.

50. The association of voice machines with the feminine is explored by Avital Ronnell, who discusses the telephone as a "maternal machine" and the corporate symbol of "Ma Bell" as the remnants of "a woman's body retransmitted through judicial procedures"; she relates a curious anecdote in which a group of New England Puritans fought to have the telephone forbidden from placement in the bedroom because it was seen as a sexually invasive device (*The Telephone Book: Technology—Schizophrenia—Electric Speech* [Lincoln: University of Nebraska Press, 1989], 339, 280, 104). See also Tim Armstrong, who considers how modernism transformed women's bodies into machines, in *Modernism, Technology, and the Body: A Cultural Study* (Cambridge: Cambridge University Press, 1998), 159–83.

51. George Du Maurier, *Trilby*, ed. Elaine Showalter (Oxford: Oxford University

Press, 1998), 299. One Dr. William Channing had prophesized that "the electrotyped cylinders ... will be put into the hand-organs of the streets and we shall hear the actual voices of our best singers ground out at every corner!" (quoted in Preece, *The Phonograph*, 56). Du Maurier's *Punch* cartoon provides a subliminally sexual interpretation of this comment.

52. Charles Grivel, "The Phonograph's Horned Mouth," in *Wireless Imagination: Sound, Radio, and the Avant-Garde*, ed. Douglas Kahn and Gregory Whitehead (Cambridge, Mass.: MIT Press, 1992), 33. Villiers's *L'Eve future* has been translated as *Tomorrow's Eve* by Robert Martin Adams (Chicago: University of Illinois Press, 1982). Grivel discusses Villiers's work, as well as the phonograph in shorter fin-de-siècle works by Marcel Schwob and Alfred Jarry.

53. Felicia Miller Frank, *The Mechanical Song: Women, Voice, and the Artificial in Nineteenth-Century French Narrative* (Stanford, Calif.: Stanford University Press, 1995), 167. Verne's novel has been translated as *The Castle of the Carpathians* (London: Sampson Low, 1893), and more recently as *Carpathian Castle*, ed. I. O. Evans (New York: Ace, 1963). This was possibly the first literary representation of a phonograph used for musical purposes; it would have been timely, as the first commercial catalog of cylinder recordings was issued by Columbia only the previous year, with over one hundred musical selections, including marches, waltzes, voice and orchestra, instrumental duets, and ever-popular (because easy to record and reproduce) whistling (Roland Gelatt, *The Fabulous Phonograph, 1877–1977* [New York: Collier, 1977], 48).

54. Verne's combination of sound and image in the spectacle of the posthumous La Stilla prefigures motion pictures, as others have noted. See, especially, Ian Christie, "Early Phonograph Culture and Moving Pictures," and Tom Gunning, "Doing for the Eye What the Phonograph Does for the Ear," both in *The Sounds of Early Cinema*, ed. Richard Abel and Rick Altman (Bloomington: Indiana University Press, 2001), 7–8, 22–26. The analogy between the phonograph and the camera was common—the amateur photographer Lewis Carroll made the link, with the wisdom of technological experience: "Went to the 'Phonograph' again, at the end of the lecture, to hear the 'private audience' part.... It is a pity that we are not fifty years further on in the world's history, so as to get this wonderful invention in its *perfect* form. It is now in its infancy—the new wonder of the day, just as I remember Photography was about 1850" (entry for 13 August 1890, in *The Diaries of Lewis Carroll*, ed. Roger Lancelyn Green [London: Cassell, 1953], 2:479).

55. A. Conan Doyle, "The Story of the Japanned Box," *Strand Magazine* 17 (1899): 3; hereafter cited in text. The story was later included in his *Round the Fire Stories* (1908). Conan Doyle's final (and least effective) use of the "phonograph trick" was in "The Adventure of the Mazarin Stone," of questionable authorship and included in *The Case-Book of Sherlock Holmes* (1927): Holmes uses a gramophone record of his violin-playing as a decoy to outfox the villain.

56. T. A. L. Du Moncel, *The Telephone, the Microphone, and the Phonograph* (New York: Harper, 1879), 237.

57. Neil Baldwin, *Edison: Inventing the Century* (New York: Hyperion, 1995), 72–73 (emphasis in original); hereafter cited in text. Connor also mentions Edison's distinctive mode of hearing in *Dumbstruck*, 359.

58. Bram Stoker, *Dracula*, ed. Maurice Hindle (New York: Penguin, 1993), 51; hereafter cited in text.

59. Jennifer Wicke, "Vampiric Typewriting: *Dracula* and Its Media," *ELH* 59 (1992): 467.

60. Rainer Maria Rilke, "Primal Sound" (1919), in *Where Silence Reigns: Selected Prose*, trans. G. Craig Houston (New York: New Directions, 1978), 51–56. Kittler reprints Rilke's essay and discusses it at length in *Gramophone Film Typewriter*, 38–51.

61. According to Alfred Baker in *The Life of Sir Isaac Pitman* ([London: Sir Isaac Pitman and Sons, 1908], 355–71), the first edition of *Phonography* technically was the *second* edition of the system set forth in Pitman's *Stenographic Sound-Hand* (1837), which was the very first edition of Pitman's shorthand system; *Phonography* was incorporated in the title from the second (1840) edition on. In an odd convergence of the phonograph and phonography, in October 1891, the nearly eighty-year-old Pitman recorded an address to the National Phonographic Society in London, congratulating the first recipients of shorthand teacher certificates (Baker, *Life*, 284).

62. Garrett Stewart writes that Dracula's telepathic powers are "the necromantic counterpart of the new telegraphic and phonographic technologies of electrically displaced origin which labor together to outmode and obliterate him" (*Dear Reader: The Conscripted Audience in Nineteenth-Century British Fiction* [Baltimore, Md.: Johns Hopkins University Press, 1996], 379). I take up this doubling effect below.

63. In a valuable essay that often has been overlooked in criticism on *Dracula*, Kittler interestingly, though with less relevance to the tropes of the novel, claims Mina becomes "merely a sensor or radio transmitter" prefiguring British naval intelligence ("Dracula's Legacy," in *Literature, Media, Information Systems: Essays*, ed. John Johnston [Amsterdam: G+B Arts, 1997], 79, while in another context, Lisa Gitelman discusses the cultural significance of typewriting with reference to *Dracula*, particularly the peculiar "noiselessness" of the typewriter in conjunction with its eminent visibility. According to Gitelman, typewriters, phonographs, and shorthand systems all became "buffers between aural experience and inscribed fact" (*Scripts, Grooves, and Writing Machines: Representing Technology in the Edison Era* [Stanford, Calif.: Stanford University Press, 1999], 215–18).

64. Gelatt, *The Fabulous Phonograph*, 40.

65. Kittler, "Dracula's Legacy," 71, 73.

66. Stephen Arata, "The Occidental Tourist: Stoker and Reverse Colonization," *Fictions of Loss in the Victorian Fin de Siècle* (Cambridge: Cambridge University Press, 1996), 107–32.

67. In this I largely concur with Carol A. Senf, who argues that the novel "revolves, not around the conquest of Evil by Good, but on the similarities between the two" ("*Dracula*: The Unseen Face in the Mirror," *Journal of Narrative Technique* 9 [1979]: 160).

68. Garrett Stewart, "Modernism's Sonic Waver: Literary Writing and the Filmic Difference," in *Sound States: Innovative Poetics and Acoustical Technologies*, ed. Adalaide Morris (Chapel Hill: University of North Carolina Press, 1997), 241.

69. Kreilkamp, "A Voice without a Body," 227, 229.

70. Edward Said, *Culture and Imperialism* (New York: Knopf, 1993), 29.

71. Krielkamp, "A Voice without a Body," 233.

72. "The Phonograph in Africa," *New York Times*, 19 January 1885, 4. I am indebted to William Pietz's "The Phonograph in Africa: International Phonocentrism from Stanley to Sarnoff," in *Post-Structuralism and the Question of History*, ed. Derek Attridge, Geoff Bennington, and Robert Young (Cambridge: Cambridge University Press, 1987), 263–85, for drawing my attention to this article.

73. Pietz, "The Phonograph in Africa," 269–70. As Michael Taussig puts it in a different context, "to take the talking machine to the jungle . . . is to reinstall the mimetic faculty as mystery in the art of mechanical reproduction" (*Mimesis and Alterity: A Particular History of the Senses* [New York: Routledge, 1993], 208).

74. *The Federal Cylinder Project*, ed. Erika Brady et al. (Washington: Library of Congress, 1984), 1:3. See also Brady, *A Spiral Way*, 31, 54.

75. The opening installment of *Heart of Darkness* appeared, as it turned out, only one month after Conan Doyle's rather benign treatment of the machine in "The Story of the Japanned Box."

76. Joseph Conrad, *Heart of Darkness*, ed. Robert Hampson (New York: Penguin, 1995), 79; hereafter cited in text.

77. Kreilkamp calls Kurtz's last words "autonomous, detachable phonemes" that are inherently "quotable" ("A Voice without a Body," 211). The same might be said for any of the sound bites from the novella.

78. T. S. Eliot, "The Love Song of J. Alfred Prufrock," *Collected Poems 1909–1962* (San Diego: Harcourt, 1970), 4; William Faulkner, *Absalom, Absalom!* (New York: Random House, 1936), 378; Woolf, *Between the Acts*, 198.

79. T. S. Eliot, "The Hollow Men," *Collected Poems*, 81.

80. Clare Kahane, *Passions of the Voice: Hysteria, Narrative, and the Figure of the Speaking Woman* (Baltimore, Md.: Johns Hopkins University Press, 1995), 134.

81. Quoted in Peter Martland, *Since Records Began: EMI, the First Hundred Years* (Portland: Amadeus, 1997), 32. The most thorough documentation of Nipper and Barraud's painting can be found in *The Story of "Nipper" and the "His Master's Voice" Picture Painted by Francis Barraud* (Bournemouth: Talking Machine Review, 1983), by the (appropriately named) Leonard Petts.

82. Barraud, quoted in Petts, *The Story of "Nipper,"* n.p.

83. Taussig claims that "the power of this world-class logo lies in the way it exploits the alleged primitivism of the mimetic faculty" (*Mimesis and Alterity*, 213). Connor, however, notes that the replacement of the phonograph with a gramophone "is an interesting early proof of attempts to exercise a commercial mastery over the voice," but since his interest resides more in the connections that voice machines had with spiritualism, he focuses on the apocryphal story that the painting originally depicted Nipper on a coffin (*Dumbstruck*, 386–87). Gunning, meanwhile, writes that the painting "highlights th[e] ambivalence surrounding recorded sound," and that the image represents "the modern separation of the senses and its inherent confusions" ("Doing for the Eye," 27).

84. Or, as Eisenberg puts it, "That we feel like dumb animals before the phonograph, cocking our ears in consternation[?] That we are not masters of the voice, but the other way around?" (*The Recording Angel*, 63). According to Taussig, the image has been reinterpreted in Central American folk art as "The Cuna Talking Dog," which "magically endow[s] . . . the hound with the human faculties of the talking machine" (*Mimesis and Alterity*, 224).

85. For more on phonographs and gramophones as centerpieces of early home entertainment systems, see Holly Kruse, "Early Audio Technology and Domestic Space," *Stanford Humanities Review* 3 (1993): 1–14.

APPENDIX

1. Second version reads: "*Now publishing*,".

2. Manuscript excludes *American Notes* and lists the works in the following order, with number divisions and prices: *The Pickwick Papers*, about 32 numbers, 4s.; *Nicholas Nickleby*, 32 numbers, 4s.; *The Old Curiosity Shop*, 16 numbers, 2s.; *Barnaby Rudge*, 16 numbers, 2s.; *Martin Chuzzlewit*, 32 numbers, 4s.; *Sketches by Boz*, 28 numbers, 3s. 6d.; *Oliver Twist*, 16 numbers, 2s.

3. Second version reads: "was".

4. Second version reads: "in the course of publication,".

5. Second version reads: "CHEAP EDITION in no way clashes or interferes".

6. Second version reads: "add, constitute".

7. Second version reads: "was".

8. Second version adds: "JAMES MACLEOD, GLASGOW;".

9. On a separate sheet included with the prospectus manuscript, Dickens wrote this unused dedication, excerpted in John Forster's *Life of Charles Dickens*, ed. J. W. T. Ley (London: Palmer, 1928), 448–49:

> This "Cheap Edition" of my books
> Is dedicated to the English People.
> In whose approval, if the books be true in spirit,
> They will live:
> And out of whose memory, if they be false,
> They will very soon die.

London. March 1847.   [signed] Charles Dickens

✎ BIBLIOGRAPHY ✐

Ackroyd, Peter. *Dickens*. London: Sinclair-Stevenson, 1990.

Altick, Richard D. *The English Common Reader: A Social History of the Mass Reading Public, 1800–1900*. Chicago: University of Chicago Press, 1957.

———. "Four Victorian Poets and an Exploding Island." *Victorian Studies* 3 (1960): 249–60.

———. "Varieties of Readers' Response: The Case of *Dombey and Son*." *Yearbook of English Studies* 10 (1980): 70–94.

Andrews, Frank. *The Edison Phonograph: The British Connection*. London: City of London Phonograph and Gramophone Society, 1986.

Arata, Stephen. *Fictions of Loss in the Victorian Fin de Siècle*. Cambridge: Cambridge University Press, 1996.

Armstrong, Nancy. *Fiction in the Age of Photography: The Legacy of British Realism*. Cambridge, Mass.: Harvard University Press, 1999.

Armstrong, Tim. *Modernism, Technology, and the Body: A Cultural Study*. Cambridge: Cambridge University Press, 1998.

Atlas, Allan W. *The Wheatstone Concertina in Victorian England*. Oxford: Clarendon, 1996.

Attali, Jacques. *Noise: The Political Economy of Music*. Trans. Brian Massumi. Minneapolis: University of Minnesota Press, 1985.

Auerbach, Emily. *Maestros, Dilettantes, and Philistines: The Musician in the Victorian Novel*. New York: Lang, 1989.

Auerbach, Nina. "Dickens and Dombey: A Daughter After All." In *Romantic Imprisonment: Women and Other Glorified Outcasts*, 107–29. New York: Columbia University Press, 1986.

Aural History: Essays on Recorded Sound. London: National Sound Archive, British Library, 2001.

"Auscultation Extraordinary." *Lancet* (1829): 1.96.

Babbage, Charles. "A Chapter on Street Nuisances." In *Passages in the Life of a Philosopher*. Vol. 11 of *The Works of Charles Babbage*, ed. Martin Campbell-Kelly, 253–71. 11 vols. New York: New York University Press, 1989.

———. Correspondence, 1806–1871. British Library.

———. *The Ninth Bridgewater Treatise: A Fragment*. London: Murray, 1837.

———. *The Ninth Bridgewater Treatise: A Fragment*. Vol. 9 of *The Works of Charles Babbage*, ed. Martin Campbell-Kelly. New York: New York University Press, 1989.

Bacon, Francis. *Sylva Sylvarum: or, a Natural History*. Vol. 4 of *The Works of Francis Bacon, Lord Chancellor of England*, ed. Basil Montagu. 16 vols. London: William Pickering, 1825–1834.

Bailey, Peter. "Breaking the Sound Barrier." In *Popular Culture and Performance in the Victorian City*, 194–211. Cambridge: Cambridge University Press, 1998.
——. *Leisure and Class in Victorian England*. London: Routledge and Kegan Paul, 1978.
Bailin, Miriam. *The Sickroom in Victorian Fiction: The Art of Being Ill*. Cambridge: Cambridge University Press, 1994.
Baker, Alfred. *The Life of Sir Isaac Pitman*. London: Sir Isaac Pitman and Sons, 1908.
Baker, William. *George Eliot and Judaism*. Salzburg: Institut für Englische Sprache und Literatur, Universität Salzburg, 1975.
——. *The George Eliot–George Henry Lewes Library: An Annotated Catalogue of Their Books at Dr. Williams's Library, London*. New York: Garland, 1977.
——. "A New George Eliot Manuscript." In *George Eliot: Centenary Essays and an Unpublished Fragment*, ed. Anne Smith, 9–20. Totowa, N.J.: Barnes and Noble, 1980.
Baldwin, Neil. *Edison: Inventing the Century*. New York: Hyperion, 1995.
Ballantyne, R. M. *Blown to Bits; or, The Lonely Man of Rakata*. London: Nisbet, 1889.
Baron, Lawrence. "Noise and Degeneration: Theodor Lessing's Crusade for Quiet." *Journal of Contemporary History* 17 (1982): 165–78.
Bass, Michael T. *Street Music in the Metropolis: Correspondence and Observations on the Existing Law, and Proposed Amendments*. London: John Murray, 1864.
Baumgarten, Murray. "Railway/Reading/Time: *Dombey & Son* and the Industrial World." *Dickens Studies Annual* 19 (1990): 65–89.
Beales, Derek. *England and Italy, 1859–60*. London: Nelson, 1961.
Beer, Gillian. "'Authentic Tidings of Invisible Things': Vision and the Invisible in the Later Nineteenth Century." In *Vision in Context: Historical and Contemporary Perspectives on Sight*, ed. Teresa Brennan and Martin Jay, 85–98. New York: Routledge, 1996.
——. *Darwin's Plots: Evolutionary Narrative in Darwin, George Eliot and Nineteenth-Century Fiction*. London: Routledge and Kegan Paul, 1983.
——. *George Eliot*. Bloomington: Indiana University Press, 1986.
——. "Helmholtz, Tyndall, Gerard Manley Hopkins: Leaps of the Prepared Imagination." In *Open Fields: Science in Cultural Encounter*, 242–72. Oxford: Clarendon, 1996.
——. "Wave Theory and the Rise of Literary Modernism." In *Open Fields: Science in Cultural Encounter*, 295–318. Oxford: Clarendon, 1996.
Bell, A. Graham. "The Telephone." *Journal of the Society of Arts* 26 (1877–1878): 17–24.
Bernstein, Charles, ed. *Close Listening: Poetry and the Performed Word*. New York: Oxford University Press, 1998.
Berry, Laura C. "In the Bosom of the Family: The Wet-Nurse, the Railroad, and *Dombey and Son*." *Dickens Studies Annual* 25 (1996): 1–28.
Bodenheimer, Rosemarie. *The Real Life of Mary Ann Evans: George Eliot, Her Letters and Fiction*. Ithaca, N.Y.: Cornell University Press, 1994.
Booth, Alison. *Greatness Engendered: George Eliot and Virginia Woolf*. Ithaca, N.Y.: Cornell University Press, 1992.
Brady, Erika. *A Spiral Way: How the Phonograph Changed Ethnography*. Jackson: University Press of Mississippi, 1999.
Brady, Erika, et al. *The Federal Cylinder Project*. Washington, D.C.: Library of Congress, 1984.
Brewster, David. *Letters on Natural Magic Addressed to Sir Walter Scott, Bart*. New York: Harper and Brothers, 1843.
Brewster, Scott. "*Tintern*abulation: Poetry Ringing in the Ears." In *Sensual Reading: New Approaches to Reading and Its Relation to the Senses*, ed. Michael Syrotinski and Ian Maclachlin, 69–82. Lewisburg, Pa.: Bucknell University Press, 2001.

Brock, W. H. "The Selection of the Authors of the Bridgewater Treatises." *Notes and Records* 21 (1966): 162–79.

Brogan, T. V. F. "Sound." In *The New Princeton Encyclopedia of Poetry and Poetics*, ed. T. V. F. Brogan and Alex Preminger, 1172–80. Princeton, N.J.: Princeton University Press, 1993.

Brooks, Peter. *Body Work: Objects of Desire in Modern Narrative.* Cambridge, Mass.: Harvard University Press, 1993.

Browning, Robert. [How they brought the good news from Ghent to Aix: Robert Browining reciting the first four lines of his poem]. Library of Congress Recorded Sound Reference Center, LWO 8527, reel 87.

Bruce, Robert V. *Bell: Alexander Graham Bell and the Conquest of Solitude.* Boston: Little, Brown, 1973.

Burgan, Mary. "Heroines at the Piano: Women and Music in Nineteenth-Century Fiction." In *The Lost Chord: Essays on Victorian Music*, ed. Nicholas Temperley, 42–67. Bloomington: Indiana University Press, 1989.

Burnett, John. *A Social History of Housing, 1815–1985.* 2d ed. London: Methuen, 1986.

Butt, John, and Kathleen Tillotson. *Dickens at Work.* London: Methuen, 1957.

Buxton, H. W. *Memoir of the Life and Labours of the Late Charles Babbage Esq. F.R.S.* Ed. Anthony Hyman. Cambridge, Mass.: MIT Press; Los Angeles: Tomash, 1988.

Byerly, Alison. *Realism, Representation, and the Arts in Nineteenth-Century Literature.* Cambridge: Cambridge University Press, 1997.

Bynum, W. F. *Science and the Practice of Medicine in the Nineteenth Century.* Cambridge: Cambridge University Press, 1994.

Cage, John. *Silence.* Middletown, Conn.: Wesleyan University Press, 1961.

Cahan, David. "Introduction: Helmholtz at the Borders of Science." In *Hermann von Helmholtz and the Foundations of Nineteenth-Century Science*, ed. David Cahan, 1–13. Berkeley: University of California Press, 1993.

Calder, Jenni. *The Victorian Home.* London: Batsford, 1977.

Cannon, Walter. "The Problem of Miracles in the 1830's." *Victorian Studies* 4 (1960): 5–32.

Carlson, W. Bernard. "Electrical Inventions and Cultural Traumas: The Telephone in Germany and America, 1860–1880." In *Elektrizität in der Geistesgeschichte*, ed. Klaus Plitzner, 143–54. Bassum: Verlag für Geschichte der Naturwiss. und der Technik, 1998.

Carlyle, Jane Welsh. *Letters and Memorials of Jane Welsh Carlyle.* Ed. James Anthony Froude. 2 vols. London: Longmans, Green, 1883.

Carlyle, Thomas, and Jane Welsh Carlyle. *The Collected Letters of Thomas and Jane Welsh Carlyle*, ed. C. R. Sanders, K. J. Fielding, et al. 29 vols. to date. Durham, N.C.: Duke University Press, 1970– .

Carroll, Lewis. *The Complete Works of Lewis Carroll.* New York: Modern Library, 1936.

———. *The Diaries of Lewis Carroll.* Ed. Roger Lancelyn Green. 2 vols. London: Cassell, 1953.

[Chambers, Robert]. *Vestiges of the Natural History of Creation.* London: John Churchill, 1844.

Chase, Karen, and Michael Levenson. *The Spectacle of Intimacy: A Public Life for the Victorian Family.* Princeton: Princeton University Press, 2000.

"Cheap Literature," *British Quarterly Review* 29 (1 April 1859): 313–45.

Cheyette, Bryan. *Constructions of 'The Jew' in English Literature and Society: Racial Representations, 1875–1945.* Cambridge: Cambridge University Press, 1993.

Christ, Carol T., and John O. Jordan, eds. *Victorian Literature and the Victorian Visual Imagination*. Berkeley: University of California Press, 1995.

Christie, Ian. "Early Phonograph Culture and Moving Pictures." In *The Sounds of Early Cinema*, ed. Richard Abel and Rick Altman, 3–12. Bloomington: Indiana University Press, 2001.

Clark, Robert. "Riddling the Family Firm: The Sexual Economy in *Dombey and Son*." *ELH* 51 (1984): 69–84.

Clarke, Norma. "Strenuous Idleness: Thomas Carlyle and the Man of Letters as Hero." In *Manful Assertions: Masculinities in Britain since 1800*, ed. Michael Roper and John Tosh, 25–43. London: Routledge, 1991.

Clarke, William. *The Secret Life of Wilkie Collins.* London: Allison and Busby, 1988.

Clayton, Jay. "Hacking the Nineteenth Century." In *Victorian Afterlife: Postmodern Culture Rewrites the Nineteenth Century*, ed. John Kucich and Dianne F. Sadoff, 186–210. Minneapolis: University of Minnesota Press, 2000.

———. "The Voice in the Machine: Hazlett, Hardy, James." In *Language Machines: Technologies of Literary and Cultural Production*, ed. Jeffrey Masten, Peter Stallybrass, and Nancy Vickers, 209–32. New York: Routledge, 1997.

Clerk-Maxwell, James. "The Rede Lecture." *Nature* 18 (6 June 1878): 159–63.

Cohen, Jane R. *Charles Dickens and His Original Illustrators*. Columbus: Ohio State University Press, 1980.

Cohen, Robin. *Frontiers of Identity: The British and the Others*. London: Longman, 1994.

"Col. George Gouraud Dead." *New York Times*, 20 February 1912, 3.

Colby, Robert A. "That He Who Rides May Read: W. H. Smith & Son's Railway Library." *Wilson Library Bulletin* 27 (1952): 300–6.

Coleridge, Samuel Taylor. *The Friend*. Ed. Barbara E. Rooke. Vol. 4:1 of *The Collected Works of Samuel Taylor Coleridge*. London: Routledge and Kegan Paul, 1969.

[Collins, Charles]. "An Unreported Speech." *All The Year Round* 6 (16 November 1861): 179–81.

Collins, Philip. *Reading Aloud: A Victorian Métier*. Lincoln: Tennyson Society, 1972.

Colpi, Terri. *The Italian Factor: The Italian Community in Great Britain*. Edinburgh: Mainstream, 1991.

Connor, Steven. *Dumbstruck: A Cultural History of Ventriloquism*. Oxford: Oxford University Press, 2000.

———. "The Modern Auditory I." In *Rewriting the Self: Histories from the Renaissance to the Present*, ed. Roy Porter, 203–23. London: Routledge, 1997.

Conot, Robert. *A Streak of Luck*. New York: Seaview, 1979.

Conrad, Joseph. *Heart of Darkness*. Ed. Robert Hampson. New York: Penguin, 1995.

Corbin, Alain. *Village Bells: Sound and Meaning in the Nineteenth-Century French Countryside*. Trans. Martin Thom. New York: Columbia University Press, 1998.

Crary, Jonathan. *Techniques of the Observer: On Vision and Modernity in the Nineteenth Century*. Cambridge, Mass.: MIT Press, 1990.

Cuddy-Keane, Melba. "Virginia Woolf, Sound Technologies, and the New Aurality." In *Virginia Woolf in the Age of Mechanical Reproduction*, ed. Pamela L. Caughie, 69–96. New York: Garland, 2000.

Curtis, Gerard. *Visual Words: Art and the Material Book in Victorian England*. Aldershot, U.K.: Ashgate, 2002.

Dale, Peter Allan. *In Pursuit of a Scientific Culture: Science, Art, and Society in the Victorian Age*. Madison: University of Wisconsin Press, 1989.

Dalziel, Margaret. *Popular Fiction 100 Years Ago*. London: Cohen and West, 1957.

Darwin, Charles. *The Autobiography of Charles Darwin, 1809–1882*. Ed. Nora Barlow. New York: Norton, 1969.
——. *The Correspondence of Charles Darwin*. Ed. Frederick Burkhardt and Sydney Smith. 12 vols. to date. Cambridge: Cambridge University Press, 1985– .
Davidoff, Leonore. *The Best Circles: Society, Etiquette and the Season*. London: Cresset, 1986.
Davidoff, Leonore, and Catherine Hall. *Family Fortunes: Men and Women of the English Middle Class, 1780–1850*. Chicago: University of Chicago Press, 1987.
De Morgan, Sophia Elizabeth. *Memoir of Augustus De Morgan*. London: Longman, Green, 1882.
Derrida, Jacques. *Of Grammatology*. Trans. Gayatri Chakravorty Spivak. Baltimore, Md.: Johns Hopkins University Press, 1976.
Dickens, Charles. "Address in the Cheap Edition of *Pickwick Papers*. 1847." In *Collected Papers*, ed. Arthur Waugh, Hugh Walpole, Walter Dexter, and Thomas Hatton. 2 vols. Bloomsbury: Nonesuch, 1937. 2:64–66.
——. [Cheap editions of the works of Mr. Charles Dickens]. Autograph manuscript. Henry W. and Albert A. Berg Collection, New York Public Library.
——. *Dombey and Son*. Ed. Alan Horsman. Oxford: Clarendon, 1974.
——. *Dombey and Son*. Ed. Alan Horsman. With an introduction and notes by Dennis Walder. Oxford: Oxford University Press, 2001.
——. "A Flight." In *"Gone Astray" and Other Papers from Household Words 1851–59*, ed. Michael Slater, 26–35. London: Dent, 1998.
——. *The Letters of Charles Dickens*. Ed. Walter Dexter. 3 vols. Bloomsbury: Nonesuch, 1938.
——. *The Letters of Charles Dickens*. Pilgrim edition. Ed. Madeline House, Graham Storey, Kathleen Tillotson, et al. 12 vols. Oxford: Clarendon, 1965–2002.
——. "Mrs Lirriper's Lodgings." In *Christmas Stories*, ed. Ruth Glancy, 500–535. London: Dent, 1996.
——. *The Mystery of Edwin Drood*. Ed. Margaret Cardwell. Oxford: Clarendon, 1972.
——. *Our Mutual Friend*. Ed. Michael Cotsell. Oxford: Oxford University Press, 1989.
——. "A Preliminary Word." In *The Amusements of the People and Other Papers: Reports, Essays and Reviews 1834–51*, ed. Michael Slater, 175–79. London: Dent, 1996.
——. *The Public Readings*. Ed. Philip Collins. Oxford: Clarendon, 1975.
——. "Review: *The Rising Generation*." In *The Amusements of the People and Other Papers: Reports, Essays and Reviews 1834–51*, ed. Michael Slater, 142–47. London: Dent, 1996.
——. *The Speeches of Charles Dickens*. Ed. K. J. Fielding. Oxford: Clarendon, 1960.
——. "The Uncommercial Traveller: Night Walks." In *The Uncommercial Traveller and Other Papers 1859–70*, ed. Michael Slater and John Drew, 148–57. London: Dent, 2000.
Dickens, Charles, and Mark Lemon. "A Paper-Mill." In *Charles Dickens' Uncollected Writings from Household Words 1850–1859*, ed. Harry Stone. 2 vols. Bloomington: Indiana University Press, 1968. 1:137–42.
Dickens, Charles, and Wilkie Collins. "The Lazy Tour of Two Idle Apprentices." In *Christmas Stories*. Oxford Illustrated Dickens, 663–758. Oxford: Oxford University Press, 1956.
[Dodd, George]. "Music in Poor Neighborhoods." *Household Words* 12 (8 September 1858): 137–41.
Dowling, Andrew. "'The Other Side of Silence': Matrimonial Conflict and the Divorce Court in George Eliot's Fiction." *Nineteenth-Century Literature* 50 (1995): 322–36.

Doyle, Arthur Conan. "The Adventure of the Mazarin Stone." In *The Case-Book of Sherlock Holmes*, 75–97. London: Murray, 1927.

———. "The Story of the Japanned Box." *Strand Magazine* 17 (1899): 3–11.

———. *The Unknown Conan Doyle: Uncollected Stories*. Ed. John Michael Gibson and Richard Lancelyn Green. London: Secker and Warburg, 1982.

———. "The Voice of Science." *Strand Magazine* 1 (1891): 312–17.

Drinka, George Frederick. *The Birth of Neurosis: Myth, Malady, and the Victorians*. New York: Simon and Schuster, 1984.

Du Maurier, George. *Trilby*. Ed. Elaine Showalter. Oxford: Oxford University Press, 1998.

Du Moncel, T. A. L. *The Telephone, the Microphone, and the Phonograph*. New York: Harper, 1879.

Duncan, Ian. *Modern Romance and Transformations of the Novel: The Gothic, Scott, Dickens*. Cambridge: Cambridge University Press, 1992.

Dyos, H. J. "Some Historical Reflections on the Quality of Urban Life." In *Exploring the Urban Past: Essays in Urban History by H. J. Dyos*, ed. David Cannadine and David Reeder, 56–78. Cambridge: Cambridge University Press, 1982.

Edison National Historic Site (ENHS). *Experimental Recordings*. Online. Available: http://www.nps.gov/edis/experimentgenre.htm. 1 December 2002.

Edison, Thomas A. "The Perfected Phonograph." *North American Review* 146 (1888): 641–50.

———. "The Phonograph and Its Future." *North American Review* 126 (1878): 527–36.

"Edison's Loud-Speaking Telephone." *Illustrated London News* 75 (15 November 1879): 462–63, 465.

Eisenberg, Evan. *The Recording Angel: Explorations in Phonography*. New York: McGraw-Hill, 1987.

Eliot, George. *Collected Poems*. Ed. Lucien Jenkins. London: Skoob, 1989.

———. *Daniel Deronda*. Ed. Graham Handley. Oxford: Clarendon, 1984.

———. *Daniel Deronda*. Ed. Graham Handley. Oxford: Oxford University Press, 1998.

———. *Felix Holt, The Radical*. Ed. Fred C. Thomson. Oxford: Clarendon, 1980.

———. *The George Eliot Letters*. Ed. Gordon S. Haight. 9 vols. New Haven, Conn.: Yale University Press, 1954–1978.

———. *Impressions of Theophrastus Such*. Ed. Nancy Henry. London: Pickering, 1994.

———. *The Journals of George Eliot*. Ed. Margaret Harris and Judith Johnston. Cambridge: Cambridge University Press, 1998.

———. *The Lifted Veil*. London: Virago, 1985.

———. *Middlemarch*. Ed. David Carroll. Oxford: Clarendon, 1986.

———. *The Mill on the Floss*. Ed. Gordon Haight. Oxford: Clarendon, 1980.

———. *Romola*. Ed. Andrew Brown. Oxford: Clarendon, 1993.

———. *Scenes of Clerical Life*. Ed. Thomas A. Noble. Oxford: Clarendon, 1985.

———. *Some George Eliot Notebooks: An Edition of the Carl H. Pforzheimer Library's George Eliot Holograph Notebooks, MSS 707, 708, 709, 710, 711*. Ed. William Baker. 4 vols. Salzburg: Institut für Englisch Sprache und Literatur, Universität Salzburg, 1976–1985.

Eliot, T. S. *Collected Poems, 1909–1962*. San Diego: Harcourt, 1970.

———. *The Letters of T. S. Eliot*. Ed. Valerie Eliot. San Diego: Harcourt, 1988.

Field, Kate. "Recollections by Kate Field." *New York Daily Tribune*, 24 December 1880, 5.

Field, Kate, ed. *The History of Bell's Telephone*. London: Bradbury, Agnew, 1878.

"The First Interview Recorded by the Phonograph." *Pall Mall Gazette* 48 (24 July 1888): 1–2.

Flint, Kate. *The Victorians and the Visual Imagination*. Cambridge: Cambridge University Press, 2000.

Forster, John. *The Life of Charles Dickens*. Ed. J. W. T. Ley. London: Palmer, 1928.

Freeman, Michael. *Railways and the Victorian Imagination*. New Haven, Conn.: Yale University Press, 1999.

Freud, Sigmund. "Recommendations to Physicians Practising Psycho-Analysis." Vol. 12 of *The Standard Edition of the Complete Psychological Works of Sigmund Freud*, 109–20. Trans. James Strachey. London: Hogarth, 1953–1974.

Frith, W. P. *John Leech: His Life and Work*. 2 vols. London: Richard Bentley, 1891.

Froude, James Anthony. *Froude's Life of Carlyle*. Ed. and abr. John Clubbe. Columbus: Ohio State University Press, 1979.

Frow, George L. "The Cylinder Phonograph in Great Britain." *Phonographs and Gramophones: A Symposium*, 49–55. Edinburgh: Royal Scottish Museum, 1977.

Gager, Valerie. *Shakespeare and Dickens: The Dynamics of Influence*. Cambridge: Cambridge University Press, 1996.

Galilei, Galileo. *Dialogues Concerning Two New Sciences*. Trans. Henry Crew and Alfonso de Salvio. New York: McGraw-Hill, 1963.

Gane, Gillian. "The Hat, the Hook, the Eyes, the Teeth: Captain Cuttle, Mr. Carker, and Literacy." *Dickens Studies Annual* 25 (1996): 91–126.

Gay, Peter. *Freud: A Life for Our Time*. New York: Norton, 1988.

———. *The Naked Heart*. Vol. 4 of *The Bourgeois Experience, Victoria to Freud*. New York: Norton, 1995.

Gelatt, Roland. *The Fabulous Phonograph, 1877–1977*. New York: Collier, 1977.

Gilbert, W. S. *H.M.S. Pinafore*. In *The Savoy Operas*, 63–102. Ware, Hertfordshire: Wordsworth, 1994.

Gitelman, Lisa. *Scripts, Grooves, and Writing Machines: Representing Technology in the Edison Era*. Stanford, Calif.: Stanford University Press, 1999.

Gladstone, W. E. Gladstone Papers. General Correspondence, 1826–1898. The British Library.

Glover, Stephen, and J. E. Carpenter. "What Are the Wild Waves Saying?" 1849.

Glover, Stephen, and Richard Ryan. "A Voice from the Waves." 1851.

Goodman, D. C. "Wollaston, William Hyde." *Dictionary of Scientific Biography*, vol. 14, 486–94. Ed. Charles Coulston Gillispie. New York: Scribner's, 1976.

Gouk, Penelope. "Some English Theories of Hearing in the Seventeenth Century: Before and After Descartes." In *The Second Sense: Studies in Hearing and Musical Judgment from Antiquity to the Seventeenth Century*, ed. Charles Burnett, Michael Fend, and Penelope Gouk, 95–113. London: The Warburg Institute, 1991.

Gouraud, Colonel. "The Phonograph." *Journal of the Society of Arts* 37 (30 November 1888): 33.

Gourvish, T. R. "The Rise of the Professions." In *Later Victorian Britain, 1867–1900*, ed. T. R. Gourvish and Alan O'Day, 13–35. New York: St. Martin's, 1988.

Gray, Beryl. *George Eliot and Music*. New York: St. Martin's, 1989.

Green, David R. "Street Trading in London: A Case Study of Casual Labour, 1830–60." In *The Structure of Nineteenth-Century Cities*, ed. James H. Johnson and Colin G. Pooley, 129–51. London: Croom Helm, 1982.

Green-Lewis, Jennifer. *Framing the Victorians: Photography and the Culture of Realism*. Ithaca, N.Y.: Cornell University Press, 1996.

Greenwood, James. "The Private Life of a Public Nuisance." *London Society* 11 (1867): 223–33.

Griffiths, Eric. *The Printed Voice of Victorian Poetry*. Oxford: Clarendon, 1989.

Grivel, Charles. "The Phonograph's Horned Mouth." In *Wireless Imagination: Sound, Radio, and the Avant-Garde*, ed. Douglas Kahn and Gregory Whitehead, 31–61. Cambridge, Mass.: MIT Press, 1992.

Grosvenor, Edwin S., and Morgan Wesson. *Alexander Graham Bell: The Life and Times of the Man Who Invented the Telephone*. New York: Abrams, 1997.

Gunning, Tom. "Doing for the Eye What the Phonograph Does for the Ear." In *The Sounds of Early Cinema*, ed. Richard Abel and Rick Altman, 13–31. Bloomington: Indiana University Press, 2001.

Haight, Gordon. "George Eliot's Klesmer." In *Imagined Worlds: Essays on Some English Novels and Novelists in Honour of John Butt*, ed. Maynard Mack and Ian Gregor, 205–14. London: Methuen, 1968.

Haley, Bruce. *The Healthy Body and Victorian Culture*. Cambridge, Mass.: Harvard University Press, 1978.

Hall, N. John. *Trollope: A Biography*. Oxford: Oxford University Press, 1991.

[Halliday, Andrew]. "The Battle of the Barrels." *All the Year Round* 11 (11 June 1864): 421–24.

Hancher, Michael, and Jerrold Moore. "'The Sound of a Voice That Is Still': Browning's Edison Cylinder." *Browning Newsletter* 4 (1970): 21–33; 5 (1970): 10–18; 6 (1971): 8–39.

Hatfield, Gary. "Helmholtz and Classicism: The Science of Aesthetics and the Aesthetics of Science." In *Herman von Helmholtz and the Foundations of Nineteenth-Century Science*, ed. David Cahan, 522–58. Berkeley: University of California Press, 1993.

Hatton, Joseph. *In Jest and Earnest: A Book of Gossip*. London: Leandenhall, 1893.

Haweis, H. R. *Music and Morals*. New York: Harper, 1872.

——. "Robert Browning's Voice." *Times*, 13 December 1890, 10.

Hearder, Harry. *Cavour*. London: Longman, 1994.

Helmholtz, Hermann von. "The Physiological Causes of Harmony in Music." In *Selected Writings of Hermann von Helmholtz*, ed. Russell Kahl, 75–108. Middletown, Conn.: Wesleyan University Press, 1971.

——. *On the Sensations of Tone as a Physiological Basis for the Theory of Music*. Trans. from 3rd ed. (1870) by Alexander J. Ellis. London: Longmans, Green, 1875.

Henkle, Roger B. "The Crisis of Representation in *Dombey and Son*." In *Critical Reconstructions: The Relationship of Fiction and Life*, ed. Robert Polhemus and Roger B. Henkle, 90–110. Stanford, Calif.: Stanford University Press, 1994.

Herschel, J. F. W. "Sound." *Encyclopaedia Metropolitana*, 2d division, vol. 2, 747–824. Ed. Edward Smedley, Hugh James Rose, and Henry John Rose. London: Fellowes, 1845.

Hill, T. W. "The Staplehurst Railway Accident." *Dickensian* 38 (1942): 147–52.

Hill, Thomas. *Geometry and Faith: A Fragmentary Supplement to the Ninth Bridgewater Treatise*. New York: Francis, 1849.

Hitt, Jack. "Eavesdropping on History." *New York Times Magazine*, 3 December 2000, 132–36.

Hollander, John. *Images of Voice: Music and Sound in Romantic Poetry*. Cambridge: Heffer, 1970.

——. *Vision and Resonance: Two Senses of Poetic Form*. New York: Oxford University Press, 1975.

——. "Wordsworth and the Music of Sound." In *New Perspectives on Coleridge and Wordsworth*, ed. Geoffrey H. Hartman, 41–84. New York: Columbia University Press, 1972.

Holme, Thea. *The Carlyles at Home*. London: Oxford University Press, 1965.

Holmes, Colin. *John Bull's Island: Immigration and British Society, 1871–1971*. London: Macmillan Education, 1988.

Holmes, Oliver Wendell. *The Complete Poetical Works of Oliver Wendell Holmes*, ed. Horace E. Scudder. Boston: Houghton Mifflin, 1908.

Holroyd, Michael. *Bernard Shaw*. 4 vols. New York: Random House, 1988–1992.

Hood, Thomas. *The Complete Poetical Works of Thomas Hood*, ed. Walter Jerrold. London: Frowde, 1906.

Horton, Susan. *Interpreting Interpreting: Interpreting Dickens's* Dombey. Baltimore, Md.: Johns Hopkins University Press, 1979.

Houfe, Simon. *John Leech and the Victorian Scene*. Suffolk: Antique Collectors' Club, 1984.

House, Humphry. *The Dickens World*. London: Oxford University Press, 1941.

Hunt, Bruce J. "Doing Science in a Global Empire." In *Victorian Science in Context*, ed. Bernard Lightman, 312–33. Chicago: University of Chicago Press, 1997.

Hyman, Anthony. *Charles Babbage: Pioneer of the Computer.* Oxford: Oxford University Press, 1982.

Ingham, Patricia. *Dickens, Women, and Language*. Toronto: University of Toronto Press, 1992.

———. "Speech and Non-Communication in *Dombey and Son*." *Review of English Studies* 30 (1979): 144–53.

Jackson, Holbrook. "Listening to Reading." In *The Reading of Books*, 110–21. London: Faber and Faber, 1946.

Jacobs, Edward. "Disvaluing the Popular: London Street Culture, 'Industrial Literacy,' and the Emergence of Mass Culture in Victorian England." In *Victorian Urban Settings: Essays on the Nineteenth-Century City and Its Contexts*, ed. Debra N. Mancoff and D. J. Trela, 89–113. New York: Garland, 1996.

James, Francis Arthur. *Thomas Alva Edison: Sixty Years of an Inventor's Life*. New York: Crowell, 1908.

James, Henry. "*Daniel Deronda*: A Conversation." *Atlantic Monthly* 38 (December 1876): 684–94.

[———]. Unsigned notice in the *Nation* (24 February 1876). Reprinted in *George Eliot: The Critical Heritage*, ed. David Carroll, 363. London: Routledge, 1971.

Jay, Martin, ed. *Vision in Context: Historical and Contemporary Perspectives on Sight*. London: Routledge, 1996.

Johnson, Edgar. *Charles Dickens: His Tragedy and Triumph*. 2 vols. New York: Simon and Schuster, 1952.

Johnson, James H. *Listening in Paris: A Cultural History*. Berkeley: University of California Press, 1995.

Jones, Ernest. *The Life and Work of Sigmund Freud*. 3 vols. New York: Basic, 1953–1957.

Joseph, Gerhard. "Change and the Changeling in *Dombey and Son*." *Dickens Studies Annual* 18 (1989): 179–95.

Junior, Jehu [pseud.]. "Men of the Day—No. CCCCXXI: Colonel George E. Gouraud." *Vanity Fair* 41 (13 April 1889): 269.

Kahane, Clare. *Passions of the Voice: Hysteria, Narrative, and the Figure of the Speaking Woman*. Baltimore, Md.: Johns Hopkins University Press, 1995.

Kahl, Russell. "Introduction." In *Selected Writings of Hermann von Helmholtz*, ed. Russell Kahl, xii–xlv. Middletown, Conn.: Wesleyan University Press, 1971.

Kahn, Douglas. *Noise Water Meat: A History of Sound in the Arts*. Cambridge, Mass.: MIT Press, 1999.

Kahn, Douglas, and Gregory Whitehead, eds. *Wireless Imagination: Sound, Radio, and the Avant-Garde*. Cambridge, Mass.: MIT Press, 1992.

Kaplan, Fred. *Dickens: A Biography*. New York: William Morrow, 1988.

Kennedy, William Howland. *Recorded Music in American Life: The Phonograph and Popular Memory, 1890–1945*. New York: Oxford University Press, 1999.

Kenner, Hugh. *The Mechanic Muse*. New York: Oxford University Press, 1987.

Kittler, Friedrich. *Discourse Networks 1800/1900*. Trans. Michael Metteer, with Chris Cullens. Stanford, Calif.: Stanford University Press, 1990.

——. "Dracula's Legacy." In *Literature, Media, Information Systems: Essays*, ed. John Johnston, 50–84. Amsterdam: G+B Arts, 1997.

——. *Gramophone Film Typewriter*. Trans. Geoffrey Winthrop-Young and Michael Wutz. Stanford, Calif.: Stanford University Press, 1999.

Kleiner, M., and P. Astrom, "The Brittle Sound of Ceramics—Can Vases Speak?" *Archaeology and Natural Science* 1 (1993): 66–72.

Knight, Charles, ed. *London*. London: Charles Knight and Co., 1841.

Kramer, Lawrence. *Music and Poetry: The Nineteenth Century and After*. Berkeley: University of California Press, 1984.

Krasner, James. *The Entangled Eye: Visual Perception and the Representation of Nature in Post-Darwinian Narrative*. New York: Oxford University Press, 1992.

Kreilkamp, Ivan. "A Voice without a Body: The Phonographic Logic of *Heart of Darkness*." *Victorian Studies* 40 (1997): 211–43.

Kruse, Holly. "Early Audio Technology and Domestic Space." *Stanford Humanities Review* 3 (1993): 1–14.

Kurtz, Marilyn. *Virginia Woolf: Reflections and Reverberations*. New York: Lang, 1990.

Lamarck, Jean Baptiste. "Mémoire sur la matière du son." *An* 8 (1800). In *Hydrogéologie*, 225–58. Paris, *An* X (1802).

Lamb, Charles. "A Chapter on Ears." In *The Essays of Elia*, 44–49. London: Dent, 1923.

Lamb, Joseph F. "Symbols of Success in Suburbia: The Establishment of Artists' Communities in Late Victorian London." In *Victorian Urban Settings: Essays on the Nineteenth-Century City and Its Contexts*, ed. Debra N. Mancoff and D. J. Trela, 57–73. New York: Garland, 1996.

Lastra, James. *Sound Technology and the American Cinema: Perception, Representation, Modernity*. New York: Columbia University Press, 2000.

Leavis, F. R. *The Great Tradition*. London: Chatto and Windus, 1948.

——. Introduction to *Daniel Deronda*, by George Eliot. New York: Harper, 1961.

Leech, John. "The Organ-Grinding Nuisance." Letter. *Times*, 20 May 1864, 6.

Lewes, George Henry. "Dickens in Relation to Criticism." *Fortnightly Review* 17 (1872): 141–54.

——. *The Letters of George Henry Lewes*. Ed. William Baker. Victoria: ELS Monograph Series 65, 1995.

Lewis, Matthew G. *The Captive*. In *Seven Gothic Dramas, 1789–1825*. Ed. Jeffrey N. Cox, 225–30. Athens: Ohio University Press, 1992.

Ley, J. W. T. "John Leech: Dickens's Friendship with the Great 'Punch' Artist." *Dickensian* 13 (1917): 202–7.

Little, Jane Braxton. "Desperately Seeking Silence." *Audubon* 102 (January–February 2000): 70–73.

L[loyd], M[ary]. *"Sunny Memories," Containing Personal Recollections of Some Celebrated Characters*. London: Women's Printing Society, 1880.

London Physician. *The Nuisance of Street Music; or, A Plea for the Sick, the Sensitive, and the Studious*. London: Renshaw, 1869.

Loudon, James. "A Century of Progress in Acoustics." *Science*, n.s., 14 (27 December 1901): 987–95.

Lowell, James Russell. *New Letters of James Russell Lowell*. Ed. M. A. DeWolfe Howe. New York: Harper and Brothers, 1932.

Mack Smith, Denis. *Cavour*. New York: Knopf, 1985.

———. *Italy: A Modern History*. 2d ed. Ann Arbor: University of Michigan Press, 1969.

Mack Smith, Denis, ed. *The Making of Italy, 1796–1870*. New York: Walker and Company, 1968.

[Mackay, Charles]. "Music and Misery." *All The Year Round* 20 (15 August 1868): 230–33.

Mackay, James. *Alexander Graham Bell: A Life*. New York: Wiley, 1997.

Mackenzie, Norman, and Jeanne Mackenzie. *Dickens: A Life*. Oxford: Oxford University Press, 1979.

Maley, V. Carlton, Jr. *The Theory of Beats and Combination Tones, 1700–1863*. New York: Garland, 1990.

Mann, Karen B. *The Language That Makes George Eliot's Fiction*. Baltimore, Md.: Johns Hopkins University Press, 1983.

Marcus, Steven. *Dickens from Pickwick to Dombey*. New York: Basic, 1965.

Martin, Robert Bernard. *Tennyson: The Unquiet Heart*. Oxford: Clarendon, 1980.

Martland, Peter. *Since Records Began: EMI, the First Hundred Years*. Portland: Amadeus, 1997.

Matus, Jill M. "Trauma, Memory, and Railway Disaster: The Dickensian Connection." *Victorian Studies* 43 (2000/2001): 413–36.

Maxwell, Bennett. "The Steytler Recordings of Alfred, Lord Tennyson: A History." *Tennyson Research Bulletin* 3 (1980): 150–57.

Mayhew, Henry. *London Labour and the London Poor*. 1861. 3 vols. Reprint, New York: Dover, 1968.

McGann, Jerome J., ed. *The New Oxford Book of Romantic Period Verse*. Oxford: Oxford University Press, 1994.

McLandburgh, Florence. "The Automaton-Ear." *Scribner's Monthly* 5 (1872–1873): 711–20.

McSweeney, Kerry. *The Language of the Senses: Sensory Perceptual Dynamics in Wordsworth, Coleridge, Thoreau, Whitman, and Dickinson*. Montreal: McGill-Queen's University Press, 1998.

Medicus. "The Organ Nuisance." Letter. *Times*, 20 March 1851, 6.

Menke, Richard. "Fiction as Vivisection: G. H. Lewis and George Eliot." *ELH* 67 (2000): 617–53.

———. "Telegraphic Realism: Henry James's *In the Cage*." *PMLA* 115 (2000): 975–90.

"The Microphone." *Spectator* 51 (23 May 1878): 662–63.

Middleton, Richard. "Popular Music of the Lower Classes." In *The Romantic Age, 1800–1914*, ed. Nicholas Temperley, 63–91. London: Athlone, 1981.

Miller, J. Hillis. *Charles Dickens: The World of His Novels*. Cambridge, Mass.: Harvard University Press, 1958.

Miller-Frank, Felicia. *The Mechanical Song: Women, Voice, and the Artificial in Nineteenth-Century French Narrative*. Stanford, Calif.: Stanford University Press, 1995.

Morgentaler, Goldie. *Dickens and Heredity: When Like Begets Like*. Basingstoke, U.K.: Macmillan, 2000.

Morris, Adalaide, ed. *Sound States: Innovative Poetics and Acoustical Technologies*. Chapel Hill: University of North Carolina Press, 1997.

Moynahan, Julian. "Dealings with the Firm of Dombey and Son: Firmness *versus* Wetness." In *Dickens and the Twentieth Century*, ed. John Gross and Gabriel Pearson, 121–31. Toronto: University of Toronto Press, 1962.

"Mr. Gladstone and Mr. Edison." *Times*, 11 January 1889, 5.

MSU Vincent Voice Library Sound Samples. Online. Available: http://www.lib.msu.edu/vincent/samples.html. 1 December 2002.

Müller, Max. *Lectures on the Science of Language Delivered at the Royal Institution of Great Britain in February, March, April, and May, 1863*. London: Longman, Green, Longman, Roberts, and Green, 1864.

Musselwhite, David E. *Partings Welded Together: Politics and Desire in the Nineteenth-Century English Novel*. London: Methuen, 1987.

Music of the Streets. Audiocassette. Saydisc, CSDL 340, 1983.

Nead, Lynda. *Victorian Babylon: People, Streets and Images in Nineteenth-Century London*. New Haven, Conn.: Yale University Press, 2000.

Nelson, Harlan S. "Staggs's Gardens: The Railway through Dickens' World." *Dickens Studies Annual* 3 (1974): 41–53.

Newman, Charles. *The Evolution of Medical Education in the Nineteenth Century*. London: Oxford University Press, 1957.

Newsom, Robert. "Embodying *Dombey*: Whole and in Part." *Dickens Studies Annual* 18 (1989): 197–219.

Nightingale, Florence. *Notes on Nursing: What It Is, and What It Is Not*. New York: Appleton, 1860.

Nowell-Smith, Simon. "The 'Cheap Edition' of Dickens's Works [First Series], 1847–1852." *The Library*, 5th ser., 22 (1967): 245–51.

Observations on the Abuse of Toleration Permitted to the Itinerants Who Prowl about the Streets of London with Machines Assuming to Be Music Played Mechanically by the Hand. London: Doughty and Wilkins, 1863.

Ong, Walter J. *Orality and Literacy: The Technologizing of the Word*. London: Methuen, 1982.

——. *The Presence of the Word: Some Prolegomena for Cultural and Religious History*. Minneapolis: University of Minnesota Press, 1967.

Oppenheim, Janet. *"Shattered Nerves": Doctors, Patients, and Depression in Victorian England*. Oxford: Oxford University Press, 1991.

Otis, Laura. *Networking: Communicating with Bodies in the Nineteenth Century*. Ann Arbor: University of Michigan Press, 2001.

Panayi, Panikos. *Immigration, Ethnicity, and Racism in Britain, 1815–1945*. Manchester: Manchester University Press, 1994.

Paschen, Elise, and Rebekah Presson Mosby, eds. *Poetry Speaks: Hear Great Poets Read Their Work from Tennyson to Plath*. Naperville, Ill.: Sourcebooks Mediafusion, 2001.

Paterfamilias. "An Unneighbourly Act." *Good Words* (1864): 697–98.

Patten, Robert. *Charles Dickens and His Publishers*. Oxford: Clarendon, 1978.

"The Peace Society." *Punch* 8 (1845): 44.

Pearsall, Ronald. *Victorian Popular Music*. Newton Abbot, U.K.: David and Charles, 1973.

Pearson, Gabriel. "Towards a Reading of *Dombey and Son*." In *The Modern English Novel: the Reader, the Writer and the Work*, ed. Gabriel Josipovici, 54–76. New York: Barnes and Noble, 1976.

Peterson, William S. *Interrogating the Oracle: A History of the London Browning Society*. Athens: Ohio University Press, 1969.

Petts, Leonard. *The Story of "Nipper" and the "His Master's Voice" Picture Painted by Francis Barraud*. Bournemouth, U.K.: Talking Machine Review, 1983.

"The Phonograph and Its Future." *Nature* 18 (30 May 1878): 116–17.

"The Phonograph at the Royal Institution." *Graphic* 17 (16 March 1878): 259–68.

"The Phonograph in Africa." *New York Times*, 19 January 1885, 4.

Pietz, William. "The Phonograph in Africa: International Phonocentrism from Stanley to Sarnoff." In *Post-Structuralism and the Question of History*, ed. Derek Attridge, Geoff Bennington, and Robert Young, 263–85. Cambridge: Cambridge University Press, 1987.

Pocklington, G. R. *The Story of W. H. Smith & Son*. 4th ed. Rev. Gwen Clear. London: privately printed, 1949.

Powers, Horatio Nelson. *Lyrics of the Hudson*. Boston: Lothrop, 1891.

Preece, W. H. "The Microphone." *Nature* 18 (20 June 1878): 207–10.

——. "The Phonograph." *Journal of the Society of Arts* 26 (1878): 534.

——, *The Phonograph; or, Speaking and Singing Machine, Invented and Patented by Thomas Alva Edison, with Extracts from the Principal Journals in England and America*. London: London Stereoscopic, 1878.

Pridmore-Brown, Michele. "1939–40: Of Virginia Woolf, Gramophones, and Fascism." *PMLA* 113 (1998): 408–21.

Ragussis, Michael. *Figures of Conversion: The Jewish Question & English National Identity*. Durham, N.C.: Duke University Press, 1995.

"Railway Circulating Libraries." *Punch* 16 (1849): 61.

"Railway Literature." *Dublin University Magazine* 34 (1849): 280–91.

Rasula, Jed. "Understanding the Sound of Not Understanding." In *Close Listening: Poetry and the Performed Word*, ed. Charles Bernstein, 233–61. New York: Oxford University Press, 1998.

Read, Oliver, and Walter L. Welch. *From Tin Foil to Stereo: Evolution of the Phonograph*. 2d ed. Indianapolis: Sams, 1976.

Reader, W. J. *Professional Men: The Rise of the Professional Classes in Nineteenth-Century England*. London: Weidenfeld and Nicolson, 1966.

Redfield, Marc. *Phantom Formations: Aesthetic Ideology and the Bildungsroman*. Ithaca, N.Y.: Cornell University Press, 1996.

Rée, Jonathan. *I See a Voice: Deafness, Language and the Senses—A Philosophical History*. New York: Metropolitan, 1999.

Rilke, Rainer Maria. "Primal Sound." In *Where Silence Reigns: Selected Prose*, 51–56. Trans. G. Craig Houston. New York: New Directions, 1978.

Robson, John M. "The Fiat and Finger of God: The Bridgewater Treatises." In *Victorian Faith in Crisis: Essays on Continuity and Change in Nineteenth-Century Religious Belief*, ed. Richard J. Helmstadter and Bernard Lightman, 71–125. Stanford, Calif.: Stanford University Press, 1990.

Ronnell, Avital. *The Telephone Book: Technology—Schizophrenia—Electric Speech*. Lincoln: University of Nebraska Press, 1989.

Rosenman, Ellen B. "Women's Speech and the Role of the Sexes in *Daniel Deronda*." *Texas Studies in Language and Literature* 31 (1989): 237–56.

Rowe, John Carlos. *The Other Henry James*. Durham, N.C.: Duke University Press, 1998.

Rowe, Richard. *Life in the London Streets; or, Struggles for Daily Bread*. London: Nimmo, 1881.

Royle, Nicholas. *Telepathy and Literature: Essays on the Reading Mind*. Oxford: Blackwell, 1991.

Ruff, Lillian. "How Musical Was Charles Dickens?" *Dickensian* 68 (1972): 31–42.

Ruskin, John. "Lecture V — The Fireside: John Leech and John Tenniel." In *The Art of England: Lectures Given in Oxford*, 161–200. Orpington: Allen, 1884.

Russell, Dave. *Popular Music in England, 1840–1914: A Social History*. Montreal: McGill-Queen's University Press, 1987.

Sadrin, Anny. *Parentage and Inheritance in the Works of Charles Dickens*. Cambridge: Cambridge University Press, 1994.

Said, Edward. *Culture and Imperialism*. New York: Knopf, 1993.

Schafer, R. Murray. *The Tuning of the World*. New York: Knopf, 1977. Reprinted as *The Soundscape: Our Sonic Environment and the Tuning of the World*. Rochester: Destiny, 1994.

Schivelbusch, Wolfgang. *The Railway Journey*. Trans. Anselm Hollo. New York: Urizen, 1979.

Schmidt, Leigh Eric. *Hearing Things: Religion, Illusion, and the American Enlightenment*. Cambridge, Mass.: Harvard University Press, 2000.

Schwarzbach, F. S. *Dickens and the City*. London: Athlone, 1979.

Scott, Bonnie Kime. "The Subversive Mechanics of Woolf's Gramophone in *Between the Acts*." In *Virginia Woolf in the Age of Mechanical Reproduction*, ed. Pamela L. Caughie, 97–113. New York: Garland, 2000.

Seigert, Bernhard. "Switchboards and Sex: The Nut(t) Case." In *Inscribing Science: Scientific Texts and the Materiality of Communication*, ed. Timothy Lenoir, 78–90. Stanford, Calif.: Stanford University Press, 1998.

Semmens, Richard. *Joseph Sauveur's "Treatise on the Theory of Music": A Study, Diplomatic Transcription and Annotated Translation*. In *Studies in Music* 11. London, Ontario: University of Western Ontario Press, 1986.

Senf, Carol A. "*Dracula*: The Unseen Face in the Mirror." *Journal of Narrative Technique* 9 (1979): 160–70.

Shaw, G. B. *The Irrational Knot*. New York: Brentano's, 1905.

——. *Pygmalion*. New York: Penguin, 2000.

——. *Shaw's Music: The Complete Musical Criticism in Three Volumes*, ed. Dan H. Laurence. London: Max Reinhardt, The Bodley Head, 1981.

Shuttleworth, Sally. *George Eliot and Nineteenth-Century Science: The Make-Believe of a Beginning*. Cambridge: Cambridge University Press, 1984.

Simkin, Tom, and Richard S. Fiske. *Krakatau, 1883: The Volcanic Eruption and Its Effects*. Washington, D.C.: Smithsonian Institution Press, 1983.

Simmons, Jack. *The Victorian Railway*. London: Thames and Hudson, 1991.

Small, Helen. "A Pulse of 124: Charles Dickens and a Pathology of the Mid-Victorian Reading Public." In *The Practice and Representation of Reading in England*, ed. James Raven, Helen Small, and Naomi Tadmor, 263–90. Cambridge: Cambridge University Press, 1996.

Smith, Adolphe. *Street Life in London*. 1877. Reprint, New York: Benjamin Blom, 1969.

Smith, Bruce R. *The Acoustic World of Early Modern England: Attending to the O-Factor*. Chicago: University of Chicago Press, 1999.

[Smith, Charles Manby]. "Music-Grinders of the Metropolis." *Chambers's Edinburgh Journal*, n.s., 17 (27 March 1852): 197–201.

Smith, Mark M. *Listening to Nineteenth-Century America*. Chapel Hill: University of North Carolina Press, 2001.

Solie, Ruth. "'Tadpole Pleasures': *Daniel Deronda* as Music Historiography." *Yearbook of Comparative and General Literature* 45/46 (1997/1998): 87–104.

Somerville, Mary. *On the Connexion of the Physical Sciences*. 5th ed. London: Murray, 1840.

Spielmann, M. H. *The History of "Punch."* London: Cassell, 1895.

Sponza, Lucio. *Italian Immigrants in Nineteenth-Century Britain: Realities and Images*. Leicester: Leicester University Press, 1988.

Stallybrass, Peter, and Allon White. *The Politics and Poetics of Transgression*. Ithaca, N.Y.: Cornell University Press, 1986.

Stern, Ellen, and Emily Gwathmey. *Once Upon a Telephone: An Illustrated Social History*. New York: Harcourt Brace, 1994.

Sterne, Jonathan. *The Audible Past: Cultural Origins of Sound Reproduction*. Durham, N.C.: Duke University Press, 2003.

——. "A Machine to Hear for Them: On the Very Possibility of Sound's Reproduction." *Cultural Studies* 15 (2001): 259–94.

——. "Mediate Auscultation, the Stethoscope, and the 'Autopsy of the Living': Medicine's Acoustic Culture." *Journal of Medical Humanities* 22 (2001): 115–36.

Stewart, Garrett. *Dear Reader: The Conscripted Audience in Nineteenth-Century British Fiction*. Baltimore, Md.: Johns Hopkins University Press, 1996.

——. *Death Sentences: Styles of Dying in British Fiction*. Cambridge, Mass.: Harvard University Press, 1984.

——. "Modernism's Sonic Waver: Literary Writing and the Filmic Difference." In *Sound States: Innovative Poetics and Acoustical Technologies*, ed. Adalaide Morris, 237–73. Chapel Hill: University of North Carolina Press, 1997.

——. *Reading Voices: Literature and the Phonotext*. Berkeley: University of California Press, 1990.

Stoker, Bram. *Dracula*. Ed. Maurice Hindle. New York: Penguin, 1993.

——. *Personal Reminiscences of Henry Irving*. 2 vols. New York: Macmillan, 1906.

Stonehouse, J. H., ed. *Catalogue of the Library of Charles Dickens from Gadshill Reprinted from Sotheran's "Price Current of Literature" Nos. CLXXIV and CLXXV*. London: Piccadilly Fountain, 1935.

Storch, Robert D. "The Policeman as Domestic Missionary: Urban Discipline and Popular Culture in Northern England, 1850–1880." *Journal of Social History* 9 (1976): 481–509.

Sully, James. "Animal Music." *Cornhill Magazine* 40 (1879): 605–21.

——. "The Basis of Musical Sensation." *Fortnightly Review* 17 (1872): 428–43.

——. "Civilization and Noise." *Fortnightly Review* 24 (1878): 704–20.

——. "George Eliot's Art." *Mind* 6 (1881): 378–94.

——. "Recent Experiments with the Senses." *Westminster Review*, n.s., 42 (1872): 165–98.

——. *Sensation and Intuition: Studies in Psychology and Aesthetics*. London: King, 1874.

"The Sun-Voice." *All The Year Round*, n.s., 46 (19 February 1881): 416–20.

Sussman, Herbert. *Victorians and the Machine*. Cambridge, Mass.: Harvard University Press, 1968.

Swade, Doron. *The Cogwheel Brain: Charles Babbage and the Quest to Build the First Computer*. London: Little, Brown, 2000.

Symons, Arthur. *Amoris Victima (1897); Amoris Victimia (1940)*. New York: Garland, 1984.

——. "The Decadent Movement in Literature." *Harper's New Monthly Magazine* 87 (1893): 858–67.

Symons, G. J., ed. *The Eruption of Krakatoa and Subsequent Phenomena: Report of the Krakatoa Committee of the Royal Society*. London: Trübner, 1888.

Tambling, Jeremy. "Death and Modernity in *Dombey and Son*." *Essays in Criticism* 43 (1993): 308–29.

Taussig, Michael. *Mimesis and Alterity: A Particular History of the Senses*. New York: Routledge, 1993.

Taylor, Charles A. "Tyndall as Lecture Demonstrator." In *John Tyndall: Essays on a Natural Philosopher*, ed. W. H. Brock, N. D. McMillan, and R. C. Mollan, 205–16. Dublin: Royal Dublin Society, 1981.

Tegg, William. *Posts & Telegraphs, Past and Present*. London: William Tegg, 1878.

"The Telephone at Windsor." *Times*, 16 February 1878, 5.

Tennyson, Alfred. *Alfred, Lord Tennyson Reads from His Own Poems*. Introduced by Sir Charles Tennyson, Craighill LP, TC 1; CRS audiocassette, CR 9000.

———. *The Poems of Tennyson*. Ed. Christopher Ricks. 2d ed. Berkeley: University of California Press, 1987.

Tennyson, Charles. "The Tennyson Phonograph Records." *British Institute of Recorded Sound Bulletin* 3 (1956): 2–8.

Thomas A. Edison Papers. Rutgers University.

Thompson, E. P. "Time, Work-Discipline and Industrial Capitalism." In *Customs in Common*, 352–403. New York: New Press, 1991.

Thompson, Emily. *The Soundscape of Modernity: Architectural Acoustics and the Culture of Listening in America, 1900–1933*. Cambridge, Mass.: MIT Press, 2002.

Thompson, F. M. L. *The Rise of Respectable Society: A Social History of Victorian Britain, 1830–1900*. Cambridge, Mass.: Harvard University Press, 1988.

Thompson, Henry. "Telephone London." In *Living London*, ed. George R. Sims, 115–19. London: Cassell, 1901.

Thomson, David. *Europe since Napoleon*. 2d ed. New York: Knopf, 1962.

Thomson, William. "The British Association: Opening Address by Prof. Sir William Thomson." *Nature* 14 (14 September 1876): 426–31.

Thoreau, Henry David. *Journal 1: 1837–1844*. Ed. Elizabeth Hall Witherall, William L. Howarth, Robert Sattelmeyer, and Thomas Blandny. Princeton, N.J.: Princeton University Press, 1981.

———. *Journal 4: 1851–1852*. Ed. Leonard N. Neufeldt and Nancy Craig Simmons. Princeton, N.J.: Princeton University Press, 1992.

———. *Walden and Resistance to Civil Government*. Ed. William Rossi. New York: Norton, 1992.

Tillotson, Kathleen. *Novels of the Eighteen-Forties*. London: Oxford University Press, 1954.

Tosh, John. *A Man's Place: Masculinity and the Middle-Class Home in Victorian England*. New Haven, Conn.: Yale University Press, 1999.

Tosiello, Rosario Joseph. *The Birth and Early Years of the Bell Telephone System, 1876–1880*. New York: Arno, 1979.

Tritton, Paul. *The Lost Voice of Queen Victoria*. London: Academy, 1991.

Trotter, David. *Circulation: Defoe, Dickens, and the Economies of the Novel*. New York: St. Martin's, 1988.

Twain, Mark. *The American Claimant*. New York: Webster, 1892.

———. *Mark Twain–Howells Letters: The Correspondence of Samuel L. Clemens and William D. Howells, 1872–1910*. Ed. Henry Nash Smith and William M. Gibson. 2 vols. Cambridge, Mass.: Harvard University Press, 1960.

———. *Mark Twain's Notebooks & Journals*. Ed. Frederick Anderson et al. 3 vols. to date. Berkeley: University of California Press, 1975– .

Tyndall, John. *Sound*. London: Longmans, Green, 1867.

Van Sinderen, Alfred W. "The Printed Papers of Charles Babbage." *Annals of the History of Computing* 2 (1980): 169–85.

Verne, Jules. *Carpathian Castle*. Ed. I. O. Evans. New York: Ace, 1963.

———. *The Castle of the Carpathians*. London: Sampson Low, 1893.

Villiers de l'Isle-Adam. *Tomorrow's Eve*. Trans. Robert Martin Adams. Chicago: University of Illinois Press, 1982.

Vincent Voice Library. Michigan State University Libraries. Recordings of Florence Nightingale and Kenneth Landfrey. Online. Available: http://www.lib.msu.edu/vincent/samples.html. 1 December 2002.

Vrettos, Athena. *Somatic Fictions: Imagining Illness in Victorian Culture*. Stanford, Calif.: Stanford University Press, 1995.

Welch, Walter L., and Leah Brodbeck Stenzel Burt. *From Tinfoil To Stereo: The Acoustic Years of the Recording Industry, 1877–1929*. Gainesville: University Press of Florida, 1994.

Weliver, Phyllis. *Women Musicians in Victorian Fiction, 1860–1900: Representations of Music, Science and Gender in the Leisured Home*. Aldershot, U.K.: Ashgate, 2000.

Welsh, Alexander. *From Copyright to Copperfield: The Identity of Dickens*. Cambridge, Mass.: Harvard University Press, 1987.

———. *George Eliot and Blackmail*. Cambridge, Mass.: Harvard University Press, 1985.

Wever, Ernest Glen. *Theory of Hearing*. New York: Dover, 1970.

Wheatstone, Charles. "Experiments on Audition." In *The Scientific Papers of Sir Charles Wheatstone*, 30–35. London: Taylor and Francis, 1879.

Whitman, Walt. *Leaves of Grass: Comprehensive Reader's Edition*. Ed. Harold W. Blodgett and Sculley Bradley. New York: New York University Press, 1965.

———. *Leaves of Grass: A Textual Variorum of the Printed Poems, Volume II: Poems, 1860–1867*. Ed. Sculley Bradley, Harold W. Blodgett, Arthur Golden, and William White. New York: New York University Press, 1980.

Whyte, Arthur James. *The Evolution of Modern Italy*. New York: Norton, 1959.

Wicke, Jennifer. "Vampiric Typewriting: *Dracula* and Its Media." *ELH* 59 (1992): 467–93.

Williams, Raymond. *The Long Revolution*. London: Chatto and Windus, 1961.

Wilson, Charles. *First with the News: The History of W. H. Smith, 1792–1972*. London: Cape, 1985.

Wilson, Edmund. "Dickens: The Two Scrooges." In *The Wound and the Bow: Seven Studies in Literature*, 3–85. 1941. Athens: Ohio University Press, 1997.

Wilson, Eric. "Plagues, Fairs, and Street Cries: Sounding Out Society and Space in Early Modern London." *Modern Language Studies* 25.3 (1995): 1–42.

Wilson, Leonard G. *Charles Lyell: The Years to 1841: The Revolution in Geology*. New Haven, Conn.: Yale University Press, 1972.

Winter, Alison. *Mesmerized: Powers of Mind in Victorian Britain*. Chicago: University of Chicago Press, 1998.

Winter, James. *London's Teeming Streets, 1830–1914*. London: Routledge, 1993.

Wollaston, William Hyde. "On Sounds Inaudible by Certain Ears." *Philosophical Transactions of the Royal Society* 110 (1820): 306–14.

The Wonder of the Age: Mister Edison's New Talking Phonograph. Comp. Kevin Daly. Argo LP ZPR 122–3.

Woodbridge, Richard G. "Acoustic Recordings from Antiquity." *Proceedings of the IEEE* 57 (1969): 1465–66.

Woolf, Virginia. *Between the Acts*. New York: Harcourt Brace, 1941.

Wordsworth, William. *Wordsworth: Poetical Works*. Ed. Thomas Hutchinson and Ernest de Selincourt. Oxford: Oxford University Press, 1936.

Wright, William. *On Fishes and Fishing: Artificial Breeding of Fish, Anatomy of Their Senses, Their Loves, Passions, and Intellects*. London: Thomas Cautley Newby, 1858.

———. *On the Varieties of Deafness, and Diseases of the Ear, with Proposed Methods of Relieving Them*. London: Hurst, Chance, 1829.

———. *Practical Observations on Deafness, and Noises in the Head, and Their Treatment on Physiological Principles, Shewing the Injurious and Often Irremediable Consequences of Violent Applications, as Exemplified in the Case of Field Marshall His Grace the Duke of Wellington*. London: Wesley, 1853.

Young, Peter. *Person to Person: The International Impact of the Telephone*. Cambridge: Granta, 1991.

Zucchi, John. *The Little Slaves of the Harp: Italian Child Street Musicians in Nineteenth-Century Paris, London, and New York*. Montreal: McGill-Queen's University Press, 1992.

≥ INDEX ≤

Page numbers in *italic type* indicate illustrations.

Punch (continued)
  on railway reading, 29
  street music parody, 62
  Tenniel cartoon, 48, *49*

Ragussis, Michael, 180n.47
Railway Libraries, 29, 30
railways, 27–33
  book trade effects of, 28–30, 35
  Dickens and, 11–12, 22, 27–32, 35, 37, 39–40
  readership effects of, 28–30, *103*
  sounds of, 27, 31, 40, 78, 111, 163n.42
  symbolism of, 27
Rameau, Jean-Philippe, 178n.18
Rasula, Jed, 125
Reader, W. J., 53
reading. *See* book trade
readings. *See* public readings
recording. *See* gramophone; phonograph
Rée, Jonathan, 13, 152n.11
resonance theory. *See* sympathetic resonance
resonators, 10, 86, 100, 108
Rilke, Rainer Maria, 134
rods of Corti, 87
Romanticism, 7–8, 10, 89, 92, 153n.15, 157n.4
Ronell, Avital, 181n.55, 188n.50
Rosenman, Ellen B., 180n.44
Rossetti, W. M., 180n.49
Rossini, Gioacchino, 92
Rowe, John Carlos, 182n.65
Rowe, Richard, 77
Royal Institution, 89, 113, 178n.25
Royal Society, 4, 5, 156n.2
Royle, Nicholas, 179n.35, 180nn.44, 48
Rubinstein, Anton, 92
Ruff, Lillian, 172n.58
Ruskin, John, 4, 68

Sadrin, Anny, 162n.30
Said, Edward, 137–38
Sauveur, Joseph, 176n.11
Savoy, Duchy of, 48, 49, 169n.28
Savoyards, 45, 47–49, 51, 64
  origin of term, 48, 169nn.28, 29
Schafer, R. Murray, 13
Schivelbusch, Wolfgang, 28
Schmidt, Leigh Eric, 155n.40
science, 8–12, 83–85
science fiction, 131
Scott, Walter, 8, 9, 177n.18
séance, 123, *124*
Sedgwick, Adam, 158n.7
Seigert, Bernhard, 108

Senf, Carol A., 190n.67
senses, 6, 8, 14, 83, 174n.81
  focus shift from seeing to hearing, 83, 91
  overstimulation of, 42
  separateness with communication, 99, 100
  telephone and, *102*, 104, *105*, 107
Shakespeare, William, 162n.30, 165n.60, 186n.23
  King Lear, 23
  Macbeth, 162n.31
  Othello, 23, 162n.31
Shaw, George Bernard, 78, 108
  Pygmalion, 108–9
shilling novel, 29
shorthand system, 10, 134, 190nn.61, 63
silence
  Carlyle and, 6, 41, 43–45, 55–56
  in *Daniel Deronda*, 12, 94–95, 106
  music and, 6, 95, 152n.10, 155nn.38, 39
  "other side of," 8, 83, 95
  valuation of, 42, 43
  Victorian marital, 94–95
  Victorian propriety and, 111
  women's socialization and, 55
Silver, Henry, 73
Simms and McIntyre, 28–29
Slater, Michael, 165n.60
slavery, 14, 161n.26, 168n.19
Small, Helen, 166n.68
Smith, Adolphe, 77
Smith, Bruce, 168n.19
Smith, Charles Manby, 46–47, 48
Smith, Denis Mack, 170n.30
Smith, Mark M., 155n.40, 168n.19
Smith, W. H., 28, 29
social class
  anti–street music movement and, 42–43, 45, 52–53, 56–57, 59–60
  Cheap Edition and, 35
  defense of street music and, 46, 171n.55
  leisure activity and, 62
  musical taste and, 45, 46, 57, 60, 63, 73, 77, 92
  territorial distinctions and, 60
  See also home-based professionals; middle class
Somerville, Mary Fairfax, 8
sound, 3–9
  Eliot's valuation of, 6, 8, 83, 84, 88–89, 91–92, 96–97
  gendered conceptions of, 55–56
  Krakatoa eruption and, 4, *5*
  in literary/linguistic study, 13–14
  power relationship, 44

recording of. *See* phonograph
Romantic view of, 7–8, 10, 89, 92, 153n.15, 157n.4, 163n.42
sympathetic resonance and, 8, 86–96, 99
transmission of, 22, 108. *See also* telephone
ubiquity of, 6
Victorian awareness of, 4–5, 8, 11–12, 14, 85, 111
writing and, 134
See also hearing; noise; voice
sound imperialism, 13
soundscape studies, 13–14, 152n.11
sound waves. *See* wave motion
Spencer, Herbert, 175n.97
spiritualism, 14, 15, 123, 186n.25
Sponza, Lucio, 169nn.23, 29, 172n.57, 173n.74, 174n.95
Stallybrass, Peter, 174n.81
Sterne, Jonathan, 6, 155n.39, 181n.56
stethoscope, 6, 152–53nn.12, 13
Stewart, Garrett, 94, 137, 155n.39, 161n.25, 164n.53
Steytler, Charles, 123
Stoker, Bram, 125–26, 141, 143
Dracula, 12, 119, 126, 131, 134–37, 139
Strand Magazine, 127, 128, 131
Street Music Act (1864), 58–59, 63–64, 73, 77, 78, 172n.65, 174–75n.95
street musicians. *See* anti–street music movement; organ grinders
suburbs, 61–62, 77
Sully, James, 77–78, 90–91, 175n.97, 177n.18, 183n.79
Sussman, Herbert, 164n.51
Swade, Doron, 157n.4
Swinburne, A. C., 4
Symons, Arthur, 79, 112
sympathetic resonance
Bell's telephone invention and, 100, 101
Eliot's metaphor of, 8, 88–89, 95–96, 99
Helmholtz's theory of, 86–87, 90, 93
psychoanalysis as, 108

talking cure. *See* psychoanalysis
talking machine. *See* phonograph
Tambling, Jeremy, 161n.23
Taussig, Michael, 190n.73, 191nn.83, 84
technological imperialism, 113, 137, 138
telecommuting, 81
telegraph, 3, 10, 28, 100, 101, 104, 163n.42
first permanent transatlantic, 182n.66
phonograph vs., 111

telephone, 10, 82, 100–109, *102*, *103*, *105*, 113, 183n.2
as "maternal machine," 188n.50
phonograph vs., 111
Tenniel, John, 48, *49*
Tennyson, Alfred, 4, 22, 61, 136, 142
phonograph recordings by, 9, 11, 12, 111, 113, 123, 125–26, 143, 187n.35
Tennyson, Charles, 125, 126, 187n.35
Ternan, Ellen, 31
territorialism, 44, 52, 55, 60, 80, 171n.54
Thackeray, William Makepeace, 152n.11, 174n.86
Thomas, Dylan, 11
Thompson, David, 169n.30
Thompson, E. P., 171n.55
Thompson, Emily, 153n.20, 168n.19, 175n.97
Thompson, F. M. L., 58, 80
Thompson, Henry, 13
Thomson, William (Lord Kelvin), 101
Thoreau, Henry David, *Walden*, 163n.42, 165n.58
Tidal Express, 39, 40
Tillotson, Kathleen, 17, 159nn. 11, 12
time, as condition of work, 171n.55
Times (London), 42, 113, 123
street noise complaints in, 42, 45, 46, 56, 66–67, 77
tone discernment, 85–87, 88, 90
trademark, 142–45
trains. *See* railways
Tritton, Paul, 186n.27
Trollope, Anthony, 174n.85
Twain, Mark, 126–27
Tyndall, John, 10, 84, 91, 108, 113, 176n.10
phonograph and, 123
Sound, 22, 89–90
typewriting, 190n.63

urban noise. *See* anti–street music movement; noise

Vanity Fair (magazine), 114, *115*, 116
ventriloquism, 127, 166n.67
Verne, Jules, *Le Château des Carpathes*, 131, 132, 136, 139
vibrations. *See* acoustic vibrations; sympathetic resonance
"Victor Dog, The," 142–45
Victoria, queen of Great Britain, 7, 15, 101, *103*, 111, 186n.27
Victor Talking Machine Company, 142, 145
Villiers de l'Isle-Adam, *L'Eve future*, 130–31